BEYOND THE NARROW GATE

BEYOND THE NARROW GATE

THE JOURNEY OF
FOUR CHINESE WOMEN
FROM THE MIDDLE KINGDOM
TO MIDDLE AMERICA

LESLIE CHANG

A DUTTON BOOK

DUTTON
Published by the Penguin Group
Penguin Putnam Inc., 375 Hudson Street, New York, New York 10014, U.S.A.
Penguin Books Ltd, 27 Wrights Lane, London W8 5TZ, England
Penguin Books Australia Ltd, Ringwood, Victoria, Australia
Penguin Books Canada Ltd, 10 Alcorn Avenue, Toronto, Ontario, Canada M4V 3B2
Penguin Books (N.Z.) Ltd, 182–190 Wairau Road, Auckland 10, New Zealand

Penguin Books Ltd, Registered Offices: Harmondsworth, Middlesex, England

First published by Dutton, a member of Penguin Putnam Inc.

First Printing, May, 1999
10 9 8 7 6 5 4 3 2 1

From *Collected Poems* by Wallace Stevens. Copyright © 1954 by Wallace Stevens.
Reprinted by permission of Alfred A Knopf Inc.
The epigraph on p. ix is a selection from the poem "Dead Water" by Wen Yi-to, pub-
lished in *Anthology of Chinese Literature, Volume 2,* edited by Cyril Birch, Grove Press,
Inc. Copyright © 1972. Reprinted with permission of Grove/Atlantic, Inc.

REGISTERED TRADEMARK—MARCA REGISTRADA

LIBRARY OF CONGRESS CATALOGING-IN-PUBLICATION DATA

Chang, Leslie.
    Beyond the narrow gate : the journey of four Chinese women from
the Middle Kingdom to Middle America / Leslie Chang.
        p. cm.
    ISBN 0-525-94257-2 (alk. paper)
    1. Chinese American women—Biography.   2. Women immigrants—United
States—Biography.   3. Taipei (Taiwan)—Biography.   I. Title.
E184.C5C445   1999
305.48'8951073'0922—dc21   98-33267
                                                            CIP

Printed in the United States of America
Set in Sabon
Designed by Leonard Telesca

This book is printed on acid-free paper. ∞

for my mother

AUTHOR'S NOTE

Many attempts have been made to transliterate the Chinese language by many different people—from learned scholars to random immigration officials—with decidedly mixed results. Because no single system is perfect, I have decided not to pick one over another, choosing instead to use the method preferred by the specific person or place to which I am referring. Thus, I write of Beijing rather than Peking and, by the same token, the Kuomintang instead of the Guomindang. For everyday words, I have used my own best judgment, preferring to impart a sense of the sound of the word to an English speaker rather than hewing to one particular form.

With the exception of my own family, all the principal people in this work and some of the secondary ones have been given different names in order to protect their privacy.

So this ditch of hopeless dead water
May well boast a certain splendor;
Then if the frogs can't bear the silence
Out of dead water a song will rise.

—WEN YI-TO

BEYOND THE NARROW GATE

PROLOGUE

Water belongs to everyone and to no one. For this reason, I have always had a particular affinity for it, which may strike some as mysterious. Westerners ask me where my parents were born, as though the answer will enable them to glean some knowledge. The answer is Beijing and Luoyang. The truth is that this response signifies nothing. The meaningful question would be to ask where my ancestors lived. The answer to that is inland. My father's people came from Wuhan, birthplace of the Chinese republic and the capital of Hubei, that sweltering province sandwiched between Sichuan and Anhui. My mother's father was, amazingly even to me, from Inner Mongolia, land of desert and grassy plains.

Yet water calls to me. I remain convinced that I would find peace if I could only have a house by the ocean or even just a lap pool. I insisted on being married near the sea. This attraction does not come from my father. He does not even know how to swim. A celebrated family anecdote involves his falling from a sailboat and losing his glasses. A true inlander, he prefers to hunker down where it is warm and safe, preferably in a medium-to-large-size city with good Chinese takeout and daily access to the *New York Times*. There is nothing wrong with this instinct. It pulls me too. But I also love open water, and this bond, I know, comes from my mother.

She longs for a view more than anything else. Once, staying at the Mandarin Oriental in San Francisco, she insisted on seeing three different rooms before she found one with which she was satisfied. It was on a floor so high it made me dizzy, with a corner window overlooking the bay. Even so, my mother spent most of her time on the bridge linking the elevator bank to our wing. The bridge consisted almost entirely of windows. It offered a view in either direction that was brilliant and blinding. If there had been a chair, she could have sat forever, letting the gold sun and blue sea overwhelm her through the glass.

My mother may have descended from inland people, but they were also nomads. Her father once rode his horse practically the length of China, from Inner Mongolia to Guangzhou, a distance of some twelve hundred miles. Whether it is due to this heritage or to the chaotic circumstances of her childhood, I do not know, but my mother could only become a nomad herself—forever moving, changing and going, yet always retaining some essential part of her being, recognizable and intact in spite of all the places she has been. In this, she is like water, not dead water but fearsomely alive. When she gazes out on its shimmering expanse, she sees her own reflection. When I gaze out, I see her, my mother, always pulling away, returning and pulling away again. I drink from her, and she slips between my fingertips. She has borne me all this way from the stagnant pond of her own birth. I cannot decide whether I want her to stay or go. When she is here, I wish she would leave. When she is gone, I wish she would return. She pulls away again, a force as elemental as the ebbing tide. I remain a child on the shore, eagerly collecting the sea glass and driftwood she has left behind.

My mother never talked about her childhood when my siblings and I were growing up, and we never asked. From her, we learned that family history was not of interest, and in our ignorance we turned our backs on what had gone before. We lived on a plateau in a land of canyons, separated from our past by chasms of time, language, and culture. My mother was a native guide who could have led us along the sheer cliff walls and dangerous riverbeds of the old days, but she never did.

For her, the past was divided into parts, each occupying a separate memory bank, some of which she tried never to visit. For me, her past was just a hopeless jumble, like a creaky, junk-ridden attic to which I was not allowed entry. China, America, and somewhere, hazily, in between, Taiwan: I could not comprehend how the three came together to form the person who had formed me.

My mother never told stories; she only dispensed facts and casual references to her past. She described the most thrilling events as casually as she would a trip to Finast, the local supermarket. "When we left China, I had to wear gold bars sewn into my belt. They were so heavy." She might as well have been talking about a bag of groceries for all the emotion she displayed. When she happened to mention the fact that her grandmother had been an opium addict with bound feet, I accepted the news with equal equanimity. Her delivery was so matter-of-fact I assumed everyone's grandmother had a hookah collection and wore shoes that measured a mere three and a half inches.

Now, when I read essays by the descendants of Holocaust survivors, I begin to understand. Their parents and grandparents had also lived in fear of their memories. To dwell on the past is to reexperience it. A onetime high-school quarterback remembers the touchdown that won the state finals in vivid detail. Doting parents tirelessly and tiresomely recount the same dull anecdotes from their children's lives. The consumption of a madeleine takes Proust back to a time of absolute contentment. But the process works in the negative as well, and the terror that wakes my mother up at night, gasping and pressing hand to heart, is very real. She did not want to share it with me. Perhaps she wished to protect me. Her secrecy was a gift that I, in turn, did not want to receive.

My physical features marked me as a stranger in my own country, but I knew nothing of the land of my ancestors. I could not even converse with the various relatives and old family friends who crowded around the dinner table at holiday times. Their jokes and discussions swirled meaninglessly about my head. Among aliens, I myself was an alien. I grew up, self-contained and removed from the world around me, unable to explain anything to anyone because nothing had ever been explained to me. At the same time, I longed to—a bird beating its head against glass, wanting only to be let inside. If I could somehow capture my mother's essence, the glass would disappear. The path forward would be clear.

I had not always felt this way. As a child in a nearly all-white community, I had wanted only to hide the Chinese in me.

I remember answering telephone calls from my mother's high-school friends when I was little. "Han Man-li?" they would ask eagerly into the receiver.

"I don't speak Chinese," I would answer rudely. It was a stock reply, one which I employed often. "I don't speak Chinese," I even used to say in response to the basic query *"Ni hao ma?"*

"Ahh." The voice would pause and continue more cautiously, "Is Mary there?"

"Hold on. I'll get her."

Mary is my mother's name, but I was in college before I made the connection. Han Man-li is my mother's name too. It is her Chinese name, her first name. Only now does it seem strange that she never bothered to explain this to me. Perhaps she had told me once, and I was the one who had not listened.

I was an adult and a writer in search of a subject when I finally asked her to talk about her life. That first conversation, she spoke practically in monosyllables. "Yes" and "No" were the only responses I could coax out of her. If a question begged a more elaborate answer, she responded by saying, "I don't know." I was the customer at an information store; she was its surly clerk. Eventually, I ended up inventing my own time frame for the paltry trickle of memories she reluctantly let drip forth. She did not care if the dates were accurate or not. The conversation took on a surrealistic tinge. She would mention that she had moved to a certain city in 1943. "Oh no," I would respond, "it had to be 1945." She would shrug. Together, we were reinventing her past, not exploring it as I had wished. The process left me so frustrated that when she got up to go to sleep, I badgered her all the way to her bedroom. She lay on one side while I hovered in a chair over her.

"Tell me more," I pleaded. "What do you remember?"

"*Ai-you,*" she finally snapped, her eyes blinking open. "I just don't want to remember."

The sound of her cry still reverberated in my head when I walked home that evening. "I just don't want to remember."

I think my mother was sorry she could not help me more. She gave me something before I left. At the time, I doubted that it would do any good. It was a list of names of the same eager voices who used to call asking for her in Chinese. Much later, I would realize it was a map to my mother's heart. At the time, I simply had no other direction to follow. I began returning the phone calls from my mother's past.

In the process, I found three other women—Dolores Fung, Suzanne Koo, and Margaret Li—who had been high-school classmates of my mother's in Taiwan. Each was linked in her own special way to my mother, but each had taken a different path in life, a path my mother might have also taken but had not. Today, Dolores is an ex–math professor living in Queens in a cramped three-bedroom house with her husband and adult son. She has abandoned a tenured position at a local university to follow a dream that those around her call crazy. Suzanne splits her time between helping out at her physician husband's office, located in Silicon Valley, and more leisurely activities—taking tennis lessons, gardening, seeing friends. It is a very different life from the one she left behind a few years ago. Margaret teaches biology at a small women's college in Los Angeles, a position that neither inspires her nor does much to support her comfortable existence in expensive Palos Verdes. She neither needs nor particularly wants to work, but she does not know how to quit. My mother, after four decades in the United States, finds herself in Hong Kong, a corporate wife and once again a stranger among strangers. As always, she adjusts. She has been surviving for so long, I sometimes wonder if she has forgotten how to live.

In some ways these four women are so alike, and in others, so separate. Both their similarities and their differences fascinated me. I wanted to understand how the women, all of whom had started from the same place, could have ended up so completely unalike. They would have developed into individuals in Taiwan, of course, but the differences would never have been so dramatic. America had changed them. If nothing else, they had become Americans, distinctly and uniquely so; Dolores, the dreamer, trapped between new fantasies and old expectations; Suzanne, the rebel, who forsook her traditional obligations to follow her heart; Margaret, a new breed of separatist, living in a gilded ghetto but letting her daughter go free; my mother, the pragmatist, the assimilationist, able to move from world to world without ever belonging to any particular one.

From these four very personal stories emerged a portrait of a larger realm, a unique segment of immigrant America. The traditional immigrant path was, as the Irish used to say about themselves, "from steerage to suburbia in three generations." These women had done it in just one: their own. I thought of them as pioneers. Not only had America changed them, but they had changed it. And in spite of these changes, my mother had maintained a bond with each of the women that defied the years and distance between them. I began to realize that their stories, similar and dissimilar as they were, were intimately and inextricably entwined. I was a writer no longer in search. I had found my subject.

CHINA

The Battle of Siping, which happened in May of 1947, changed everything. China had been at war, off and on, for an entire decade already. At first the country had been battling the Japanese, but after the American bombing of Hiroshima and Nagasaki, China began fighting itself. A long and bloody civil war followed. It would kill millions of people and ruin the lives of hundreds of millions more. It was as if the sleeping dragon, goaded by the samurai, finally woke up to turn and bite its own tail.

The two sides in the struggle divided along every possible fault line: politics, economics, social class. To the right were Chiang Kai-shek and the Kuomintang party. The top American military advisor to China, "Vinegar Joe" Stilwell, used to call Chiang "Peanut" behind his back. Peanut preferred the title "Generalissimo." His Nationalist government claimed to be the rightful heir to the republic that Sun Yat-sen had founded in 1911. It had the support of the capitalist rich, the urban professionals, and, most importantly, the United States.

On the left were the broad-faced, pandalike Mao Zedong and his ragtag People's Liberation Army. They used Russian weapons and wore crude sandals hand-made of straw. They introduced the local peasantry to the joys of land reform. Much of their support came from the impoverished and the idealistic. At the end of World War II, they had fewer than half as many troops as the Kuomintang. On paper, the Communists seemed like a longshot at best. A seasoned gambler would shake his head and walk away at the sight of their odds. But odds only tell part of the story.

In truth, the Kuomintang was beginning to founder. By 1947, inflation had risen thirtyfold since the end of World War II. Corruption and ineptitude ran rampant in the ranks. Many of the army's vaunted numbers came from peasant conscripts who were involuntary, ill treated, and ill trained. The Communists hunkered down in the countryside to the north and west, patiently waiting for the Kuomintang to come to them. Chiang, more interested in the symbolic reunification of the country than in strategically consolidating his power base in the south, did just that.

He sent his best troops to Manchuria to wrest its resource-rich lands away from Mao. For a year and a half, fierce fighting mingled uneasily with American-negotiated cease-fires. Then, in January of 1947, the American mediators threw up their hands and left. For the first time in over a century, China was on its own.

Full-scale war resumed in Manchuria. A series of Communist-led attacks began that spring, culminating in the Battle of Siping. It was an unremarkable place save for the fact that it was a railway junction. Victory there allowed the Communists to go on the offensive. They boldly severed supply lines and cleverly isolated the Nationalist forces in the cities. The war would drag on for two more years, but the Kuomintang would never recover. At the time, few in China realized the import of Siping, but its outcome would change the course of all their lives.

Much has been written about what happened to the Chinese people in China after the civil war, but this is the story of four Chinese girls who left. At the time of the Battle of Siping, they were still children and strangers to one another. A few short years later, they would be neither.

Xiao Mei was only eight years old in 1947 and living in the Nationalist capital of Nanjing, where her mother was a representative in the National Assembly. Everyone called the girl Xiao Mei, or Little Younger Sister, because her own sister and only sibling was almost a decade older. She was a friendly, happy child, unusual only in that her parents were divorced and that she was very precocious. Two years later, in Taiwan, she would enter junior high school at the age of ten. Most of her classmates were already twelve. This was all right with her. She was used to being the youngest. She was used to being taken care of. Many years later in America, she would become Dolores Fung, but in some ways she would always remain Xiao Mei.

In the southern city of Guangzhou, another little girl, named Ling, lived in a two-story Western-style house with six servants and a guard at the front gate. Her father served as senator for Guangdong province. He was so busy he did not know the birthdays of his six children or even what ages they were. In contrast, Ling's mother flawlessly attended to every detail of the household, including deciding what clothes the children would wear each day. She kept the home deadly calm, a vast, cool tomb of silence. In spite of her large family, Ling felt adrift and alone. Later, when she was a young adult, she would move to America, where she soon became Suzanne Chen and then, years afterwards, Suzanne Koo. Still, as hard as Suzanne tried to shake her off, the girl Ling would remain, a constant presence, like a guilty conscience, in the back of her head.

Much farther north, in Beijing, known under the Kuomintang as Beiping, lived another family with six children, all girls. The middle child was known as Ma-hua, a name that later smoothly anglicized into Margaret. The ease of the process and the name itself both fit the girl. She was sensible, practical, and always suitable. She could adapt to any situation without complaint. It was a useful skill, one that she may have acquired in part from her father, a man of many different trades—banker, academic, businessman, and even high-school principal. But it was also a skill that would take her where she did not want to go. Much later on, after she had left China and settled in America, she would realize that she had spent so much time living up to other people's expectations that she had never had the chance to live up to her own.

To these girls, the Battle of Siping was a hazy news item from a faraway place, in spite of the consequences the Communist victory would eventually hold for them all. It was not so for a fourth girl, who lived in an elegant walled compound on the site of what is now Tiananmen Square in Beijing. Her name was Han Man-li, and she is my mother. Her father was a general in the Kuomintang army, stationed in Manchuria. He was killed in the Battle of Siping. My mother still remembers kneeling in white burlap at a railroad station on a warm May afternoon, waiting for the train that would bring her father's bullet-riddled body home. She became weightless that day, a leaf to be blown about by the wind. Eventually, she would land in America, where she would become Mary Chang and, almost twenty-three years to that day at the train station, give birth to me. By then, she would already have three other children, a husband, and numerous friends, but some part of her would forever remain unsettled.

The China that these four girls had been born into no longer exists. Back then, the country was in a period of transition, marked, as many transitions are, by the coming together of the old and the new—ancient customs at loggerheads with radical ideas. Imperialism, republicanism, factionalism, communism, fascism all vied for power in a world that was still largely dominated by the hierarchical system proposed by Confucius two thousand years before. In this hierarchy, scholarship dominated. Accomplishment in this arena gave even emperors greater stature than they otherwise would have enjoyed. The path to power, prestige, and even wealth lay in the government; and for centuries, entry to the government had been granted through the Imperial Examination system. Government positions in ancient China were wholly unlike those in America, which are in place to serve the people. In China, rather, the people were in place to serve the government. Tax dollars and tributes all flowed upwards, not down. In America, the wealthy entrepreneur is paramount—the robber barons of the Gilded Age, the oil magnates of TV soap operas, the cyberkings of Silicon Valley. In China, hard as it may be for a Westerner to believe, it was the government official.

Although the fall of the Qing dynasty in 1911 led to the dismantling of the ancient system, the prominence of scholars still did not wane. It merely transferred from those who had passed the Imperial Examinations to those who had studied abroad.

Graduates from American and European universities studded the upper ranks of the Nationalist government. An anecdotal statistic from the book *Family, Fields, and Ancestors* by Lloyd E. Eastman reveals how, even in the private sector, returned scholars, as they were known, were accorded the utmost respect. In the 1920s, a graduate from a Chinese college could only with experience hope to get a position at a commercial press for 80 Chinese dollars a month. He would also get a 3-by-1½-foot desk. A graduate from a Japanese college would receive 100 to 120 Chinese dollars and a 3-by-2-foot desk, while a graduate from the Japanese Imperial University could expect 150 Chinese dollars, a 4-by-2½-foot desk, a bookshelf, a crystal inkstand, and a rattan chair. A graduate from any Western college would receive the same plus an additional 50 Chinese dollars. Finally, if the graduate came from Harvard, Yale, Oxford, or Cambridge, he would get 250 Chinese dollars, the bookshelf, the crystal inkstand, the rattan chair, and, most importantly, as could only befit such an accomplished scholar, a custom-made desk—all this without any experience required.

In more serious matters, the value of such an education, as my own family history reveals, could literally be priceless. After returning to China, my paternal grandfather parlayed his studies at Harvard into a place with the State Department of the Nationalist government. Eventually, he rose to head the desk of North American Affairs during World War II and then to serve as a delegate to the United Nations. It was this position which eventually gave him the diplomatic passport that would allow him, his wife, and their three children—my father among them—to enter America during the civil war. At the time, millions were struggling to leave China. In the United States, there existed an immigration quota of 105 Chinese per year.

Returned scholars occupied a special niche in Chinese society, one that was without analogue in the West. Even including ones who had studied in Japan, they still numbered in the mere tens of thousands, a minuscule minority in a country that by the mid-twentieth century had a population of well over 500 million. An enormous gulf separated these scholars from the masses. They lived in cities. They espoused Western thinking. Often, their wives were also college graduates. With the exception of those who had gone to school in France—Chou En-lai was the most notable of this number—they almost all supported the Nationalist government. It was into this milieu that Dolores, Suzanne, and Margaret were born.

Both of Dolores's parents had studied in America, her mother at Berkeley. Suzanne's father had attended the University of Heidelberg. Margaret's father had gone to Oxford. Even if, like Margaret's, they did not have a great deal of money, the families that made up this unique world still benefited from the enormous prestige that accompanied their degrees. In a country with a deposed emperor and court, they formed a sort of aristocracy.

My mother's situation was somewhat different, but in some ways even more privileged. Traditionally in China, the soldier occupied one of the lowliest positions on the social totem pole, but, since the fall of the Manchu dynasty, militarism had dominated the country. The chaos of the era demanded it. In fact, the first president of the republic was not Sun Yat-sen, who had founded the revolutionary movement, but a general named Yuan Shi-kai, whose claim to the position lay largely in the fact that he controlled the army. For years after Yuan's own downfall, warlords waged territorial battles, dividing the country into numerous fighting factions. Into this fray stepped Chiang Kai-shek and his band of elite military officers from Whampoa Academy, the West Point of China. Their Northern Expedition of 1927 subjugated the warlords and united the country at a time when internationally, military might was becoming crucial. In this way, the army gave Chiang his true legitimacy as China's leader, not the people nor his principles. During the 1930s and 1940s, with the Japanese invasion and the advent of World War II, military officers enjoyed a level of prominence and prestige in China which surpassed even that of the intellectuals. Scholars may have regarded soldiers with the same sort of disdain with which old money views new, but in those violent times they looked to them for protection.

My mother's father was an army general and a graduate of Whampoa. It was to attend school there that, as an eighteen-year-old, he had left his home and ridden his horse twelve hundred miles. Growing up, I had known none of this. The strongest images I had had of my maternal grandparents came not from any memory of my mother's but from two photographs that sat on the piano in our living room. One was of my grandfather in his army uniform. He stands tall, his jaw set. On his feet are dusty leather boots, which proclaim his rank as clearly as any epaulets or medals. In the Nationalist army, no one under the rank of a general wore boots. In Mao's army, no one did. In the photo, my grandfather is standing next to a smiling, handsome man sitting in a camp chair. I had known since I could speak who he was, but I was startled when someone, a white person, picked up the picture one day and said with surprise in his voice, "That's Chiang Kai-shek." Of course, I had thought, who else would it be? The two men were inextricably linked in my mind.

In the other picture, my grandparents stand together. Again my grandfather wears his army uniform. At six feet, he towers over my grandmother, who is wearing a white dress and has large, worried eyes. Her face is shaped like a square with rounded edges, and I used to imagine that I saw a hint of her jaw-line in my own. I grew two grandparents out of those black-and-white images—he dashing and stern, she beautiful and childlike. I had no real idea. They had both died long before I was even born, when my mother was still a girl. I knew nothing of them save what I could glean from those two old photographs and the scraps of information that my mother almost incidentally tossed my way.

When my mother had said "I just don't want to remember" to me, she meant this, her childhood. I had to pry bits and pieces from her like a hunter digging buckshot out of a pheasant's dead carcass. In the same way, she gave her memories up—inertly but still unwilling. Only now that I have reassembled them can I understand why.

The first important corner of the puzzle came to me one fall afternoon. My mother and I had just eaten lunch together in Chinatown and were walking down the street towards East Broadway. I was going to the library, she to the brokerage house where she traded her stocks. It was a mild day, but windy, and as we walked, the detritus of Chinatown life swirled about our feet—

pieces of red crepe paper, cabbage leaves, a napkin from the Häagen-Dazs on Bayard Street. We stepped aside to let a man carry a bucket of fish into a store. Water splashed over the sides.

"My father killed a man," my mother said suddenly.

I stared at her. It was so unlike her to volunteer any information, much less something so shocking, that, for a moment, I wondered if she was kidding. Perhaps the atmosphere of Chinatown had gotten to me. By now, we had arrived at Pell Street, where Chuck Connors, the self-anointed "mayor of Chinatown," had once held court a century before. He had specialized in taking credulous white people on tours of the area, complete with staged knife fights, phony opium dens, and appropriately exotic slave girls. Now, a hundred years later, I was a tourist here too, this time to my mother's past. Perhaps she, like Connors, was just giving me what I had come for.

She was not. Her father had really killed someone. He was a soldier, after all. It was his job. But she was remembering one time in particular because it happened while she was there.

As an army man, my grandfather moved constantly, taking his wife and children with him. Once, during World War II, he was transferred from Ningxia to Gansu, and the whole family went by way of the Yellow River. Along one empty stretch, they encountered another boat with two men on board. One of the men was a deserter from my grandfather's division. My grandfather ordered him on board and saw that the soldier was just a boy. He could not have been more than fifteen years old, and he begged on his knees for mercy.

"Let him go," my grandmother said.

Instead, my grandfather commanded two guards to take the boy to shore. They dragged him into the woods. Beyond that, my mother could not see, but she could hear. At the time, she was about eight or nine. The sound of the pistol shot cracked across the loess-filled waters that make the river so famously yellow, and lodged itself in her brain. It remains there today.

"A fifteen-year-old boy," she said to me. "Imagine."

Old women pushed past us on their way to market. A car stereo blared a Hong Kong pop song.

"Somehow," my mother said, "this is all connected."

"What do you mean?" I asked.

"I think," she said, "my father shot this boy, and then the things that happened later . . ." Her voice trailed off.

"It's all connected," she repeated.

"Like karma?" I asked, trying to understand. I still did not know to what things she was referring.

"What's karma?"

"It's energy," I explained. "You create energy by your actions and send it out into the world. That energy eventually comes back to you. If your actions are positive, the energy is positive. If they're negative, the energy is negative."

We had reached East Broadway, where we stood on the corner, waiting for the light to change so we could go our separate ways. The wind blew dust into our eyes.

"In Chinese, we have a different word for it," my mother said. "We call it revenge."

Two years after the killing by the banks of the Yellow River, my grandfather was dead. When my mother and the rest of her family, which included an older brother and two younger sisters, went to the station to greet the train that carried his body from Manchuria to Beijing, they knelt respectfully on the platform. Dressed in coarse burlap robes of mourning white, they bowed their heads to pay obeisance to their most recently departed ancestor. That train station no longer exists, but my mother remembers the moment clearly. She was not yet eleven at the time. She had closed her eyes and was trying not to fidget in the warmth of the late-spring afternoon when she felt someone pull her up from behind. Startled, she looked around, but there was no one there. Her relatives knelt nearby, oblivious to what was happening. She shrugged and closed her eyes again.

At the time of my grandfather's death, the family was living a privileged existence in Beijing. They owned a traditional walled compound known as a *si hu yen*. Theirs was built around two courtyards, the sort of aristocratic home that has rapidly disappeared under the modernizing plans of the Communists. My mother's house, the deed to which she still holds, was razed years ago, along with scores of other similarly elegant and ancient homes, to make way for Tiananmen Square. The family summered in Manchuria and had servants of every sort—a cook for the kitchen, maids for the other rooms, amahs for the children. My mother studied piano with a White Russian émigré. A Jeep and driver waited at my grandfather's disposal. Army guards stood at attention by the compound gates. They even followed my mother and her brother to the park where the children went skating. My grandmother feared that someone would try to kidnap the boy, her only son. If my mother went to the park by herself, no guard would go along. A girl held no value.

All of that changed after my grandfather's death. The Jeep and driver disappeared along with the summer home, the piano lessons, the army guards, and many of the servants. Now when the children went to the park, one of their mother's brothers would take them. The only thing that did not change was my uncle's position in the family as the oldest child and only son. If anything, my grandmother increasingly pinned her hopes on his success.

One day in October of the same year, my uncle came home from school to find his mother waiting for him. My mother was in another room, but she could hear the sounds of an argument. And then there was a loud noise and then screaming.

When my uncle had gone into the room where his mother was, she had begun to reprimand him for getting poor marks. She wanted him to switch schools and study harder. The scolding had escalated into a fight. They say that my uncle always carried a revolver with him. It had belonged to his father. Suddenly, he drew it from the heavy cotton jacket that he had put on that morning for protection from the autumn chill.

"Stop," he said, "or I'm going to shoot myself."

I don't know if my grandmother did not believe him or if she reached for the gun too quickly or not quickly enough or if my uncle simply felt he had to carry out his threat or he would lose face. At the age of thirteen, face means everything. But in an instant, before his mother could stop him, he had stuck the gun in his mouth and pulled the trigger before her horrified gaze. My grandmother never once mentioned the incident after it happened. My mother heard the news from a servant.

The day at the train station, five months earlier, came back to her. She remembered the mysterious tugging on her shoulders.

"I think," she told me, years later, "it was my father lifting me up, telling me that I was going to be the oldest in the family." Or what was left of it. A younger sister had already died of food poisoning some years before. Now only my mother and two other little sisters remained.

I was many months into my book research before she mentioned this story. She had never even told me before about her brother's existence. My sister had told me. Once, as a teenager, I had asked my mother outright if she had once had an older brother.

"No," she had said, shaking her head and feigning confusion. "No, I didn't."

This time, she let the information slip in her typically casual way; but as she spoke, her face grew more expressive. She told me about how the newspapers had circulated stories about her brother after his death, how they had reported on his good looks and popularity, on how his classmates would miss him. They had written that he had killed himself out of grief over his heroic father's death. At this last, her voice grew heavy with feeling, the first time I detected such a note thus far in our conversations, but it was not the emotion I expected.

"He was spoiled," she said. "He always got everything he wanted. Then the papers say he killed himself because he's sad about our father? That's not true. I know. He killed himself because of bad grades."

For a moment, I could not place her tone. Then I realized, with a start, that she was disgusted. What seemed so obvious and so sad to me, raised as I was on an American diet of talk shows and psychobabble—that her brother had killed himself from pressure and grief, that the argument over grades was only the catalyst, not the reason—seemed merely pathetic to my mother. She needed to despise her brother for his weakness, needed for all these years to believe that he had committed suicide over something so trivial as a report card. If this was the case, then her brother was abnormally fragile, incapable of survival under any circumstances. If this were not so, then she would have had to confront the fact that she did not live under just any circumstances but under inconceivable ones. Time and again she would face tragedy without flinching because she had convinced herself that tragedy was normal.

The year following my grandfather's death marked a turning point, not just in my mother's life but in China's history. The chaos at home matched the chaos outside. By the time of my uncle's death in the fall of 1947, the Communists controlled virtually the entire northeast countryside from Manchuria to Shandong while the Kuomintang clung to their power in the cities. Inflation swept the nation and destroyed fortunes in single strokes. Families who relied on a fixed income or kept their savings in paper money were ruined. By the end of one six-month period in 1948, prices were 85,000 times higher than they had been at the beginning. In Shanghai, a bottle of Coca-Cola cost 250,000 yuan, which worked out to about $83 U.S. That was if one changed money at the black-market rate of 3,000 yuan to one dollar. The finance minister T. V. Soong, brother of Sun Yat-sen's widow and Madame Chiang Kai-shek, used his power to change money at the official rate of 20 yuan to one U.S. dollar and then resold the dollars on the black market, using the profits to buy gold. Ordinary citizens did not have that option. They simply carried around unwieldy bundles of paper currency. Transportation authorities had to put a weight limit of forty pounds on the amount of money travelers could carry on board. People carted their bills around in wheelbarrows just to do the morning shopping. When they returned home, the wheelbarrows would be empty—unless, of course, there was nothing to buy. Often there was not. Shopkeepers hoarded their goods rather than sell them for paper money, the value of which lessened with each passing hour.

Unlike many others, the families of the women in this book did not go hungry. Their special status protected them from the worst. Even my mother's fatherless family owned gold, ensuring that they would have a place to sleep and rice to eat. But the relative wealth and privilege of these people did not protect them from the violence that daily threatened to crash in on them. If anything, they were even more vulnerable, because they were marked. They were families whose members either worked directly for the Kuomintang or at least supported them. They lived off money gained, more likely than not, from Kuomintang corruption. Not surprisingly, they feared that when the Communists came, they would come for them. They fled ever southward, looking for refuge. Each family's story is different but somehow still the same. Fear, flight, desperation, confusion mark them all.

In April of 1948, Luoyang, the city of my mother's birth, fell to the Red Army. May saw the almost certain defeat of Chiang in Manchuria. My mother's family moved constantly that year, ever southward in search of a haven. The first airplane flight my mother ever took was from Beijing to Nanjing. She came down with cholera that summer and spent three months in a hospital. She was the youngest in a ward of twenty patients. One night, she woke up screaming: a rat had chewed through the mosquito netting which covered her bed. Outside, the Communists continued to grow in strength and number. By the end of that long summer, they had a complete stranglehold on the areas surrounding the Nationalist-held cities. It was only a matter of time before the cities fell too.

Inflation continued to skyrocket. The price of a seventy-one-pound sack of rice, according to historian Jonathan Spence's book *The Search for Modern China*, rose from 6.7 million yuan in early June to 63 million yuan in August. A forty-nine-pound bag of flour went from 1.95 million yuan to 21.8 million yuan, and a twenty-two-gallon drum of cooking oil soared from 18.5 million yuan to 190 million yuan. In the summer of 1937, these prices had stood at 12, 42, and 22 yuan respectively. Discontent with and distrust of Chiang's regime grew almost as rapidly as inflation. In July of 1948, five thousand students marched on the residence of the president of the municipal council in Beijing to protest the government's indifference to refugee conditions. Troops fired at the demonstrators, killing fourteen students and wounding over one hundred others. The cracks had appeared long before. The foundations had already started to shift. The social order was crumbling into dust.

The autumn proved even worse. My mother's family fled to Fuzhou, where my grandmother's sister lived with her husband and children. My great-aunt behaved like a character out of Dickens toward her sister and her sister's children, treating them like unwanted orphans. Without a husband to protect her and give her status, my grandmother was at the mercy of others. In her sister's household, she and her three girls were not quite servants, but they were not family either.

Outside, the cities had begun to fall: Jinan, Mukden, Changchun. In December of 1948, French photographer Henri Cartier-Bresson took his famous photograph of panicked people crushing against each other in line at a bank in Shanghai, desperate to change their money before it depreciated any further. In Fuzhou, my mother paid her school tuition in rice because the administration refused to take paper currency. The Communists captured Tianjin in the first weeks of the new year. And on January 31, 1949, the Red Army entered the walled city of Beijing, ancient seat of China's emperors. By now, my grandmother, her sister, and her brother-in-law were making preparations to leave along with masses of other Kuomintang loyalists. Overcrowded trains arrived daily from northern cities bearing refugees, many of whom sat on the roofs of the cars because there was no room inside. Only the very lucky had the resources to escape abroad.

My grandmother's two younger brothers were living in Shanghai with their mother, the tiny-footed opium smoker. The brothers were young men who, like so many other youths, had lost faith in the Kuomintang. Although they had lived in my grandmother's household since she was first married, they decided not to leave China with the rest of the family. My great-grandmother chose to stay with them. According to Confucian tradition, sons look after their parents in old age. One brother agreed to meet the family in Fuzhou, sail to Taiwan with them, and then return to Shanghai. At the time my mother did not expect that she would never see her other uncle or her grandmother again. But that is what happened. Nor did she predict that she would see the uncle who accompanied them across the strait so soon after he left them in Taiwan. But that, too, is what happened.

They set sail in March on a boat that carried just four families. Traveling with them were my grandfather's Japanese concubine and her baby son, my mother's half-brother, who had been born after my grandfather's death. The trip lasted three days. The boat was so small and the waters so rough that the passengers threw up the entire way. My great-aunt feared that they would sink. At the end of the voyage, my grandmother stepped off the boat and vowed that she would never travel again.

"I will die in Taiwan," she said.

Shortly afterwards, the Communists took the Kuomintang capital of Nanjing. In May, they captured Shanghai. Xian, Lanzhou, and Changsha fell in August. In October, Mao declared the founding of the People's Republic of China from the Gate of Heavenly Peace in front of the Forbidden City in Beijing. His army had rolled like a cartoon snowball from the top of China to the bottom, gathering speed and strength as it went. It had crushed some in its path and collected others—peasants, ex–Kuomintang backers, and the indifferent—into its giant mass. Ahead of it ran Chiang Kai-shek and his ever-smaller band of supporters. It looked certain that the snowball would crush them too. But on December 8, Chiang fled across the Strait of Taiwan with the ragged remains of his army and government, and in a classic cartoon ending, the snowball stopped short at the water's edge. Behind it lay a gaping wound of a country. Before it, a leaf-shaped smear, an island that had never even been a nation in its own right, waited 150 miles away.

Like that, childhood had vanished: the oranges tucked under my mother's pillow every New Year, the tennis court on the grounds of Suzanne's grandfather's estate, the plump and ancient amah who would care for Dolores while her mother was away on business, the sisters in Margaret's family who were shipped by ones and twos farther and farther south to safety. But like the frogs in Wen Yi-to's poem "Dead Water," the girls had managed to survive in spite of the waste and destruction around them. They remained the privileged ones. Wen, a leading poet, intellectual, and activist of the earlier republican movement, had himself died in 1944, shot down in the street for daring to criticize the increasing authoritarianism of the Kuomintang. In the time since, still greater devastation had occurred. An era had ended, to be followed by one of an even harsher regime, one of the worst the world has ever known. For the next quarter century, no song would rise from the dead water of China's mainland— only from those frogs who had managed to leave. These lucky few numbered a scant two million; people with the means and connections to fashion an escape. For those who remained behind, life was only to get worse. For themselves, they hoped, life could only get better.

EXILE

The refugees arrived in Taipei like conquerors rather than the conquered. Taiwan had been a Japanese colony for the past fifty years, and after the end of World War II, its natives were treated like enemy collaborators. Anything worthwhile that the Japanese had accomplished on the island—from building a prosperous sugar-cane industry to offering quality elementary-school education to all—was rapidly undone by Nationalist forces in the first years after the war. The army ruled like despots. They seized property and possessions for personal gain. An officer who hit someone with his Jeep would curse the hapless victim for denting the fender. In February of 1947, government troops gunned down a group of Taiwanese protesters, unleashing a campaign of violence against locals that lasted several days and killed as many as ten thousand.

This was the scene when mainlanders began arriving by the hundreds of thousands in 1948 and 1949. They, who had never regarded Taiwan as anything but a resort, at best, and a Japanese colony, at worst, now found it to be their new home. The entire island contained just ten million people. Taipei, the largest city, had 455,000. Fifty-two percent of the population made their living by farming, but they only managed to produce enough rice to satisfy one-fourth of the island's minimum needs. The gross national product stood at less than four hundred million American dollars, or forty dollars a head. As late as 1949, it was still possible to contract smallpox and the bubonic plague. Indoor plumbing remained a novelty.

Most of the mainland remained backward as well, but the people who came from there to Taiwan were far from typical. They had lived in cities like Beijing and Shanghai. Many of them had studied abroad. They belonged to a group who had headed universities and engineered the restoration of the Burma Road with General Stilwell. They had commanded armies and were hailed in *Life* magazine for their military victories. They had been government advisors and cabinet ministers. With the exception of the handful who managed to go to the United States, the two million who landed in Taiwan represented the elite of China, a country of over five hundred million people. To them, well-educated and once powerful, Taiwan offered no prospects for the future.

They tried to convince themselves that all was as it had been. They ignored the Taiwanese, who, wisely, after a half-century of colonization and two years of brutality, tried to behave as submissively and unobtrusively as possible. The loudest noise they seemed to make was click-clacking down the streets in their Japanese-style wooden shoes. For the most part, they lived in different neighborhoods and went to different schools. The Kuomintang made Mandarin the official language. The mainlanders may have left China, but they were determined not to let China leave them.

"The people who left mainland China," Peter Kwong, a leading scholar in the field of Asian-American studies, told me, "were a very homogenous group—high government officials, military people, relatively successful businesspeople. The very rich went to the U.S., Hong Kong, even to Park Avenue in some cases. But the people who went to Taiwan, they were important enough, vulnerable enough to have to leave but not rich enough or smart enough to get to America."

None of them thought Taiwan was forever. Even today, Taipei is referred to as the provisional seat of the government of the republic, a definition that suggests that one day a permanent government will be reinstated in Nanjing. For years, senators in the

Taiwanese congress participated in the fiction that they still represented their home provinces, places like Sichuan, Hubei, and Hunan where Mao and his minions had long held absolute sway. Some of my parents' friends still blanch when I refer to the island as "Taiwan." "China," they correct me. What I think of as China is "the mainland" to them or, on occasion, "Communist China." Even if they no longer believe the Kuomintang will vanquish the Communists, they refuse to acknowledge their disillusion publicly. They will neither cede China nor give Taiwan its own identity. To do so would be to admit to wasting half a century on an impossible dream.

"Taiwan was a way station," the professor, who had briefly stopped there on his own journey to the United States, said to me.

At first it seemed a way station en route to a Nationalist victory on the mainland. As time passed, it became a way station on the road to a better life. The two million people who had fled to the island shared one goal: to leave. With the possibility of returning to China looking ever dimmer, they turned to America for hope.

More specifically, they turned to their children and to the only way they knew how to succeed: through education. Not only was this group steeped in the Confucian ideals of learning, but also, in the days before the immigration reforms of 1965, practically the only way for a Chinese to gain entry to the United States was as a student. It was to this end that parents pushed their children to succeed academically.

In those years, only about 3 percent of the secondary-school population went on to institutes of higher learning. In total, there were 6,665 students and seven institutes of higher learning, four of which concentrated solely on research. This meant there were only 1,666 students per class year spread among four colleges. The largest and best, and the only university in this group, was Taiwan National University, known to all as Tai Da. Going to Tai Da practically paved the way for graduate study in the States. Of the students there, a disproportionate percentage were graduates of my mother's high school, called simply the First Girls' School because it was the best girls' school in the city, and by extension, the country. Informally, it was known as Beiyinyu. People have likened it to Eton in England, a comparison that is both hyperbole and understatement, but one that will have to suffice. Unlike Eton, Beiyinyu is state-run. When my mother was a teenager, no private schools even existed at the time, which meant that everyone went into the public school system and that almost every girl wanted to get into Beiyinyu. Dolores, Margaret, Suzanne, and my mother were no exceptions.

One classmate of theirs told me that 90 percent of their graduating class had received scholarships to Tai Da and that more than 90 percent had passed a test administered to students who wished to attend college abroad. The school loomed as such an important force in their lives, the students even had a term for it. "We call it the narrow gate," the same classmate explained. "*Zai men.* Everybody go through the same channel, you see. Once you're in the good high school, you know you have more opportunity than the regular. It's a narrow gate. Not everybody can get into there, so when you get there, it seems like an easier path for you to go. Once you're in there, you're safe. You go to college or you go abroad. The main goal is go to United States."

Girls had to attend cram school just to get into Beiyinyu. The summer after my mother arrived in Taipei, she went to cram school every day to prepare for the entrance exams. To her surprise, she ran into some of the girls she had known on the mainland. In those final frantic months before the exodus, children had simply disappeared from classrooms with no explanation. Each day had brought still more absences. And every vacant seat was like another hole in the tattered fabric of my mother's childhood. Finding old schoolmates safe in Taipei brought a measure of relief, proof that some of those rips could still be mended.

By then, my grandmother had bought a Japanese-style house, a legacy of Taiwan's recent past. The family slept on the floor on tatami mats as if on an extended holiday. A sense of normalcy began to return to my mother's home. The concubine became my grandmother's best friend. They hired a maid. They shopped in the stores. The children played games and went to the movies. The clock of everyday life resumed ticking.

My mother worked all summer long to pass the entrance exams. In the evenings, my grandmother would shush the younger children to keep them quiet. When my mother finished her work every day, my grandmother made sure to give her a special treat, a piece of candy or a pastry. This was in a country where Hershey bars represented indescribable luxury. On the day of the entrance exams, my mother woke to a hot, humid summer morning. Breakfast consisted of a bowl of soupy rice and leftovers from the day before. Her mother, her father's concubine, whom she called "Auntie," her two younger sisters, and her half-brother gathered around her to wish her luck and wave goodbye. It was a patchwork quilt of a family that had been made up of odds and ends, but together it formed a beautiful pattern. My mother mounted her bicycle and rode to a nearby school, where she spent the morning answering questions about literature, history, geography, math, and science. All across the city, girls were taking the same test at the same moment.

The next week my mother pedaled back to the school to see the results of the exams, which were written on long streamers and posted at the entry. Each person's name was listed along with her score and the school she had gotten into, long stark lines in black and white, dictating one's fate: First Girls' School, Second Girls', and so on. If a girl did not get into the First or Second school, it hardly mattered where she went.

My mother jostled her way through the crowd of other girls who were anxiously trying to find their names on the lists. She gave a little cry when she saw her name and covered her mouth in surprise. Not only had she gotten into the First Girls' School, but she had made it into the first section of five; the one reserved for students who had achieved the highest scores. Girls standing around her clapped in delight when they found their own names. Some smiled quietly to themselves. But other girls pretended that the bright sunlight hurt their eyes. They shielded their faces with their hands and turned away. Nearby, two friends stood, one with an arm around the other's shoulder. My mother witnessed this all, but the scene barely registered. She biked home quickly, ignoring the hot sun as it beat down on her hatless head. She could hardly wait until school started. She could hardly wait to tell her mother the news. For the first time in a long time, she felt hopeful. The year ahead held promise instead of fear. How wrong she would be.

THE NARROW GATE

In the China the girls had come from, life had revolved around the village, as it had for millennia. There, every family had its place, and every family member his or hers. It was a system that had both sustained and restrained the country. It promoted a strong social structure yet subjugated the individual. Harmony, rather than progress, prevailed.

Beiyinyu girls were already one or more steps removed from this ancient way of life. Their grandparents' generation had overthrown the imperial dynasty. Their parents had studied in the West and returned infused with a hodgepodge of radical ideas from Voltaire to Freud. The girls hoped to study abroad themselves one day. One might think that the Ministry of Education, staffed as it was with returned scholars—including, by then, Suzanne's own father—would seek to incorporate Western styles of teaching in their best schools.

Instead, Beiyinyu, which had been founded by the Japanese to educate their own daughters, remained inflexibly traditional. Western curricula, particularly in the sciences, were pragmatically introduced, but the teaching methods and many of the other courses came straight from those for the Imperial Exams. Girls learned by rote instead of by thinking. They obeyed their teachers absolutely. In this way, the school was almost a throwback to that earlier age. Like the ancient cities of Xian and Beijing, it was even self-contained, surrounded by a high gray wall, its chalky yellow buildings rising fortresslike from behind. Hard by the Presidential Palace and the National Assembly, the school was located right in the center of Taipei; but inside the serene sanctity of its confines, the bustle of the city seemed far away. Beiyinyu became a village of sorts for its students, who, raised in war and chaos, turned to its reassuring stability with relief. At the school, as in the villages of old China, everyone and everything had a proper place. Some of the girls, among them Suzanne, would rebel against such strictures; but most, like Margaret, simply accepted them as a matter of course. For my mother, the school's very constancy would prove her salvation.

Three months into my mother's first year at Beiyinyu, my grandmother died. She had been battling uterine cancer since the family had lived in Beijing. At that time, she had spent many months in a hospital in Shanghai undergoing a cure. The doctors had proclaimed her to be well. In Taipei, when the cancer recurred, she went to a public hospital, where she was misdiagnosed and sent home with many reassurances that whatever it was she had, it was not serious. She had resisted seeking superior private care for a long time, mindful of the straitened circumstances in which the family now lived. She still had a small fortune in gold, but that she was saving for her children. When she finally checked into a private hospital, the doctors told her it was too late.

She lingered in the hospital for a month or more. My mother saw her only once during that time.

"I wanted to go see her," my mother told me many years later. "My aunt kept me away."

When she told me this, we were sitting in a McDonald's on Fordham Road in the Bronx waiting for a garage to finish servicing her car. I was drinking coffee. She was eating a biscuit and eggs. Around us, people sat alone or in pairs. An old man read one of the daily tabloids, not pausing to look up as he bit into his Egg McMuffin. It was a bright, windy fall day, and people walked by on the street outside with their hair streaming behind them, eyes focused straight ahead. My mother's eyes had the same intensity. I felt her looking not at me but through me.

Her mother had become very religious since the death of her son and had started going to a modest Presbyterian church near their home. One day, a woman from the church came running up to the house.

"You better go to the hospital," the woman told my mother. "Right now."

When my mother arrived, my grandmother spoke to her briefly.

"Write to your uncle," she instructed her daughter. "He will come take care of you."

Then she told her about the store of gold she had saved. At this point, accounts of the story diverge. My mother claims that her mother left the money with her sister, my mother's aunt, for safe-keeping. Whenever the children needed money, my mother was to go to her aunt to ask for it. My aunt, one of my mother's sisters, insists that my grandmother left the money at her church and that their aunt later stole it. The truth may never be known, but these two versions are important because of what happened later.

When my grandmother was done speaking, she closed her eyes. Not long after, the words she had spoken on leaving the boat from the mainland nine months before came true. She died in Taiwan.

Tears welled in my mother's eyes, and the woman from the church turned to her.

"You should be happy for your mother," she said. "She doesn't have to suffer anymore."

As I listened to my mother's story forty-five years later, I wondered how I would have reacted in the same situation. I asked her what she had done.

"So," my mother said to me matter-of-factly, "I stopped crying."

She was thirteen years old when her mother died, and she became an orphan with three younger siblings to look after. At that age, the thing I wanted most in the world was cable TV. My mother cannot understand me. I cannot understand her. In the McDonald's, we sat across a plastic table from each other, not even touching. I pushed my coffee cup toward her eggs, wanting something to connect between us. At thirteen, she had already learned to expect only the worst from life. At thirteen, I had thought the greatest tragedy was losing a contact lens.

She could not describe the hospital to me or even what her mother had looked like as she lay dying. The most vivid memory she retained of the event was the moment when the church friend had come for her.

"I was in the yard," she said. "Rake the leaves."

It was the sound of bare twigs scratching against hard dirt that she remembered. The simple chore. The tidy lawn. The refreshing breeze of the late fall air. The soothing pleasure of creating order out of disorder. She could spend a lifetime raking the leaves of every tree in the world and tying them all into neat bundles, but she would never know that feeling again.

My mother wrote to her uncle, and he agreed to come. The Communists were beginning to tighten controls at the border, but he managed to slip out and get passage on a small boat. He arrived in Taiwan not even a year since he had been there last to wave goodbye to his sisters and their families. My mother could not contain her happiness and excitement. She told her friends at school.

"She was really looking forward to that," a classmate remembered. "She told me her uncle is coming from China, would come and take care of them."

Instead, the blows continued to fall. A few days after her uncle's arrival, my mother came home from school to find him missing. The maid told her the news. The police had come to the house and arrested him for being a Communist spy. In those days, the level of paranoia in Taiwan surpassed that created by McCarthyism in the United States. Another relative of my mother's was a famous Nationalist general who had been captured by the Communists near the end of the civil war. His family managed to flee to Taiwan, but for decades to come, the government refused to allow them to leave the country in order to guarantee General Tu's silence from his prison cell in Red China. If such a fate could befall the family of a war hero, then anyone was suspect in those precarious times. My mother says that neighbors reported her uncle to the police simply because he had come from the mainland.

Shortly after the arrest, my grandfather's concubine married and left the family and her own son behind.

"We didn't go to the wedding," my mother told me. "We were so mad at her. 'How could you do this to us? My mother just died, and you go off.' "

A different account also exists to explain what happened. According to my aunt, the older of my mother's two younger sisters, the concubine had wanted to stay. My grandmother's sister had forced the concubine to marry and leave her boy behind. And more likely than not, my aunt believed, my grandmother's sister had also reported her own brother to the police. The way my aunt tells it, my great-aunt operated from one motive only: greed.

"Before my mother died," my aunt said to me, "she bring all the money—all the gold bars—put in the church, give to those ministers, tell them to hold it until she coming back. She didn't know she was going to die. My father's concubine told me they put it in a trunk and had it sealed. After my mother died, my aunt has the right to take it back if my father's concubine is no longer live there. That's why they want her to leave."

Whether or not their aunt was responsible for the fates of their uncle and their father's concubine, my mother and her sister agree on one thing: their mother had not wanted them to live with her sister.

"She did not trust her," my mother said with typical understatement.

My aunt revealed much more.

"After my mother died," she told me, "the first time I saw my aunt was just before New Year's. I was playing with my neighbor's kids, and she came in. First she slapped my face. She said, 'Your mother, why did she do this? Why she died? Why she left all of you?' Then she go in and grab all my mother's makeup that we brought from Hong Kong. And also I remember that time my mother had a Waterford crystal fruit bowl. It was ten U.S. dollars. At that time, you buy a house for thirteen dollars, and that was a crystal bowl. My aunt took it. Packed all those things and left."

My mother had already learned to expect the worst from life. Now she discovered that she could trust no one—not her neighbors, not her father's concubine, not even her mother's sister. To this day she doubts everyone else's motives, including those of her own family. Betrayal has covered her heart in scar tissue and scabs. Paradoxically, almost perversely, as mistrustful as she is, she remains open and giving. Like a child, she cannot resist picking open her wounds to reveal the flesh underneath. And each time she does so, it seems as if someone else is waiting to take advantage of her vulnerability.

Her uncle stayed in jail for a year. During that time, my mother tried to run the household. Every month she went to her aunt's for gold, which she would then trade on the black market for cash. She hated going to her aunt's and would sometimes send the older of her two younger sisters instead. On those days, my aunt used to walk around the neighborhood for hours and return to the house with some excuse—the aunt wasn't home; she had refused to give her any money—in order to avoid going. My aunt told me that often they did not have enough to eat. One day, she said, the maid quit, saying, "I cannot come to your house anymore. There's no food for me to cook." But my mother denies that they went hungry.

"We were poor," she said, "but not starving."

The truth of these stories may never come to light. But even with enough food, there was plenty else to worry about. The faucet in their house dripped constantly. My mother did not know how to fix it. The drip ran up an enormous water bill. When my mother went to the water company to complain, no one would listen. She was a young girl, barely into her teens. The rest of the world had no time for her.

Her grades suffered. She who had scored so well on the entrance examinations, sank to the bottom of the class.

"After my mother died," she told me, "my schoolwork was just terrible. I fell apart."

In spite of that, she loved school. Beiyinyu let her live the life of an ordinary girl every day, six days a week. She would wake

up in the morning and put on her uniform, which consisted of
a black, pleated skirt and white blouse. During her third year,
the white shirt changed to dark green when Chiang Kai-shek
himself decreed that the white made the girls too easy a target
for enemy bombers. My mother's friends would come to meet
her, and they would ride their bikes to school. Together, they
saluted the flag and sang the national anthem every morning,
standing in the grassy expanse of the athletic field. My mother
took tests and practiced calligraphy. She studied the Chinese
classics and puzzled out geometry. She learned how to swim.
Even military instruction class, which all the students derided
because it was dull, unimportant, and proved to be an exercise
in brainwashing, provided her with reassurance. While the
teacher droned on about Sun Yat-sen's three principles, my
mother rolled her eyes with boredom and passed notes to her
friends. In the classroom, she became just another naughty
schoolgirl who was so carefree she did not even bother to pay
attention to the lecture at hand.

Lunch was her favorite period. The students ate at their desks
out of tin boxes they had brought to school that morning. They
usually contained leftovers from the evening before, and when
the students arrived, they would put their boxes into large net
bags, which two of the girls would carry to the kitchen. At noon,
the girls would go back to the kitchen to pick up the bags, which
had been thrown into giant steamers to heat the food inside. The
students would identify their boxes by the names written on
them in white paint and pull them out of the bag. Then the excitement began. The girls could only wander around the classroom at lunchtime, and wander they did. My mother, who
inevitably had the worst food, went from friend to friend, pok-
ing her nose into their lunches and wheedling a taste here and
there. Decades later, she remembered those meals with a rarely
displayed level of emotion. She smiled. Her voice rose enthusiastically. When she mentioned old classmates, the relative merits of
their lunchboxes were never far from the top in their list of dis-
tinguishing characteristics. "She had a good lunch," she might
say, sighing over the memory of roast chicken or *hong xiao* pork.
The lunches she remembered most fondly were the ones that ar-

rived, piping hot, at the school just as the students were about to eat.

"Some have maids to bring their lunch at lunchtime," she told me. "One had a really good lunch. Her maid would bring layers and layers of boxes all stacked up."

The midday meal popped up often in the minds of the classmates I talked to. People who could not remember what classes they took or what their teachers' names were remembered other students' tin boxes with a level of detail that defied the forty years that had passed since graduation. "She always had four ounces of meat," one woman sighed wistfully as she described a friend's lunch. "And two hard-boiled eggs. That was just . . ." Her voice trailed off, as if such luxury were impossible to describe. Another lucky girl had uncles who lived in Hong Kong. They sent her bars of chocolate, which she generously shared with her friends. Forty years later, coming across the girl's name on the list of alumnae brought a smile to my mother's face.

"Oh," she said, "Veronica was always so nice to me. She always gives me chocolate."

My mother cobbled a family life for herself out of such simple gestures. In the sharing of a friend's lunch she could taste the warmth and security of a home in which two adults lived, nourishing food appeared at dinner, and a young girl only had school marks to worry about. My mother began spending more and more time with her friends. She ate dinner with their families and hung around their houses on the weekends. They saw movies together on Saturdays and rode their bikes to the park. When my mother walked arm-in-arm with her Beiyinyu friends, dressed in their school uniforms, and saw the admiring, envious glances passersby shot their way, she felt as though she belonged somewhere. Nothing distinguished her from the other girls with their regulation-length bobs, white socks, and tennis shoes. No one could tell that she was anything but a well-scrubbed, fresh-faced student at the best girls' school in the country. No one would guess that she was an orphan with three younger siblings at home, an uncle in jail, and an aunt straight out of a Grimm Brothers fairy tale. When she stepped within the iron gates that closed the school off from the rest of the world, my mother stepped outside of reality.

When she returned home, the problems came raining down. She felt guilty because she spent so little time with her family. My aunt claims that she and the youngest sister had to forage in garbage cans for food to eat. She thinks my mother spent their money on movie tickets and other outings with her friends. My mother says there was always enough money for both. But I sense that even if there was enough money and food at home, my mother made little effort to replace her mother in the lives of her younger siblings. She survived in whatever way she knew how. She let her sisters and her half-brother do the same. I do not know if this is the truth. I only know that no thirteen-year-old girl should ever have to find herself in that position.

The next year, her uncle was released from jail and, according to my mother, the situation improved. Small moments of pleasure illuminated her world. My aunt remembers an outing their uncle took them on to celebrate one of my mother's birthdays. Several of her Beiyinyu friends joined them. They took a train to the nearby mountains and ate a picnic lunch. Photos survive of that day. They show her friends smiling, their faces turned to the sun. They show my mother sitting in a field of tall grass, laughing.

"Oh," my aunt said to me, remembering that day, "your mother was so happy."

Then she added, surprisingly to me, "It was the happiest day for me too."

That was how little they had had growing up.

One of my mother's principal strengths lay and still lies in her ability to connect with all people. It is a mechanism for survival that has served her well. Others have told me that my mother ran with a fast crowd—the social leaders, the girls who had money, the ones who even had the temerity to attend the occasional dance party. The class president was one of her best friends. But, as my mother put it, "I was just friendly whoever wants to be friendly with me." At the time, those people included most everyone she came into contact with, including Dolores, Suzanne, and, to a much lesser extent, Margaret. If in high school my mother was not best friends with Dolores and Suzanne and barely even knew Margaret, some measure of her warm spirit would shine through in her encounters with them. They would meet her again at different points in their lives and recognize that same spirit like a slender but strong thread connecting them to their own past.

Beiyinyu was divided into two parts: junior high and senior high. Each lasted for three years, and students stayed in the same section for all three. At the end of junior high, they took another entrance examination along with all the other girls in the city to see if they could get into the senior high. There were coeducational junior high schools that equaled Beiyinyu in academic stature, but all education was single-sex in high school. At that level, Beiyinyu indisputably provided the best education a girl could receive in Taiwan. According to my mother, some sort of miracle occurred when she took the entrance exams for the senior high. She passed, although her grades had plunged and she rarely studied.

When she entered high school, she was assigned to the same section as Dolores. Dolores claimed to me later that it had also been a miracle that she had managed to pass the entrance exams. Like my mother, she had spent much of the previous three years just scraping by. But Dolores had a mother, and my mother did not. What is more, Dolores had a mother who was good friends with the school principal, who warned her in advance about her daughter's performance.

After a conversation in which her friend told her that Dolores might not pass the senior-high exam, Dolores's mother tested her daughter. She asked a geography question. Dolores could not answer. She asked her a history question. Again she received no response. Dolores's mother grew irate. Every girl in Taipei wanted to go to Beiyinyu, and her daughter looked as if she was about to fail out. To pass the exams, Dolores would need to know not only geography and history but also math, science, and Chinese. At the moment, it appeared that she knew nothing.

"You will not leave the house," her mother commanded, "until you're ready for the exams."

Dolores did nothing for three weeks but study. Her mother's vigilance paid off in the end. Dolores managed to pass. Looking back, she might have thought the exertion hardly warranted. Half a year later, she would be in America.

The classrooms at Beiyinyu were long and narrow. The teacher stood at the far end in front of a blackboard mounted on the wall. Rows and rows of wooden desks stretched from this starting point back past the windows, with their many diversions, toward the door, which held the promise of escape. The air in Taiwan feels like a steaming towel. A room of fifty teenagers quickly grows as close and oppressive as a non-air-conditioned subway car in August. In those conditions, with sunlight bathing her head, a girl could easily fall asleep if she sat tucked into the back of the room, out of the teacher's direct line of vision.

A student's height dictated where she sat. The taller girls perched in the back, the shorter ones in the front. Ways existed to circumvent the system, and students employed them often. But where in an American school every pupil would clamor to sit at the back, at Beiyinyu everyone wanted to sit in the front. Decades later, my mother, who was one of the taller students, still complained about the injustice of the situation.

"Some girls," she said indignantly, "pretend they can't see. They say they have to sit in the front. It's not true. They can see. They just want to be near the teacher."

The ones in front heard the lessons more clearly. The teacher called on them more often. Not surprisingly, the shorter girls at Beiyinyu seemed always to be the smarter ones.

Dolores sat in the back with my mother. By virtue of their placement, they were friends, but not best friends. In fact, they differed in many ways. My mother was a year older than most of the students. Her peripatetic childhood had led to many missed days, sometimes even weeks, of schooling. Standards in China varied widely from place to place. She had attended schools in the hinterlands and schools in the most sophisticated cities and almost always left, as she put it, "right before the final exams." When she arrived in Beijing after World War II, she was held back a grade. It took much prompting on my part to get her to admit to this fact half a century later, and she did so only with great reluctance and shame.

Dolores, in contrast, had skipped two grades and was only ten when she first entered the Beiyinyu junior high, a fact that she related proudly. The first year of senior high, she was thirteen. My mother was sixteen. Not surprisingly, the first word that came to Dolores's mind when describing my mother was "mature."

"I always sensed in school," she said to me, "that your mom is somehow different. She's not as giggly."

Dolores was the opposite. She fairly bubbled over with giggles. She epitomized her nickname, Xiao Mei, Little Younger Sister. She had a round face and a wide smile that charmed everyone. People often treated her like a pet. Her sister was almost a decade older and already studying in the United States, so Dolores was the only child at home. Her mother regarded her like a little grown-up and often took her to dinner parties and other adult gatherings. For years, her mother sent the family maid to school with Dolores's lunch at noontime until, embarrassed, Dolores finally implored her to stop.

My mother slouched around the school halls with her shirttail flopping outside the waistband of her skirt. At Beiyinyu, such an act was tantamount to smoking cigarettes in the bathroom of an American school. Shoes and socks had to be white. Skirts had to hang to the knee. Hair had to be worn above the chin. Perms, jewelry, and makeup were all strictly forbidden. One reckless girl curled her hair during winter break. When she returned to school, a teacher ordered her home. The next day she returned with a marine's crewcut. Some of the wealthier girls tried to edge around the rules by eschewing plain cotton for their uniforms and trying silk. Or they cut their skirts on a bias in imitation of Grace Kelly. But only those with extra money for luxuries could do so, and very few girls of that sort existed. In any case, my mother's nonconformity was dictated not by fashion or vanity but by the opposite. She had no mother at home to press her clothes or remind her to act like a lady. Time and again when I have asked her schoolmates to describe her to me, they have said "She was like a boy."

The pampered darling and the tomboy formed a bond because, in spite of their differences, they shared one defining characteristic: they each faced unusual situations at home. In fact, Dolores's family life, while more stable than my mother's, was actually more scandalous. Her mother and father were divorced. They had been since World War II, when she was still very young. Dolores rarely saw her father. Her mother had raised her alone. Fortunately, Dolores's mother had more resources at her disposal than the average Chinese woman of the era. The government had sent her to Berkeley to study. Study abroad was reserved for the very privileged or the very talented. In 1923, there were only twenty-six hundred Chinese students in the United States and thirty-one hundred in Europe. Few enough young men ever received the opportunity to go abroad. To give the chance to a woman seemed almost irresponsible.

Dolores's mother became a professor and ultimately a legislator in the National Assembly. While growing up, Dolores had known only the privileges the world had to offer and none of the hardships. Her home in Nanjing had bustled with servants. A limousine carried them around the city. Dolores's childhood may have lacked the emotional comfort a father can provide, but it never lacked the material.

Dolores's mother had studied psychology and sociology at Berkeley. Social welfare had been her main area of interest, the care of children in particular. In addition to serving as a senator, she also ran a large orphanage on the outskirts of Taipei. Not surprisingly, she took an interest in my mother and encouraged her own daughter to invite her over for dinner. The two girls grew closer, perhaps each recognizing in the other the crooked seams that imperfectly stitched their torn selves back together. At that age, many of their other classmates still remained whole.

Today Dolores claims that not having a father meant little to her. I once asked her how the others had viewed her parents' divorce, and she tried to toss back an answer with a casual shrug of her shoulders. But something in her indifference seemed studied. As she spoke, her response grew lengthier and more complicated, as though she were trying to rationalize the situation to herself.

"It's funny," she said, "I didn't really feel unusual, because, you see, probably the average Chinese would not divorce, but the people my mom and my dad associate with they're sort of the cream of the crop. How do I say? They belong to the top 10 percent of the country's young people, and most of them studied in the U.S. Some studied in France. Some studied in Germany. Most of them have some education abroad.

"And so," she continued, "many of them have very liberal ideas. Within their circles, divorce is not uncommon, because most of them have very, very liberal ideas, and a lot of them—a lot of my mom's friends—even, they, you know, they joined the revolutionary parade. My mom was jailed, she told me. She went to jail because she was in the revolutionary parade, and Bei Da— you know, the university in Beijing? A lot of her friends, including her, were students of Bei Da, and they were very liberal, very intellectual, and so in their circle, divorce is not something uncommon, and so because of her views, I never thought it was something weird or unacceptable."

Dolores groped toward a conclusion. Her voice remained calm as she spoke, but the sheer length of her explanation belied her nonchalance.

"So," she summed up, a little breathless but still game, "in that sense, you know, uh, I just accepted it."

She laughed nervously, and I nodded, pretending to believe her. I thought about something my father often said to me. His father, my paternal grandfather, had won a scholarship to Qinghua College, a school whose main purpose was to prepare students to study in the United States. He had gone to Harvard in the 1920s. When he became a father, he rejected the centuries-old tradition, based on a poem, that his family used for naming their children. The first character of the poem became the generation name for the first generation, and so on. When the poem ended, the cycle was repeated. That my grandfather eschewed this venerable tradition was a deliberate and shocking act of rebellion against his social class and lineage. Instead, he gave his own children simple, one-character first names. He had espoused such radical views, in fact, that he had opted to live in New York after the war instead of blindly following the Kuomintang to Taiwan, even though he had served as one of Chiang's advisors. He was undoubtedly an intellectual and, relatively speaking, a liberal, the sort of person to whom Dolores was referring when she spoke of her mother's circle. Later on, my grandfather had even insisted that his son attend Oberlin instead of Harvard, which is about as revolutionary as a Chinese parent can get. My father deeply respected my grandfather's opinions and adopted many of his views. I remember one in particular because of the consequences it would have on my own family. "The Chinese," my father liked to state firmly in the midst of proving some point or another, "don't believe in divorce."

As is their wont, the women in my mother's class identify people by the most scandalous gossip attached to their names.

"Hmm," they say when I mention Dolores. They struggle to remember her. Then their faces brighten. "Oh yes," they say triumphantly, "she's the one—her mother's divorced."

Even if, as Dolores stated, divorce was acceptable in certain circles, a woman who was divorced two times would have raised eyebrows in any society, Eastern or Western, in the 1950s.

Dolores had led me to believe that no acrimony existed, that her parents had simply drifted amicably apart in the casual way that modern couples do. I could not reconcile Dolores's version of events with the perception I had of the straitlaced Chinese from her parents' generation. My own grandmothers had died before I was born, but memories of other children's grandmothers flooded my mind. They stooped at the shoulders and shrank with each passing year. They had wispy white hair and smiled ceaselessly at me in an attempt to bridge our language barrier. When that failed to produce the desired effect—often they just wanted a smile in return—they resorted to stuffing me with sweets instead. Xiao Mei, they called me too, and I could not for a moment imagine any of them doing something so upsetting to the balance of family harmony as running away from their husbands. I refused to believe that this generation accepted divorce with such equanimity.

One old classmate remembered visiting Dolores's house in high school. Dolores's father stopped by to see his daughter. He brought a basket of fruit and smiled wide when Dolores appeared at the door. She refused to let him in.

"She closed the door real tight," the woman said, "because she was on her mother's side."

So Dolores had lied to me, or, more charitably, concealed the truth—about the ease with which people divorced in her parents' day. Whether she had done so consciously or not, I did not know. It would not be the last time I would wonder. If nothing else, her studied indifference reminded me of the all-important value of saving face. If her parents' divorce did bother her, she refused to let it show.

Like the other students, Dolores spent most of her time at school. It could hardly be avoided. Classes ran six days a week. Mondays through Fridays, students arrived at the high-walled compound before eight in the morning. Academic subjects lasted until four and sometimes five in the evening. Saturdays were half-days, but after classes, students were required to stay after and clean not only their own classrooms but also the entire school. Each classroom formed a work brigade led by someone, usually one of the better students, who had been elected chair of the cleaning committee. Such positions abounded in the school, obsessed as it was with hierarchy and order. One heady semester, my mother even served as the chair of the entertainment committee. She arranged to play a movie one weekend at school, and the event drew hundreds of paying students. It's the one event she remembers from high school that makes her beam with pride.

The cleaning chair did not have so glamorous a task. If she was particularly ineffective, she even had to shoulder much of the cleaning herself. But usually students pitched in to help. Feelings of pride and competition ran high among the different classrooms, and girls were graded not just on their academic records but on their comportment and appearance, a category that also extended to their rooms. Also, divided among fifty pairs of hands the work did not seem that bad. One girl might be assigned to clean just one window, and clean it she would, outside and in, the panes of glass almost blinding in their brilliance when the sun shone through. The students also polished the red-colored wood railing that ran along the stone stairway and rubbed off the dirt that collected on the mint-green institutional tiles that rose a third of the way up the walls of the hallways. They occasionally even had to clean out the bathrooms, a memory that still makes my mother shudder. Beiyinyu had no toilets, just ceramic-lined holes in the ground—what the French so characteristically refer to as "Turkish toilets," the origin of which the Turks probably attribute to the Greeks. But the toilets at school were even worse than the standard squat variety. Instead of having separate holes in their own individual stalls, the bathrooms contained one long trench, which everyone used and which emptied at only one end.

Aside from cleaning, the students had extracurricular activities to keep them occupied when classes were over. One student remembered staying late into the night to take her turn practicing on the school's lone piano. She claimed she used to walk home alone at one or two in the morning. That was how safe Taipei was back then. There were endless competitions to ascertain which section had the cleanest room, which the most school spirit, which could create the best-looking banner. The students formed committees to tackle these projects too, and the hapless but duly honored chairs stayed after school using pots of sticky paste to glue colored pieces of paper to board. My mother most enjoyed swimming in the school's pool, where the water provided some relief from the constant heat. Beiyinyu even had some athletic teams, the prim appearance of their students notwithstanding. The best of these was basketball.

Dolores played on the basketball team. Nearly every day she had practice, to which she wore voluminous bloomers which hung to the knee. The girls put rubber bands around the bottoms to make the material balloon out even more. Whether the school dictated such modesty or the girls considered the look stylish, I do not know. But I smile at the image of the slight girls in baggy, saggy, bulging bloomers, white cotton tennis shoes, and identical haircuts doing three-man weaves and grapevining up and down the length of the wooden court, which had been polished that morning, no doubt, by one of their number.

Dolores may not have been the team's best player, but she stood out in another way. One of the coaches developed a crush on her. Not only was he ten years older, but also he was a member of the national basketball team and something of a teen idol in Taipei. Years later, my mother told me the story while Dolores giggled in the background. She likened the man to Michael Jordan. Dolores interrupted eagerly.

"All the girls adored him," she said. "He had a big name."

Beiyinyu sits in the center of Taipei. In those days, the national basketball team practiced nearby. They were the closest thing that Taipei schoolchildren, who lived in a country with no film or television industry to speak of, would ever get to a celebrity. In their spare time, girls liked to run across the way to watch the men practice. Rebellious ones did not always wait for moments when they were free but sometimes went instead of attending classes. Dolores rarely did the former and never the latter. She held her coach in awe because of his authority and his fame, but she was too good, too young, and too naive a girl to respond to his advances. When he started writing her letters and following her home from school, she was frightened rather than enchanted.

Not long after, Dolores's mother pulled her out of Beiyinyu, and the two left for North America. Her classmates assumed that Dolores's mother wanted to get her daughter away from the basketball coach. Dolores gave me a different reason. Her mother had enemies in the legislature who were spreading rumors about her, and Dolores's sister was already studying in the States. When the United Nations offered to send Dolores's mother on a trip to Canada to report on the country's social welfare system, she decided to take her younger daughter with her and settle in the States after her work was done.

A few nights before Dolores left, a classmate hosted a goodbye party for her. A dozen or so students, including my mother, gathered at the classmate's home. And then Dolores was gone, the first in her class to emigrate. She did not realize what she was leaving behind. She regretted little, feared less, and anticipated much. The others sighed enviously when they thought of her. Xiao Mei. So pretty, so popular that a famous basketball player had fallen in love with her. Now she was going to live in America. Her life was a romantic adventure. She attracted good fortune like a magnet did metal. Perhaps her friends would follow her one day; but whatever they thought the United States had to offer—the squeaky-clean charm of Doris Day, the sweeping passion of Rhett and Scarlett, Gregory Peck's handsome cleft chin—Dolores would experience it first. She could buy saddle shoes and curl her hair. She could order chocolate ice cream in any restaurant. She could live in a house with a pool. She could drive a Cadillac, star in a movie, marry a millionaire. Their dreams, big and small, were endless and infinitely possible. In a way, it was fitting that Dolores be the first to go. She would turn out to be the biggest dreamer of them all.

Among the girls she left behind was Suzanne, a teammate. Suzanne was also a dreamer. She used to walk the halls with a basketball tucked under her arm and a vacant expression on her face. When the teacher called on her in class, she rarely knew the answer. Instead she would stand with hunched shoulders and blink rapidly like a nocturnal creature woken in daylight. If the question was very hard or the teacher particularly merciless, Suzanne would stick her tongue out nervously and twist her hands as if by rubbing she could magically produce an answer.

Among many of the other girls, she was the source of much gossip and laughter. She had come to Beiyinyu from a junior high school in Hong Kong. She arrived in the middle of the semester still thinking in her native Cantonese and mystified by why she was even in Taipei at all. In 1948, the rest of Suzanne's family had moved to Taiwan from Guangdong, but her parents had sent her to Hong Kong instead. She lived there for three blissful years with her indulgent grandmother, who, in spite of her age and bound feet, had some unusually liberal child-rearing methods by the standards of the day. She encouraged Suzanne to learn Western arts like the piano and ballet. The two went bowling. She let Suzanne, who was not yet a teenager, wear lipstick and face powder. Whenever her granddaughter was sick, she took her to a Western doctor, never to a Chinese one. Ashamed of her malformed feet, she always wore thick socks, even in the most oppressive Hong Kong weather.

At the same time, Suzanne's grandmother held some old-fashioned ideas. Her husband had gone to Canada and made some wise business decisions. By the end of World War II, he was a very rich man. When she could not bear him a son, Suzanne's grandmother found him another wife. She felt it was her duty, even if by doing so she was disinheriting herself from her husband's wealth and property. She accepted her fate. She never complained—not about her hurting feet, not about her ungrateful husband.

"Always give," she once told her granddaughter. "It's better that someone owe us things than we owe anybody."

A good and generous philosophy, the words had a nice ring. But in a culture in which the young deferred to the old, the female to the male, they had a devastating effect on a girl of twelve. Her grandmother's words remained embedded in Suzanne's mind and heart for years, influencing practically every action for better and worse. It is easy to think little of yourself when everyone else appears to think little of you as well. Suzanne never once heard from her parents during the three years that she lived in Hong Kong with her grandmother. She claims she never missed them. She claims, in fact, that she simply forgot about them, the same way that they appeared to forget her. They never wrote her a single letter, not even a postcard.

But they came crashing back into her life as abruptly as they had left it. A man came to Suzanne's home in Hong Kong one day with no advance warning. Standing in the doorway, he broke the news to her.

"Your parents have bought a ticket for you to come to Taiwan," he said. "They sent me over to pick you up. We are leaving."

One imagines that Suzanne's parents had informed her grandmother beforehand, but she had not yet told Suzanne. In any case, neither of them expected someone to simply show up at the door to take Suzanne away that very afternoon. The grandmother left the room with her typical stoicism and immediately began to pack. But after folding the first items of clothing into a camphor-lined steamer trunk, she began to cry.

"You go first," she told Suzanne. "And I'll follow after I take care of the house."

Suzanne accepted the news calmly in the same way that my mother had watched her mother die, in the same way that Dolores had learned that she was moving to America.

"I think I believe her, so I wasn't sad," Suzanne told me. "She says she has a lot of business to take care of in Hong Kong."

She paused for a moment. When she spoke again, I detected a tremble in her voice. In her intonation lay a note of regret, of the hindsight the years had given her.

"But she didn't come for another four or five years," Suzanne said. "By then, I already come to the United States."

That experience set the pattern for years to come. People she loved slipped out of reach. She missed opportunities. She lived in limbo. If the dictates of other people did not always make her happy, at least they saved her from having to make her own decisions.

She settled into her family's home as noiselessly as a leaf slipped between the pages of a book, belonging and yet not. Her siblings all spoke fluent Mandarin, a language that felt strange on her tongue. They excelled in their studies. Suzanne did not. They treated her politely, like a guest.

At school, she fared little better. She received notice only for the things she did not accomplish. She often skipped classes. Her grades always remained at the bottom. Classmates started to gossip. Suzanne's father was an undersecretary of education. Everyone agreed that he had pulled strings to get his daughter into Beiyinyu. It was a farce. The girl could not answer a simple question. The only thing she did well was dribble a basketball.

But that she did with far more talent than most of the girls displayed in their studies. And she did not just dribble. She had uncanny intuition when it came to passing the ball. On offense, she slipped past the defense like a mouse down a hole. She dropped baskets with the aim of a sharpshooter. The few friends she had were almost all on the basketball team. The sport became her identity, her means of expression. It even taught her how to want something.

When she cut classes, it was to watch the national team practice at their stadium nearby. When she deigned to appear in school, it was always with a basketball. Eventually, like Dolores, she attracted the attention of one of the men on the national team. Unlike Dolores, she did not dissuade him. They began to date, and Suzanne added more gossip to her name. Only a handful of girls dated, and it was always without the knowledge of their parents. They even invented code names for their boyfriends so they could talk about them with their friends without other people knowing whom they meant. In a world without drugs, alcohol, or tobacco, dating was the most scandalous road to rebellion a teenage girl could take. The issue was certainly not sex. It was probably not even kissing. The girls were so sheltered that dating consisted mostly of being friends with a boy. If the rare and also illicit opportunity to attend a dancing party arose, the couple might try a demure turn or two. Suzanne's relationship involved simply talking to her boyfriend on the phone while she hid in one of the closets in her home. She claimed that she never even held hands with him.

Even so, dating a boy was enough to bring shame on any parent's head. On top of that were all of Suzanne's other, more minor, but still egregious sins. She constantly misplaced her book bag. She lost her bicycle three times, a particularly extravagant display of absentmindedness. She never did her homework. Suzanne's parents hired her a tutor for every single subject, including history, which was commonly thought to be the easiest of all the classes. Still, she struggled—or, rather, did not struggle enough. She was not stupid. She was simply uninterested. Some of her teachers began telling her in advance what would be on the exam just so she would pass. Even so, she managed to fail math and English, the irony of which probably escaped her years later in America when she married a mathematics professor and became a librarian.

At the time, Suzanne's parents could not foresee such a satisfactory end to their tribulations. Suzanne presented a problem, which might have seemed minor to some parents but was excruciatingly embarrassing for hers. Not only was her father prominent in the government, but her mother prided herself on being the perfect wife and mother. Appearance counted for everything in their household. The children were not even allowed to pick out their own clothes. Instead a tailor came to the house twice a year and laid out bolts of fabric for Suzanne's mother to examine. She chose the ones she wanted and then ordered the clothes for the whole family.

One day, the school principal approached her. "Tell me," she said, "do you play mah-jongg all day long?" The principal's insinuation—that she could not raise her daughter properly because she devoted all her time to the gaming tables—horrified Suzanne's mother. Mah-jongg was not a proper occupation for a lady.

The family lived in a Japanese-style house of the same sort that my grandmother had bought when she first arrived in Taipei.

They were low, with gently pitched roofs and sliding doors. Today, the houses of that type, which still exist, have high walls built around them, but back then they had open yards, and people could look across to their neighbors' homes and wave greetings at passersby. Not Suzanne's house. It had a front gate and a bell just like the *si hu yen* my mother used to live in when she was a child in Beijing. Whenever visitors arrived, a servant would appear to open the gate and usher them in. My mother, who went there a few times during high school, remembered the place as being unnaturally quiet. She always went directly to Suzanne's room instead of sitting about the main rooms the way she would in other friends' houses. In fact, she did not recall ever even seeing any of the other members of the family during her visits.

Suzanne and my mother were friends but not intimates. They shared a bond primarily because they sat at the back of the class, along with their grades. They also both enjoyed cutting school when they could, a notion the more diligent students at the front of the room would never have entertained. That was then. But the tie that would bring them back together years after their brief friendship in high school stemmed from something else entirely. They both understood what it was to be alone, to want help but not to know how to ask for it. In spite of the gossip she generated and the seeming disregard with which she passed through the hallways, Suzanne was actually quite aware of certain situations at school that her classmates never even considered.

Taiwan was a poor country, but the majority of Beiyinyu students, while not rich, came from families who had some money and often prominent positions. Even my orphaned mother had her store of gold and a government subsidy paid to the families of Kuomintang soldiers who had died in battle. She owned a bicycle, something of a luxury to the rest of the islanders. There was not much money, but there was always enough for the basics and even for such simple pleasures as a Saturday matinee, an occasional ride in a pedicab, or a bowl of noodles on the street. But some students had even less money. My mother never poked her nose into their *bien dan* at lunchtime. She knew she would find slimmer pickings than in her own tin box. These students could barely scrape together the money required to buy the cloth for a school uniform. Beiyinyu was a public school, but certain fees came with going there. There were books to buy, a student activity charge to pay, and class outings to go on. Certain students brushed off the trips to the mountains and the beach that each class indulged in at holiday time. They were too busy. Their parents wanted them to stay home. They simply did not want to go. Their classmates thought the last excuse excessively odd, but they accepted it with as much gullibility as the other ones. Not Suzanne. The truth was, those students could not afford to go. More than once, Suzanne stepped in and paid for their trips with her own allowance. She never mentioned doing so to anyone else. I learned of her generous deeds through others who had found out somehow over the years. During high school, no one, not even the girls for whom she was paying, suspected. When I confronted Suzanne with what I had learned, she shrugged me off.

"Yes," she admitted, looking slightly sheepish, "I give some money. It's true. But it's only a little bit."

I imagined my fifteen-year-old self—my extreme narcissism, my lack of empathy. I would not even have possessed the perceptiveness to realize that someone else needed my help unless she asked for it directly. The idea of willingly forgoing pocket money, which represented everything fun—magazines, junk food, concert tickets, train trips to New York—would have struck me as unnecessarily generous. Hardest of all for me to understand was not that Suzanne did so without prompting but that she did so without seeking any credit. This spoke of a sincere heart, the kind I recognized in my own mother. It was this bond, above all, that would ultimately draw the two together. Suzanne recognized it too, maybe as far back as high school, although she probably did not realize it at the time. Instead, she tucked that knowledge into her subconscious, where it would lie dormant for decades. It would resurface at a moment when Suzanne felt more absolutely alone than she had ever felt before—more so, even, than when she lived all those years in that quiet vault of a house in Taipei, more than when her closest sibling died in a devastating car crash, more than her first isolated year in America at a school in Davenport, Iowa. It was then, at that low moment, that Suzanne would call my mother, seeking in her a savior of the kind she herself had once been.

But in high school, they had felt only friendly affection. When Suzanne did not return to Beiyinyu after the summer break, my mother did not question her absence. She assumed correctly, like the rest of the school, that Suzanne had finally failed out. But according to Suzanne, there was more to the story. Her parents had found out about her boyfriend and decided to ship her out of Taipei. Her father had even wanted to deport the boy. Instead, they sent Suzanne to a small Catholic girls' school in Taichung, a city near the island's center. And just as she had gone to Taiwan and to Beiyinyu, Suzanne went without protest. My mother, used to people disappearing with no warning, barely noticed. The two girls met a few years later, shortly before my mother was to come to the States. Ten years would pass before they saw each other again. This time, it would be in America, where, to my mother's astonishment, Suzanne had become the decorous wife of a promising young mathematician and the devoted mother of a bright little boy. The defiant, slack-jawed basketball player had been replaced by a paragon of suburban domesticity. Or so it seemed.

Of the three women—Dolores, Suzanne, and Margaret—Margaret was the only one to graduate from Beiyinyu with my mother. Ironically, she was also the one my mother knew least well. They were not in the same section. They had some friends in common and knew each other well enough to wave in the hallways at school. The relationship ended there. They did not study at one another's homes. They did not eat dinner together. I doubt that even if they had been in the same classroom, they would have become friends. Margaret was a short girl, the kind who sat in front, near the teacher, and got good grades. Yet, many years later, they would come together again, and, observing them, I would think that of the three classmates, Margaret had the most in common with my mother.

Dissimilar as they were at the time, the common thread that connected the lives of many of the girls at Beiyinyu connected theirs as well. Margaret also had an unusual family situation. She lived in Taipei with her mother and three of her sisters. Two of her sisters had already left the family and were studying in England. Her father resided in Hong Kong. It was another variation on the same theme of wartime upheaval that all the girls from the mainland knew so well.

I asked Margaret once if she had ever missed her father during those years. "No," she said bluntly, and then amended her answer. "I guess I never really thought about it. That's just what Chinese families did back then."

What they did was scrape by any way they could. That may seem a disingenuous way to describe a family headed by a husband who held degrees from Oxford and the London School of Economics and a wife who served in the national assembly, but in those days practically everyone struggled. Margaret's family fled to Taiwan in 1948, where her father began working in the timber business. In December of 1949, Chiang Kai-shek and the remnants of his government followed. On New Year's Day, 1950, Margaret's family moved to Hong Kong. The timing was not a coincidence.

During the 1930s, Margaret's father had presided over a university in Manchuria known as Dong Bei Da Xue, of which a man named Chang Hsueh-ling was the official, if nominal, head. Chang Hsueh-ling was more famously known as the Young Marshal, warlord of Manchuria, sworn enemy of the Japanese and the mastermind behind the notorious Xi'an Incident of 1936. It was in this ancient, walled capital that Chang's Manchurian forces collaborated with Communist troops to kidnap Chiang Kai-shek with the intention of forcing him to fight the Japanese. Chang was imprisoned for life for his role in the affair. His protégés were not looked upon kindly, either. After Chiang's arrival in Taipei, Margaret's father could not find work.

In Hong Kong, he began teaching at a high school. He would work there for the next seventeen years and eventually become the principal. During that time, he never learned a word of Cantonese. His daughter was a different story. Even though she had spoken Mandarin, the lingua franca of the Nationalist elite, all her life, Margaret had no problem learning Cantonese.

"I picked it up like that," she told me. "At first I didn't understand the words. I just imitated them. Then one day I did."

Then, in an uncharacteristically immodest way, she added: "I've always been good at languages."

What she really excelled at, and still does, was making friends. She adjusted to life in Hong Kong with a typical minimum of fuss. And two years later, when she learned that she would be moving back to Taipei, she equally did not complain. Her father felt that Hong Kong was a bad influence on a young girl. When they had first moved there, he had used his savings to send his two oldest daughters to England to study. By the time Margaret reached high school, he could not afford to do the same for her. Even Hong Kong had become too expensive. If the family moved back to Taipei, Margaret's mother could count on the steady salary and extra ration coupons that came with her position as a member of the national assembly. The girls could go to good public schools, which did not exist in Hong Kong. Margaret's father made a decision. He would stay in Hong Kong, where he had a decent job and no fear of government repercussions; his wife and four youngest daughters would return to Taiwan. It hardly mattered where Margaret ended up. She accepted her fate with a shrug of her practical shoulders and readjusted to Taipei as easily as she had to Hong Kong. She did well in school, which was important in gaining the respect of the other students, but she was not a grind. In fact, she had a sharp sense of humor, which could have been interpreted as cutting but rarely was. Somehow her jokes did not sting as much as other people's, because she reserved her harshest judgment for herself. During one of our conversations, she once acidly described the majority of people as mediocre. "Writers too," she said, not sparing me from her biting observation. But she swept away any anger I could have harbored with the very next sentence.

"Me," she said cheerfully, "I'm probably most mediocre of them all." It was impossible to take offense.

In fact, Margaret was not mediocre, at least not in school. She did well in all of her classes. In Taiwan at that time, such a happy situation could mean only one thing to any responsible parent: the child would study science. So it happened that in Margaret's rambling, multitalented family of six girls, five of them would end up in science or medicine. This fact is general proof of the obedience instilled in Chinese children of that era. Specifically, it stands as testament to the iron will of Margaret's father. He ruled his brood like an army general, dispatching directives from his Hong Kong headquarters to remote outposts in England and Taiwan, knowing that his commands would be followed absolutely. When his children wrote him letters, he returned them with corrections in red ink. He required Margaret, who was in high school, to write him in English. He corrected those letters just as strenuously. Only his youngest daughter, schooled in America, managed to foil him. She became a lawyer. Eventually, Margaret's father accepted the decision, even grew to like it. But Margaret could not disobey him. The thought did not even occur to her. Good parents told their children what to do. Good children listened.

"A doctor, an engineer," her father told her, "they will always have work."

Students sat for college entrance exams the summer after they graduated. Practically from the moment Margaret walked in the door of the examination hall, she had to know what she would study in college. Not only were people interested in humanities given one test and people interested in science another, but also a student had to specify exactly which field she wanted to study. She could not switch once she had made the decision. That day, Margaret wrote "engineering." And so she found herself on the road to a career in science before she even really knew what other paths existed. Even had she known, it would hardly have made a difference. For the most part, successful students studied math and science, regardless of where their natural talents lay. There were some exceptions, but Margaret would not be one of them in spite of her many other interests. Her fondness for music, her appreciation of the visual arts, her talents for learning languages and getting along with others would all remain secondary. Later in life, she might listen to Tchaikovsky for pleasure or dabble in painting for fun, but she could not follow those roads to their ultimate conclusion. She had never been given a map. To her dismay, she would never learn how to get one. Later in life, my mother would regret that she had not had enough guidance when she was young. Margaret would rue that she had had too much. But when they met again, they would discover that they had much in common. They had both tried to prepare their daughters for the lessons they had once learned.

Margaret headed to Tai Da to study chemical engineering, not because she particularly wanted to but because her parents did. My mother, a weak student, set off to America to become a nurse, also not because she wanted to, but because she did not know what else to do. If, as their classmate had told me, Beiyinyu was a narrow gate to this country, it worked in different ways for different people. Margaret's path was linear and direct. After Tai Da, she would win a scholarship to do graduate work in America. The rest of the family even immigrated with her, providing her with a home to go to during the holidays and a sense of continuity in a strange country. My mother's was more complicated. She once described herself to me as a leaf. "I go here, there," she said, "wherever the wind takes me."

A leaf may skitter along the pavement or float on the breeze, but its landing will always be soft. A leaf lacks direction. It cannot control its destiny. But it also lacks substance, making it seem, in some ways, as inviolable as the air itself. In those days, my mother was so light, so paper-thin, she simply opened her arms and let herself be borne aloft by the currents. Her leaf analogy fit well. The wind would pick her up and blow her across the water.

Other girls had happy memories of home and family. My mother had only Beiyinyu. In the mornings when she walked her bike past the forbidding iron gate that separated the school from the rest of the world, she felt relieved, not restless. The concrete-lined bomb shelter by the administrative offices, the athletic field in the middle of the courtyard, the high wall that surrounded the school, they were all more familiar to my mother than her own home, a location that had changed twice since her mother had died and which now consisted of an apartment above a stationery store run by her uncle and his new wife. She could not even call the place hers. Her uncle had put the deed in his name even though he had bought the property with the proceeds from the sale of the little Japanese house her mother had bought so long ago.

My mother is the least sentimental person I know. I think in those final months in Taipei, she did not dwell on the past. She thought only of the future. The Catholic Church had given her a scholarship to study in America. She could not wait to leave. She felt neither fear nor sorrow. When she had first started the school, her mother was alive. Her father's concubine had been like an aunt to her. They had lived in a clean, comfortable home with a yard and children to play with next door. Now her mother was dead. The concubine had married and gone away. My mother lived in a cramped apartment in the business district with an uncle and an aunt who wanted to be free of their obligation to his sister's children. Taiwan offered my mother nothing.

But still, I can't help thinking that as she passed through the school gate for the last time, she must have felt some small twinge at the thought of what she was leaving behind. Her real home, her village, lay inside Beiyinyu's yellow brick walls. Her real family consisted of the girls with whom she had shared classes, lunches, summers, and studies for the past six years. It was the longest time my mother had ever gone to the same school in her entire life, the longest time she had ever lived in the same city. Only a handful of her classmates would be studying in the States. Most of them were going on to Tai Da. Leaving Taiwan meant leaving them behind. Before my mother left, her friends threw her a farewell party much like the one Dolores had been given two and a half years before. Her best friend presented her with a box. Inside lay a silk *qi pao*, a dress more familiarly known to Westerners by its Cantonese name, cheongsam. Everyone had chipped in to have it made.

"This is to wear in America," her friend said. The other girls nodded in agreement. They laughed: some because they had not yet learned to cry, some because they had already learned not to.

"Later," they said. "We will join you later."

They had all passed through the same narrow gate like a surging herd that remained intact because it followed a familiar path. Then the path ended. Like my mother, most of the classmates would eventually find their way to America, where they foraged alone in a land of wide-open, endless prairies. The old rules would no longer apply—none of the familiar regulations, hierarchies, ways of thinking that had gotten them here in the first place. As soon as they arrived, the narrow gate would clang shut behind them. No one knew on which side freedom lay. Some of the classmates would realize their dreams. Some would even surpass theirs. Some would create entirely new ones. Still others would discover only that they could not go forward and they could not go back. The one thing that bound them together was the narrow gate through which they had all passed and the fact that now, no gateposts remained to guide them.

HAWAII

Forty years later, thirty-nine students from the Beiyinyu class of 1955 met again, some for the first time, at a reunion on the Hawaiian islands of Maui and Oahu. Wordsworth once wrote that the child is father of the man. I headed to Hawaii to find out if he was right. In the unnatural time warp that a reunion creates between the past and the present, I hoped to glean a greater understanding of the girls that Suzanne, Margaret, and my own mother had once been and the adults they were now. Dolores was not attending. At the time, I did not even know of her existence. Later on, her decision not to go would reveal volumes.

For the classmates, the very idea of a reunion was a relatively recent one, first born in 1975, a full twenty years after graduation. Appropriately enough, its mother was my mother. She had held the first gathering in our house in Hartford, Connecticut. It had numbered about a dozen women, but over the years the reunions had grown, following no particular pattern. Sometimes the women met every two years; sometimes it was three. As the classmates prospered, their meetings became more elaborate. They had begun as small affairs in people's homes and local colleges, until by the 1980s the women were convening in such places as Lake Tahoe and Beverly Hills. The reunion before Hawaii had taken place on a cruise.

The first reunion and this latest one were like bookends on a particular shelf in a growing library of history, not just that of the classmates but that of Chinese America. My mother's reunion had consisted of a lonely band of women coming together from pockets of isolation in the Northeast. Back then, they had just been entering middle age. Their families and careers were still growing. They worried about mortgages and college tuition. For the most part, their America consisted of work, children, and the few other Chinese who may have settled in their community. Now, two decades later, their children were grown, some with children of their own. Many of the classmates were contemplating retirement and, for the first time, thinking about what they wanted to do, not what they had to. They had come together, fittingly, in this most diverse of states to celebrate their own diversity. Somehow, in the two decades that had passed between Hartford and Hawaii, they had ceased being Chinese in America and had become Chinese Americans. And, somehow, it was fitting that if my mother had organized the first, homespun event, this latest, most elaborate one be directed by Margaret Li.

The first day of the reunion, I arrived with my parents and Suzanne at mid-morning. In addition to myself, three other children—as our parents and their friends still called us—were attending. One of them was Wei Li, Margaret's daughter, who lived near me in New York. She and her father, Dan, had arrived the day before from Hong Kong, where they had been visiting relatives. Margaret usually opted out of her husband's annual trip back to his home city. Instead, she was coming in from their home in the Los Angeles suburbs. She had been due to arrive in the morning, but the flight, to the consternation of several of her reunion helpers, had been delayed.

A conference room had been reserved as a reception area. Sushi and turkey sandwiches comprised a uniquely Hawaiian buffet. I sat at a table and watched the women arrive. They came from all over—Singapore and Kentucky, the Philippines and Diamond Head next door. Some dressed casually in sweat pants and cross-trainers. Others wore tailored suits, stockings, leather pumps, and a vault's worth of jewelry. But no matter who appeared, the initial greeting remained the same. A woman would hesitantly enter the room and look around for a familiar face.

The first person to recognize her would scream loudly, jump up, and embrace her. The others would start clapping. This ritual repeated itself again and again. As people began to crowd in, the enthusiasm grew rather than lessened, so that I began to fear the entire room would collapse in one simultaneous, hyperventilating fit. The rest of the week progressed along similar lines. Friends who had just left each other at breakfast would shriek and run into one another's arms at lunch. The long years and physical distance separating them served only as a partial explanation. I was witnessing a biological phenomenon. The women were reverting to their infectious, enthusiastic, adolescent selves.

While everyone waited for Margaret to arrive, several of the women bustled around preparing a surprise birthday party for her husband, Dan. In his wife's absence, Dan had assumed the responsibility of greeting new arrivals in the lobby in his affable, if slightly harried, way. At one point, while I waited for my parents to finish checking in, I watched him circle the area like a bee deciding where to alight. Wei had gone to a dance class and had instructed him, before she left, to get my room number. He asked me for it three times. Each time, I acted as though it were the first. He certainly seemed to think it was.

With Dan safely out of sight below, two of the classmates fussed over the cake, arranging candles and stacking piles of plates and napkins nearby. A third woman held up a grass skirt she had found in a store across the street. The classmates laughed. When everything was ready, someone ran downstairs to find Dan. They returned, and people began to sing "Happy Birthday." Dan beamed with pleasure. He let the woman dress him in the grass skirt and then twirled becomingly. The classmates roared. Someone led him to the cake. He had just blown out the candles when Margaret walked into the expectant pause of a room about to burst into applause. When people did start clapping, it was for her, not for him.

They called to her like fans. Dressed in a white silk shirt and trim black pants, Margaret smiled and waved, a benevolent monarch greeting her subjects. She nodded at her husband. He waved back sheepishly. The tendrils of his grass skirt drooped about his ankles. She looked next at her daughter, Wei, who, with no words having passed between them, immediately moved to the cake and began taking off the candles. The room relaxed. Their leader had arrived.

Watching Margaret, I began to read the group more clearly. The sweat pants and tailored jackets that had formed one indistinguishable mass before now began to organize themselves. Invariably, the less glamorous women came from the East Coast or, as one or two did, the Midwest. The Californians dressed with, if not better taste, greater flair. They wore bright red lipstick and large sunglasses. Rubies and diamonds glowed from their fingers. The easterners looked older and more sedate. Some of them were stylish—more so, actually, than their West Coast peers, in a subdued sort of way—but they could not match the Californians for glitter. Margaret's clothes were a great deal more chic in their quiet quality than those of the other Los Angeles women, but at the same time, she looked nothing like an easterner. The chunky gold belt around her waist, the sweater tied around her shoulders set her apart physically; but there was yet another element, an intangible quality that I had never noticed in my mother's friends back home. It was the self-confidence that comes with being self-sufficient. If the dozen friends at my mother's reunion had been self-controlled, these exotic West Coast creatures were self-possessed.

When Wei began tending to the cake, the other two children in attendance, a pair of sisters, also in their mid-twenties, automatically moved to help her. Together, they began slicing pieces and passing them out. I had missed my cue. I had been sitting on a table in the back, not paying attention. By the time I realized what was happening, it was too late. One of the daughters handed me a plate. I took it guiltily and then put it down beside me, hoping no one had noticed. It would have been too obvious if I had started helping at that late moment. Wei had almost finished cutting the cake. Most people already had their slices. I sat against the wall and tried instead to look terribly busy.

Instinctively, I knew that people had noticed. I would be labeled *bu tai hua*, poorly raised. It was ironic. Finally, I was the grown adult I had always dreamed of becoming after years of talking back to my parents and behaving rudely to their Chinese friends. Instead of being beyond their censure, I simply felt the shame I should have felt as a child. I had always acted with perfect politeness to white adults. Instinctively, I too had absorbed the feeling that permeated the Chinese-American community of my youth. Whites were outsiders, whether they were to be emulated, ignored, or scorned. A part of me recognized, with absolute clarity, that every time I was with them, my behavior proved some kind of point in their minds, not just about me but about all Chinese. I could not, as the English say, let down the side. Within the Chinese community, it was different. In the Hartford of my childhood, we numbered a dozen or so families. Every man was an uncle to me, every woman an auntie. Best manners were for the outside world, not for home.

Somewhere along the way to growing up, the situation had gradually reversed itself. Out of politeness, I continued to take pains with all my elders, but I had ceased to care what the white ones thought of me. With the Chinese, however, I became overly solicitous, overly submissive, wanting always to be told what a good girl I was. When I spoke to them, my tongue fumbled trying to pronounce the truncated Mandarin phrases that my brain was frantically digging out of its darkest recesses. My embarrassment no longer stemmed, as it once had, from being associated with this loud sing-song language that turned heads in the supermarket, but from no longer being so. My exterior motive for going to Hawaii was to do research on my book. My ulterior one, hidden even from me, was to redeem myself.

The opening banquet was held the next night. No gathering this important would be complete without one. The night before, Margaret had given each woman a replica of the pine-green blouse that had comprised part of their school uniform. This version came in silk and had shoulder pads, but the women had greeted its appearance no less ecstatically for its modern refinements. Every classmate wore the shirt to the banquet, which was being held at a Chinese restaurant in the neighborhood. Walking down the Ala Moana Boulevard together, an excited, giggling mass, they looked like some sort of ragtag choir which had budgeted for only half a uniform.

After dinner, each woman stood up and gave a short speech on her life. They took turns based on some pecking order which was invisible to me but remained ingrained in them, in spite of all their years in egalitarian America. Perhaps they had learned to adapt to their new country's ways, but here, among their old schoolmates, they reverted to traditional form as naturally and easily as they had put on their green shirts. As far as I could tell, this particular hierarchy appeared to be based on a woman's relative importance to the reunion. For example, Margaret, the organizer, went first. My mother, who had brought both a husband and a child with her to Hawaii, spoke fairly early on. Suzanne went next-to-last.

I had known her long enough by then to tell that she was nervous. She would rather not have talked at all. I could not blame her. A hush had fallen over the room when she stood up. Most of the women had talked about their husbands and children. Although they had almost all worked—some for the entirety of their adult lives, and a handful very successfully—they had concentrated on their families' achievements rather than their own. It was by the former that their peers would judge them. Now they wondered expectantly what Suzanne would say, and they waited to judge her as they had been judged in turn. It was a deadly serious contest of sorts, the dark side of their small community. The closeness and affection I had admired in their warm, welcoming embraces stemmed from the same source as the silence that filled the banquet hall. The culture from which they came had stifled their own free will long ago in the interest of harmony and stability. Free will was not only unusual, it was dangerous. Suzanne had made her own choices in life, decisions that none of the rest of them, not even the Californians with their vibrant, imperious ways, would have dared to follow. Even if they did not realize it, they disapproved of her. She, in turn, made them nervous.

She had not even wanted to come to the reunion. She told me that she had done so only because my mother had asked her to. Now, she stood, her skin pale against the dark green of her shirt, her very thinness a sort of exclamation point of brittle bones. She had once been even skinnier. She wore pearls around her neck and elegant pumps on her feet. She looked both worn and perfect.

Each woman before her had started by introducing herself and then saying what class section she had been in. The class was divided into four. Suzanne followed suit but quickly faltered. "I don't know what section I was in," she admitted.

The audience tittered. Suzanne had failed out of Beiyinyu. She had graduated from a different high school. After the laughter died down, she finished quickly. She mentioned that her husband was a doctor and that she worked in his office. She said that they lived in California. She sat down. The others looked disappointed. They had been hoping for more, but they were not going to get it.

I remembered what I had hated most about being with my parents' Chinese friends or my own extended family. Nothing was ever a secret. My business was everyone's business. As far as they were concerned, pointing out that I had acne or that I had gained weight was a perfectly appropriate way to start a conversation. My sister experienced her own brand of mortification when she would appear, a blossoming adolescent, at Chinese gatherings.

"She has such big breasts!" some friend or other of my mother's would gasp.

"Yes," my mother would say, eyeing my sister as if she were livestock. "I think she drinks too much milk."

Whenever I failed at something, I felt that everyone knew. My problems had already been discussed at dinner tables throughout the community, passed around on the lazy Susan like a dish of stinky tofu. I know this because my own family did the same, and I leapt in, as eager as the next to winnow out the weak. And just as failure was oppressive, success was heady. I succeeded so seldom that I had little firsthand knowledge of those exhilarating heights, but I had ample opportunity to watch my brothers as they basked in the glory of their achievements, ones that made my own shortcomings seem even more dismal by comparison.

In Hawaii, I began to feel the same noose tightening around my neck. Seen in a different light, warmth turned into oppression, curiosity into prying. One evening, my mother and I came back to our room just before dinner, sweaty and disheveled from playing tennis. My father was waiting impatiently. He was ready to go downstairs and eat.

"Just go without us," I said.

"I can't do that," he replied.

"What?" I asked. "Why not? We'll catch up."

"You don't understand," he said. "If Mom and I don't show up at dinner together, people will start to talk."

Such were the moorings I had struggled to break free from as a child, restlessly wanting to be like my white friends who were not obliged to know every other white person in town, who could drift anonymously onwards. But I could not escape, and neither could Suzanne.

The only way was, as Dolores had done, not to show up at the reunion at all. At the time, I did not notice. I did not know that she existed, even though she lived in Queens, a mere subway ride away from my own home. Many months and many interviews would pass before I would finally meet Dolores and be struck by just how different she was from the rest of the classmates I had met thus far. Big-boned and slightly plump in a motherly way, she welcomed me with a bear hug when we met. She spoke with just the slightest hint of a Chinese accent. She tried to feed me potato chips and milk. Unlike the others, she discussed most aspects of her life with astonishing candor and then would call me later to clarify and rectify, wanting to be certain that I had understood. Most of the classmates talked freely only when they were discussing others, never themselves. With them, there was no misunderstanding. Everything, even in their own minds, was carefully censored. Dolores had not so much broken free from her classmates but, rather, had gradually become detached, so that she remained like a loose button, dangling by just a thread. She was renouncing their scorn, or in her case what would probably be pity, but in doing so she was also forgoing their allegiance.

As the reunion week wore on, the cameras never stopped clicking. The women were not recording the awe-inspiring scenery—the view from the majestic Mount Haleakala, the rusting hull of the USS *Arizona*. These places served as mere backdrops to the real subjects—themselves. Groups of women posed in front of the Royal Palace in Honolulu, at an orchid farm in Maui, by the hotel pool. They never tired of taking pictures of the same faces, preserving on film what was already etched in their hearts.

I watched in wonder as they transformed themselves. As the days went on, the women continued to shed the skins they had acquired in America. The typically retiring, painfully shy self-consciousness gave way, in the safety of numbers, to bold and silly antics. A trio of women sneaked into the hotel pool next door simply to check it out. Another plucked an orchid in plain sight. For my mother, who could already be bolder and sillier than most, the transformation reflected a difference in intensity rather than a change in her nature. Still, I watched the dark side of her personality slip away to be replaced by its opposite. I have often seen both in my lifetime and have never failed to be terrified by the one and exhilarated by the other.

They held a farewell ceremony on the last night. We dined outside next to the crashing sea and under a Fragonard sky. The tall dark palms swayed ever so slightly in the gentle breeze, inebriated sentinels keeping guard over the proceedings. But dinner proved to be a mere prelude leading up to the real action of the evening, which occurred indoors in a nondescript meeting hall. It reminded me of the Chinese gatherings of my youth—the unadorned tables, the empty spaces between, the groups of chattering women and men. The room lacked only a large sheet cake covered in white frosting and some buckets of Kentucky Fried Chicken, the greasy, salty contents of which had once been employed by our mothers to bribe us children into attending. I, for one, always refused to touch the homemade delicacies—steamers of dumplings, spicy noodles, and whole roast ducks—that my mother and her friends would prepare. But tonight, I was here of my own accord. For dinner, I had eaten the same thing as everyone else: a salad of mixed baby greens, grilled chicken, and chocolate mousse cake. The change in cuisine wasn't the only or even the most significant difference. This evening, instead of *wushu* movies imported from Hong Kong or groups of children singing the simple songs they had learned in Chinese class, the entertainment was being provided by the adults.

They had been preparing since the morning. While Wei, her parents, a handful of other adventurous souls, and myself had gone snorkeling off the coast of Lahaina, the rest of the group had remained behind, passing out song sheets and making leis out of plumeria blossoms. I returned in the afternoon to find my father busily translating a local folk song into Chinese and singing snatches of it to himself. My mother was conferring mysteriously with a giggling group of friends on a nearby patch of lawn. She waved me off as I approached. She was busy.

I found out why at the farewell banquet. She and her friends stood in the open area at the front of the room, which would serve as a stage for the evening. They were wearing leis, and some had even fashioned ersatz sarongs out of brightly colored scarves. These they had tied around the waistbands of their shorts and skirts. My mother wore neither sarong nor lei, just her usual baggy shorts, which fell to her knees, and an oversized T-shirt of almost the same length. Soft and comfortable, she looked like a giant stuffed animal I used to have when I was little. Its name, appropriately enough, was Mama Bear.

They began to hula-dance. It was a simple routine based on a song about catching fish. The women mimed drawing in lines and then swiveled their hips to the chorus, "We're going to a hula." Some were graceful and sure, and most were at least able to coordinate the movements of their arms and feet with the lyrics. Not my mother. She mimed ocean waves while the others caught fish. When they moved to the left, she moved to the right. She was so awful I began to wonder if she was misbehaving on purpose. At one point, I caught her laughing.

The dance was over in less than five minutes. Afterwards, one woman stood shaking out her legs as if she had just run a 10K and was trying to avoid cramps. My mother, still chortling to herself, ran up to the table where I was sitting.

"That was fun," she said. "Was it?"

I recognized the question. It was familiar and rhetorical. She asked it whenever she was having a great time.

The evening progressed: a trio sang a cappella; my father did the Charleston with Wei, who, at the behest of her mother, also performed a solo modern-dance routine; Dan Li enthusiastically rendered his version of "My Way," complete with hand gestures and his daughter's accompanying groans of "Oh, Jesus." Margaret cracked some jokes about Cantonese people while her Hong Kong–born husband laughed good-naturedly. One of the husbands stood up in the grass skirt from Dan's birthday party. A classmate stuck a hibiscus in his hair and put two leis around his neck. The room catcalled him, and he obligingly shook his rear. Towards the end, when yet another group of women rose to perform a hula, Wei turned to me.

"This whole thing," she said, referring to the evening's entertainment, "is about how they weren't allowed to do anything when they were young. They're living their childhood now."

I agreed with her in part. Their childhood had been abrupt and unsettled, even tragic. Their adolescence had been intensely regimented. But much of their adult lives had also been uneasy and uncertain. It was no coincidence that, now that they felt free enough to act like children, they wanted to do so with those who had known them when they were young. The look on my mother's face did not often appear in the company of strangers. I'm sure it appeared even less frequently on the faces of her classmates. They might have white neighbors and even, like my mother, many close white friends; but, in a way that I struggled to understand, they shared a bond with each other that transcended the time and distance between them. It was almost like family. Just the thought of one made the other remember from where she herself had come.

In the span of a week, the classmates had re-created the insular, gossipy, tight-knit village they had known in Taipei. When it came time to leave it, they dissolved into tears. They stood in a circle, hand clasping hand, and sang "Auld Lang Syne" again and again. All around me, women were hugging. One was crying so hard that her glasses slid off her face. She was almost sixty, with children and grandchildren, a full, happy life, but there she stood clinging to another, already mourning her friend's absence. I stood just beyond this knot of classmates, bathed, as they were, in the glow of the hotel chandelier. I watched them silently, an outsider still. This was my mother's home, not mine. I was only a visitor. The best I could do was try to understand how far she and her classmates had traveled to get back there.

IMMIGRATION

The women arrived in America in the late 1950s and early 1960s—my mother, specifically, in the fall of 1955, a dozen years after the Chinese Repealer and a decade before the groundbreaking immigration reforms of 1965. Through this brief window of time they slipped—between the dying, dwindling world of elderly Cantonese laundrymen who had helped pave the way to Gold Mountain and the vast influx of Asians to come from all parts of the world and all walks of life.

The Chinese Repealer had done away with the Chinese Exclusion Act, in place since 1882, and the first congressional legislation specifically designed to exclude a particular ethnic group. More symbolically, the Chinese Repealer had also negated an 1870 act which, while granting citizenship to former slaves, had at the same time deliberately withheld it from the Chinese. That is to say, until 1943, Chinese immigrants to the United States could not become citizens. The men who suffered through freezing winters, building the railroads that spanned the Rockies while living in fear of the snowslides which carried away their fellow laborers; the migrant workers who stooped for hot, dusty hours, planting and weeding and picking; the gold-seeking miners who were driven violently from their claims by greedy whites; the agricultural expert who produced the Bing cherry: they were all categorically denied citizenship, land, and even wives in a nation to which they had given everything, including, for many, their last, miserable days spent dying alone in cramped, cell-like rooms, far from the graves of their ancestors.

If the Chinese Repealer cracked open the door to the later compatriots of these solitary pioneers, the immigration reforms of 1965 practically ushered them in. The reforms, which did away with Eurocentric quotas, quite literally changed the face of America. Between 1965 and 1990, over seven hundred thousand Chinese immigrated, more than double the population that was already in place after over a century in America. These new immigrants were joined by growing numbers of Koreans, Filipinos, Indians, Vietnamese, and others, so that the Asian-American population in the United States has since grown from a million in 1965 to well over seven million today, from one half of one percent of the total population to more than three percent. With the new immigrants have come new languages, new cultures, and new ways, for better or worse, of viewing diversity in this country.

In California, for example, whites are rapidly becoming a minority. Eau Claire, Wisconsin, is home to a population of Hmong tribespeople. Vietnamese fishermen trawl the waters of the Gulf of Mexico. Within a five-block radius of my apartment in Manhattan, I have access to Mandarin, Cantonese, Thai, Korean, Indian, Tibetan, Burmese, Filipino, Vietnamese, and Malaysian food. The choice is practically as varied for Japanese cuisine alone, with places specializing in sushi, noodles, barbecue, shabu shabu, and even sake. Many of these restaurants are not the simple, family-run affairs of old that specialize in delivery but instead are trendy and even sometimes pricey destinations, drawing diners from all over the city who long not for the exotic but simply for the delicious.

It was not so in 1955. Back then, Chinese restaurants, if they existed at all, made chow mein with dry, hard "noodles," the likes of which have never been seen in the Middle Kingdom, and served such fare as flaming pu-pu platters, a vaguely Polynesian-inspired dish still available at the Jade Palaces and Moon Gardens of my 1970s, suburban Connecticut youth. When my mother and her classmates arrived, there were approximately two hundred thousand Chinese in the entire country. In these days of the model minority myth, admissions officers at elite universities debate whether or not to institute quotas against applicants of Asian descent, and already a decade has passed since a sign in Monterey Park implored "the last American to leave" to "please bring the flag." According to the last census in 1990, the suburb was 56 percent Asian. The numbers can only be higher by now. It is difficult to imagine a time when my mother and her fellow students were curiosities to their American peers, but that's exactly what they were. They were Chinese students and Chinese women at a time when there were few of either in this country. Eventually, they would marry and settle down, not in the Chinatowns of the inner cities but in middle- and upper-middle-class white neighborhoods across the country. At the time, they were not a large enough group to pose a threat to the establishment, as my generation later would, and, thus, definitely not great enough in number to be treated simply as individuals, as I hope the next generation will be. Instead, my mother and her friends were pioneers—mingling at block parties, going to PTA meetings, and learning to juggle work and family, all in a new and unfamiliar language. They were a lost generation too, the last remnants of a fading era in Chinese history, adrift in a strange land. Some four decades later, they remain, in a sense, still lost. The world they left behind no longer exists. The world they created is being absorbed and diluted by new immigrants, the mainstream, even their own children. That fact does not particularly dismay or disappoint them. They have never had the time or the luxury to ponder such abstractions. They have been treading water for so long, they are simply grateful for the chance to come ashore.

A friend of my mother's explained their generation's peculiar status to me: "We are a very different group of Chinese. In a way, it's sad. We're called the bamboo generation. You know bamboo sticks? There's little blocks in between. Either side, you're either Western or Chinese. Both sides, you are not. You are not one way. You get caught between because you're the tube in between two ends."

"Is that good?" I asked her. "Or bad?"

"Hollowed," she responded. "You're hollowed."

The classmates' paths had begun to diverge even before they left Taiwan. Dolores had come to America early, in 1953, with her mother. Shortly afterwards, Suzanne was sent to school in central Taiwan. Of the four, she would be the last to arrive in the States, in 1961. In contrast, my mother came almost immediately after graduating from high school. Margaret would follow in 1959 with her entire family.

These details may appear unimportant, but when the women arrived, how, and for what reason would bear directly on who they would later become. To actually immigrate with one's family, as Dolores or Margaret did, was extremely rare. The quota for incoming Chinese still hovered in the low hundreds. Most everyone who entered in those years, including my mother and Suzanne, came in on temporary student visas and simply never left, eventually becoming citizens. Dolores's mother also managed to enter and bring Dolores with her on a temporary visa through her work with the United Nations. Again, when her job was finished, she and her daughter stayed on, along with her older daughter, who was already in America studying. Of the four classmates, only Margaret officially immigrated with her family through a special program that the Eisenhower administration had instituted, which allowed four thousand families of Chinese ethnicity to enter the country during the 1950s. Chinese families from all over Southeast Asia, not just Taiwan, were eligible, but there was a catch: the head of the household had to have been educated in either Europe or the United States.

Even student visas were difficult to come by. You had to win a place at an American college or university. For my mother, Suzanne, and the vast majority of Chinese students who entered in those years, this meant winning a scholarship. They could not have afforded the tuition otherwise. It was difficult enough to scrape up the passage and the thousand dollars that the U.S. government demanded each foreign student have in the bank. One classmate told me of arriving in America with a suitcase, an old fur coat, and three hundred dollars meant to cover all her expenses for the next three years. The thousand dollars was never to be touched. My mother, whose uncle had loaned her the thousand dollars out of money he had stolen from her mother's estate, insisted that she wire it back to Taiwan as soon as she arrived in the States. Apparently the authorities did not check to ensure that the money stayed in the country after the student did.

Scholarships abounded in math and science, but only qualified students could hope for these. They were the ones, like Margaret, who had already spent four grueling years at Tai Da. My mother's only hope lay with the Catholic Church and the nursing scholarships they offered. It was a decidedly less prestigious way to come into the country. Nursing was a trade, not a profession, but even so, some five hundred students applied for one hundred spots the year my mother graduated from high school. My mother's Beiyinyu background worked to her advantage, but her grades did not. For one of the few times in her life, a family member offered to help. Her great-aunt, the wife of the prominent Nationalist general still being held captive on the mainland, knew the archbishop of Nanjing, Yu Pin, who would later become cardinal of Taiwan, the first Chinese cardinal in the Catholic Church. At the time, the archbishop was stationed in New York, where he was urged by the Vatican to keep a low profile in order not to antagonize the Communists into reprisals against Catholics on the mainland. He devoted himself in part to finding scholarships for Chinese students in the States. On one of his trips to Taiwan, my mother and a younger cousin spent a day with his entourage, following him from function to function. By the end of the day, my mother had her scholarship.

Suzanne's scholarship also involved connections. By then, her father had risen to become minister of overseas Chinese, one of the most important cabinet positions in a country that still relied heavily on the generosity of its compatriots abroad. After Suzanne finished high school, her father sent her to a small Catholic institution in Taichung. The place was basically a finishing school for the rich. The student body numbered fewer than a hundred. The tuition had to be paid in U.S. dollars. It was an exclusivity based solely on money. Anyone with any intellectual ambition, rich or poor, aspired to go to Tai Da, which was free. Private schools were for the incompetent sons and daughters of the affluent. In order to lend the place legitimacy, Suzanne's father arranged to have it accredited.

"All of a sudden," Suzanne told me wryly, years after the fact, "the school becomes a college. The sisters so nice to me, so nice to me. They even waive the tuition."

From there, Suzanne won a scholarship to another small Catholic college, this time one in the United States.

These differences in how the women arrived in America, however small-seeming at the time, would come to mean a great deal. Dolores, a teenager when she arrived, graduated from an American high school. Not surprisingly, she easily adopted many American customs. At the same time, she and her mother had arrived in this country together, her sister here to greet them. With her family still intact, she could not completely dissolve the old ties that held her to Chinese culture. She would wrestle with her dual nature for the rest of her life, torn always between the dreams of one and the expectations of the other.

Margaret came after college to study biochemistry in graduate school. By then, she was twenty-two, her formative years already behind her. In the sciences, students did not have to make the same adjustments. Schoolwork consisted of numbers and lab work, universal languages. In Taiwan, science and medicine were always taught with English textbooks anyway. In the United States, it was easy to cloister oneself in one's studies. In the bigger schools, one could even hope to find Chinese classmates. Margaret, who had finally come across a cultural barrier that she, who had never had a problem adapting to new situations before, seemingly could not penetrate, now did not have to. Whenever she spent lonely evenings studying in freezing South Dakota or, later, encountered curious stares in racist Missouri, she could always think of her family waiting for her in New Jersey.

Suzanne came to this country with no one. Her favorite brother had died in a car crash in South Bend, when she was still studying in Taichung. One of the first things she did when she arrived was look for his grave in Brooklyn. She could not find even that. Alone in Davenport, Iowa, she would at first cling to her past and, by extension, the large but cold family into which she had been born. Later, she would learn to appreciate her new home precisely because of the independence it gave her. Then, the distance separating her from her family would become not a hardship but a sort of exhilarating freedom, the kind that she could only have found in America.

Through these three stories runs the common thread of my mother. It is fitting because she is neither American, like Suzanne is, nor Chinese, in the way that Margaret remains, nor even the mix of the two that Dolores is. My mother arrived young, when she was only eighteen, but in many ways she was already grown up, too mature to be easily influenced. Still, when she arrived at her women's college in Arlington, Virginia, she quickly picked up new slang and new friends. She had no family and no home, and she had not had them for some time. She had already learned to alter her personality to suit those around her. She was as changeable as water. Unlike Dolores's, my mother's new American identity came not from being impressionable but from being wise. If she knew nothing else, she knew how to survive. She transcended national identity. I have seen her make the same easy conversation with flirtatious middle-aged men in Munich beer houses as she does with gum-cracking teenagers in New York City. My mother is the classic restless wanderer of old, eternally pushing onward. These other three women have also journeyed, but while each of them has, in her own way, come to an end point, my mother never has. She does not even know how to find one.

I wondered what had happened in the women's respective travels to make this the case. In doing so, I discovered crucial moments or themes in their pasts when each of their lives has either intersected with or paralleled my mother's. She shared her first, early student days in America, full of both novelty and uncertainty, with Dolores, on whom good fortune always seemed to smile. Years later, they would meet again to find the situation reversed. Next, my mother passed long, dreary years as a wife and mother, echoing those spent by Suzanne, until both of them were jolted, for better and worse, from their growing listlessness. With Margaret she shared the same later-life feelings of failure, which, although shaped by very different environments, had come from a similar source of self-doubt, one that was alleviated by neither work nor friends.

These were the moments I sought to explore. Like elements in a chemical reaction, the women had, at various times, bonded and then separated, emerging altered and distinct from one another. Only in America could their lives have remained so separate and yet so familiar. Only in America could their choices and circumstances have carried them to such different futures even as the past continued to connect them.

ACROSS THE BRIDGE

"My life," my mother once told me, "has always been controlled by someone else. Push me around."

She arrived in America under the auspices of the Catholic Church, which planned for her to become a nurse. Dutifully, she reported to a nursing school in Paterson, New Jersey. When it subsequently emerged that an error had occurred, and the school had only two scholarships available for three students, my mother just as dutifully left. She had not made the decision to become a nurse in the first place, and now she was not deciding not to be one either. As always, she simply took what life offered.

Archbishop Yu Pin sent her to a Catholic girls' boarding school in Niagara Falls. It was an unmemorable place save for the fact that it was unbearably cold after the subtropical climate of Taiwan and that Dolores was also there finishing high school. Since leaving Taiwan, Dolores had changed. The years in Niagara Falls had been the loneliest of her life. She needed to carry a dictionary with her at all times simply to be able to speak with other people. The only reason the school had taken her in the first place was that it had accepted two Vietnamese girls the year before she arrived. The girls were so polite and studious and China and Vietnam so close on the map that the school reasoned that a Chinese student could only be the same.

Dolores, who had once been so casual about her schoolwork,

did not disappoint. With few friends and no family to distract her, she began to study harder than she ever had before. She was at the school on scholarship and needed to maintain a certain grade point average to remain. Ironically, in spite of the poverty, life in Taiwan had been easier in many ways. The most obvious was the language, but the most important was her sense of self. At Beiyinyu, she had been known and loved. In America, she had to begin again, with none of the automatic anointing that had come with being a Beiyinyu girl. She became an outsider during the most difficult time for such a transition: adolescence. Bereft of the rest of her identity, Dolores's hallmark became schoolwork.

My mother, who was eighteen and already a graduate of one high school when she arrived in the States, did not undergo such a transformation. Instead, she allowed herself to be pulled along by the current of others. Her inner core, forged by tragedy, remained intact and unyielding even as her exterior shifted, like the changes of the day, to accommodate whatever world she happened to find herself in. Still, for one semester, she and Dolores, as different as they were already starting to become, remained inseparable.

At the end of the semester, the archbishop pulled my mother out of school.

"You need money," he said, and it was true. My mother had already sent the thousand dollars in her American account back to her uncle.

The archbishop found her a job in a medical lab at All Saints Hospital in Morristown, New Jersey, so she could save money for college. In the fall of 1956, she started at Marymount Junior College in Virginia. Again, she wound up there through someone else's decision rather than her own. The archbishop had initially intended the spot at Marymount for Dolores, but Dolores had grander visions for herself than a claustrophobic two-year college in the sanitized suburbs of D.C. Perhaps she feared a repeat of the experience she had undergone in upstate New York. Unlike my mother, she also had other options. She was a resident of New York City and had spent three years intensely studying, among other subjects, English. She now had the skills to pass the stringent entrance examinations for Hunter College, which, along with its male counterpart, City College, still shone as one of the tuition-free jewels of the City University of New York system. The Marymount opening went by default to my mother.

These days, Marymount is a coed university with four thousand students, graduate-level programs, a new library, and a second campus two miles down the road. Back then, it was a junior college all of six years old. In 1952, the first graduating class consisted of nine students. When my mother graduated in 1958, the number was eighty-three. The school catered to the daughters of upper-middle-class Catholic families, the kind of girls who came from Scarsdale, Bronxville, Grosse Pointe, Greenwich, and Darien and who wanted nothing more than to marry and raise their own small tribe of children. Practically everyone had some version of the name Mary in her own name. It is little wonder that my mother chose Mary as her own English name.

The school looked like a country club, and in fact abutted one: the Washington Golf and Country Club, whose long green fairways ran right up to the college's own grounds. The main building consisted of an old neoclassical mansion, the type that grace the South with their perfectly proportioned columns and long verandas. A broad expanse of lawn sloped gently down to the road, which in those days was a quiet two-lane country way. A thick, luxuriant hedge shielded the school from whatever traffic did go by. It disappeared long ago to make way for road expansion, but oaks, dogwoods, and even two holly trees still dot the campus, a reminder of the school's more serene past.

When I arrived there to do research, a gentle nun ushered me into the archives, where I searched for a copy of the yearbook from my mother's class. I could not find it. On a hunch, I walked in the rain over to the alumni office. A pleasant, pregnant woman greeted me. Her fertility was a startling sight in the midst of all that chastity. She had no yearbooks, but she pointed me in the direction of Sister De Sales.

"Rumor is," the woman said, as if giving me a bookie's hot tip, "she has every yearbook."

"Let me check," Sister De Sales said when I ran into her in an administrative office. She was a wizened old woman with blinding white hair. She wandered off to her office in another build-ing. I went for an appointment with yet another nun, one Sister Majella, who claimed to remember my mother.

"I'll call you at Sister Majella's office when I find it," the nun assured me.

Sister Majella turned out to be another slight, stooped, ancient woman who greeted me kindly but vaguely.

"She was a darling girl," the sister told me about my mother. "Everyone loved her, and we had no international students. She was the only one."

It seemed like a promising start. If my mother was the only in-ternational student, she must have made some sort of impression. But it turned out that one sentence was the most vivid description the nun had to offer of my mother. I prodded her gently. She had nothing more to give. It was not that her memory was faulty. She described the school as it was in the fifties with a keen sense for detail, telling me about the Georgetown boys who would pull up by the carload into the narrow driveway that wound its way through campus. They were required to wear a jacket and tie to pick up their dates but did not necessarily want to wear them all evening if they were just going to the movies or to a local diner for a burger and some fries. So the boys would carry one set in the car, and each suitor would take turns going into the dorms to retrieve his date. When the couple emerged, the jacket and tie would be handed off to the next in line.

Sister Majella spoke of those days with a fondness the old have for the past's quaint ways. She reminisced about the school's long-gone traditions—the annual May pole dance, the Magnolia Ball, the Snow Ball. Students could not leave for weekends with-out a formal invitation from the hostess of the house they were visiting. They were required to dress properly for dinner, which was served sit-down-style every evening at six. Each year, the school held a series of mandatory lessons to teach its charges such important life lessons as how to set a table, how to treat the help, how to answer a telephone, how to hold a tea party.

"Some people," Sister Majella said, fixing me with a baleful eye as if daring me to include myself in their number, "said all you had to do was know how to hold a cup of tea."

She sniffed and continued. "That wasn't it. Oh no. We had very strict classes."

I realized then why it is that I know how to eat bread at dinner properly. Tearing the bread into one manageable piece at a time, buttering that piece and putting it into my mouth in one bite is as ingrained in my habits as brushing my teeth twice a day. My mother is responsible also for the near fanatical way in which I approach writing thank-you letters. I find myself surreptitiously changing the table settings in restaurants; it bothers me so to find all the cutlery crowded to one side of the plate or on the wrong sides entirely. I was taught to say "please" when I ask for something and "thank you" when I receive it. To help clear and clean the dishes when I am a dinner guest. To bring a present when I am staying in someone else's home. My brothers were taught to stand when a woman approached or left their table at a restaurant. We were all instructed to do so when our elders entered and left the room. That we seldom do now stems, not from ignorance, but from laziness and embarrassment because we are almost always the only ones. Most of my peers, white and non-, do not seem to have ever been taught these lessons at all.

Perhaps the answer lies in my parents' unusual immigrant status. They did not disappear into an ethnic enclave but were immediately thrust into mainstream society. For my mother, all alone in this country, the situation must have seemed incomprehensible. Forget that in China, chewing loudly is a sign of appreciation for your host's cooking. Forget about sticking your eating utensil in a communal platter. Forget that young ladies do not drink, smoke, wear makeup, curl their hair, or flirt with men. At Marymount, the nuns served their charges, along with the Buzzes and Chickies who escorted them, buffet dinners before formal dances in order to counteract the effects of all the alcohol the students would later ingest. The smoker, where girls downed Pepsi, played bridge, and went through packs of Pall Malls, was the most popular meeting place on campus.

My mother absorbed these new rules with her usual flexibility, but I doubt that she ever tried to understand why they existed or what they meant. She knew only that other people acted this way, and she instilled such behavior in us. Real Americans, who had been brought up with these manners, began shrugging them off in the sixties. Many did not bother to pass them on to their children. There is also the possibility that Marymount had been more old-fashioned than the times. But, like a just-hatched duckling, my mother imprinted her new American self on the first example she saw.

The phone rang in Sister Majella's outer office. Her assistant picked up the receiver and called out to us.

"Sister," she said, "it's for the young lady in your office."

It was Sister De Sales.

"What did you say your mother's last name was?" she asked. "Han."

"I thought so. I can't find her anywhere. How do you spell it?" I spelled it for her.

"Oh," she said, comprehension dawning on her. And then, in an accusing tone, she added, "you mean 'Han.' " She pronounced it like the first three letters of the word "hand." I pronounced it like the name "Hahn," the way it is pronounced in Chinese. My own last name had undergone a similar mutilation in the course of its migration to this country. It became "Chang" to rhyme with "hang," when in fact the pinyin spelling "Zhang" was a more accurate reflection of the real pronunciation, which was actually most akin to "jahng." This has happened to other Chinese too. Clothing designer Vera Wang's last name should be pronounced "wahng" but only is by other Asians. Journalist Sheryl WuDunn's ancestor was simply given the last name "Dunn" when he reached this country because it sounded somewhat like one syllable of his name. He reinstated the "Wu," his real surname, later in his life. And so it was that when she was eighteen, my mother ceased to be Han Man-li and instead became Mary Han. A simple, common enough process, and one not limited to the Chinese, but I wondered whatever became of Han Man-li.

I found my answer in the Marymount yearbook. Page after page of the volume revealed smiling young women on the verge of adulthood. They wore tweed suits with velvet collars and skirts that hit midcalf. They posed proudly with their jowly fathers and prim mothers for photos on Parents' Weekend. They wore dresses of frothy tulle and stood by a crystal punch bowl at a dance, making small talk with men dressed in dinner jackets. A row of archers wearing simple white belted tunics aimed their arrows like so many virgin Dianas. And then I flipped to a picture of some girls dressed to perform for the school: their faces were painted in blackface, their eyes and lips ghoulishly outlined in white. I saw another photo, this one of my mother in an embroidered silk *qi pao*—the same one, perhaps, her Beiyinyu friends had given her when she left Taiwan. She was surrounded by four girls in heavy satin dresses with full skirts, the kind a small child could hide under.

I continued to leaf through the book until I reached the section reserved for the graduating class. Each page featured two students. There was a head shot, a name, a hometown, and a chatty description of the girl's preferences and personality. Spring Lake, New Jersey, was "perfectly groomed." Irvington-on-Hudson demanded, "Quick, where's my calorie book?" Meanwhile, Larchmont believed that "diamonds are a girl's best friend." One Manhattanite was dubbed a "somber sophisticate," but dowdier Greenwich was relegated to "Peck and Peck tweeds." Prophetically, West Hartford promised to be a "typical homemaker." And then there was my mother. She had "a flare [sic] for fun . . . a smile for everyone." "Mary," her paragraph concluded, "has found a place in all our hearts." The other girl on my mother's page was named Jeanne Heffernan, from Pelham, New York. The yearbook is in black-and-white, but from the looks of it, Jeanne had sandy blond hair and light-colored eyes. "Friendly oriental eyes" was the description bestowed on her.

I once asked my mother what she had thought of Marymount.

"I was very uncomfortable there," she told me. "Most students don't study. They just go to smoke, talk about boyfriends. One of the girls I know, she quit school and left because she miss her boyfriend so much."

She pursed her lips in disgust at the memory the same exact way she did at the thought of her Chinese classmates slaving over their textbooks. My mother had gone from one extreme to another, from academic overload to matrimonial obsession; and in spite of her discomfort, she adapted—the way she always did, the way I never could. She converted to Catholicism the week be-

fore graduation. The school paper ran an article on the event ti-
tled "A Big Day for Mary." The piece called her "one of the most
popular girls on campus" and described her baptism, which was
administered by none other than Archbishop Yu Pin. That year,
she was named the Queen of the Spring Prom and reigned, without irony, as the "Sayonara Queen." It did not surprise me to
learn that she had not converted for religious reasons.

"I thought the school was so nice to me," she said. "And also
the archbishop. I converted to make them happy."

When I got up to leave Sister Majella, I thanked her profusely
for her time. My cheeks ached from constant smiling, something
I do when I am trying to be extremely polite. I asked the nun if
there was anything else she remembered about my mother.

"Well," she said, smiling at me in return, "you certainly remind me of her, you do."

On May 12, 1958, my mother appeared again in the school
newspaper in a column called "The Inquiring Reporter." The
column picked a new topic each week and then asked students
for their opinions. The topic this week was life after graduation.
"This summer I will look for a job in New York City," it quoted
my mother as saying, "and in September, I will go on to school
to major in Chemistry. Upon completion of my schooling, I will
return to China."

Not a single one of those plans came true. My mother, the leaf,
went wherever the wind blew her. She spent the summer on Long
Island working at a restaurant owned by the father of one of her
Marymount friends. In the fall, she headed for Hartford, where
the archbishop enrolled her in a school to learn how to be a medical technician. She had only been in the States for three years,
but if one counted a summer spent working in the Catskills and
the summer on Long Island, Hartford marked the sixth place she
had lived during that time. Little did she know that she would
stay in the area for the next twenty-nine years of her life, longer
than she had ever lived anywhere before, longer, probably, than
she ever will live anywhere again.

She hated Hartford. After six o'clock, she could barely find a
place to buy a cup of coffee. Every weekend found her on the
train to New York City. The Marymount yearbook listed her as

coming from New York, but the school records showed an address in Taipei. As far as I know, my mother never lived in New York until many years later. Most likely, the address the school had for her in the city was the Sino-American Amity building on Riverside Drive. This was the archbishop's residence when he stayed in New York. From there, he and his assistant, Father Paul Chan, ran the Chinese Catholic Information Center, a headquarters for the students in their care.

The center did not have accommodations for students. When my mother was in New York, she stayed at Dolores's family's apartment on 120th Street. Dolores lived in one of those rambling, prewar spaces that are still prevalent in Morningside Heights. Her building had a rich-red brick front with two swaths of granite running up on either side, like white ribbons on a gift box, deviating every now and then to form a curlicue or provide a window trim. In this design, it echoed the sedately famous lines of the McKim, Mead, and White Columbia campus, just up the street. By today's standards, the apartment sounds quite large, the sort of place that spoke of an earlier, more luxurious style of living. There were three bedrooms, a living room, a formal dining room, and an eat-in kitchen. Other Chinese students lived in dorm rooms or boardinghouses. They floated from semester to semester to summer, staying wherever they could find lodging. Not only did Dolores have a permanent home, she had a mother. Not surprisingly, the apartment quickly became a gathering place for her and her sister's friends. When they were not at Sino-American Amity, Chinese students often found themselves waiting for the elevator in the ornate, wood-paneled lobby of Dolores's building. If it was Christmastime, the wind off the nearby Hudson would whip past Riverside Church and its massive carillon, down across the green-trimmed Victorian home of Columbia's Teachers College. It would shake the glass panels in the entryway to Dolores's own building and then drop off into the valley of Morningside Park below. Inside the building, a fireplace glowed. Brass sconces and doorknobs gleamed. The students rubbed their hands in anticipation. As warm as it was in the lobby, it was even warmer upstairs.

Back then, New York was still the most important city in the country, perhaps in the entire world. It was home to the sparkling new United Nations, whose "Wise Men" ruled foreign policy. Its intellectuals held sway over academia. Its abstract expressionists were producing the most groundbreaking art since before the war. The city had long since vanquished London as the world's financial capital. Its manufacturing industry was the largest in the country. Its harbor was greater than the next six biggest combined. No one doubted the mayor, Robert Wagner, when he proclaimed New York to be "the center of the universe."

The city may have been the most powerful in the world, but it was also the most democratic. In 1958, it passed the first law in the country banning discrimination in private housing. Of its eight million inhabitants, a full quarter were Jewish. Almost a tenth were black. Puerto Ricans and Eastern European refugees flooded in after the war, joining the existing substantial populations of Irish, Italians, and Germans. The city teemed with life from everywhere, even China. Most of the Chinese were laborers, concentrated in Chinatown, which was still considered exotic enough to have its own Methodist missionary; but there was also a small, yet increasingly visible, core of scholars and diplomats who had been stranded in New York after the civil war. In the enormous, sprawling mass of the city, these class distinctions did not matter nearly as much as they once had, back in Shanghai or Budapest or San Juan. Everyone paid the same fifteen cents to ride the subway. Anyone could promenade in Central Park on a lovely Sunday afternoon or soak up the sun on the fine white sand of Orchard Beach for free. Items that were considered luxuries in Asia or Europe—coffee, tomato juice, ice cream—could be found in any of the newfangled, utterly American supermarkets. Chocolate, that precious substance so coveted by the girls at Beiyinyu, emerged from subway vending machines for a mere two cents. Social hierarchies did exist, but so too did, as E. B. White once put it, "a tolerance from necessity." New York was nothing if not pragmatic. Like its original namesake, Amsterdam, the city reserved its greatest distinctions for money. Riches counted more than land, family, or even ethnicity. What was once written of Amsterdam held true in New York as well:

"The life of the place was trade." All people who adopted the city for their own eventually came to learn this lesson.

Dolores's training ground was Hunter College, a New York institution in every way. It would be difficult to find two places less similar than Hunter and Marymount in the 1950s. Instead of a gleaming white antebellum clubhouse, Hunter consisted of a modern sixteen-story tower of granite and steel, which had replaced an older structure in 1940. Its campus was the city, Sixty-eighth Street to be exact. The most telling difference between the two schools lay in the student body. Democratic and meritocratic, Hunter had been purposely founded in 1869 to instruct girls from poor, often immigrant, families. By the 1930s, the school had evolved into a full-fledged liberal-arts college with grand aspirations. If City College enjoyed a reputation as the workingman's Ivy League school, then Hunter tried hard to be a Seven Sister. Its faculty included academics with degrees from the real Ivy League and Seven Sisters, along with refugees from the universities of such wartorn cities as Bonn, Vienna, Heidelberg, and Berlin. Marymount's tea-party courses paled in comparison with the wide range of Hunter offerings, which included, among many other subjects, physics, economics, psychology, and philosophy. Hunter meant to educate its students, not simply groom them. My mother graduated with seven-or-so dozen women in twin sets and pearls, whose main ambition was to get married. Dolores's class had almost eight hundred students—whites, blacks, Latinas, Asians—whose principal goal was to have a career.

When Dolores entered Hunter in 1956, the school, like its home city, teetered on the edge of change. The GI Bill had granted men entry, and although the few there remained confined, for the time being, to an outpost campus in the Bronx, their arrival signaled greater transformations to come. The yearbook from my mother's graduating class at Marymount in 1958 had seemed to me like a relic from an ancient time. The Hunter yearbook from 1960, the year Dolores graduated, already offered a much different perspective, one still familiar to my eyes. The photographs were laid out with deliberately torn edges. A free-verse poem sprawled, graffitilike, over the opening pages.

One section, entitled "Class History," read like an Allen Ginsberg imitation: "Staccato! repercussion of a police action in a distant east; the pulse of power; the echo of a revolution. . . ." Hunter embodied New York, from the sleek chrome fixtures on its elevator banks to the Lexington Avenue subway line that ran practically to its door. Its students could not help noticing the world around them and, in turn, wishing to be noticed by it.

Dolores loved the school. There, she was busy and happy. Later, she would count those years as being among the best of her life. There were enough other Chinese students that they had their own club on campus and could even mount a production of the famous Chinese novel *Dream of the Red Chamber*. Dolores starred as Chia Pao Yu, the most important male lead, although everyone who saw her agreed that she was the prettiest girl on stage. The club advertised the play in the local papers, and the auditorium was packed on the two nights it ran. In the downtimes during rehearsal, Dolores would sneak off to study in the stairwell by the dressing rooms. Schoolwork was important to her. She maintained an almost perfect grade-point average in her math classes, and the chairman of the department urged her to go on to graduate school. New York was a city for dreamers, and Dolores, more than ever, counted herself among their number.

When I asked my mother about those days, she told me that Cardinal Yu Pin had long since died but that his assistant was still alive and in residence at the old Sino-American building. I made an appointment to meet him. Rain poured so hard the day I went that it felt like the pellets of water whipping across my face were leaving small dents in my cheeks. I hurried down the long hill toward the park, the wind blowing rain up and under my umbrella. The organization was located on the corner of Eighty-first and Riverside in a coldly magnificent limestone mansion, once the home of Douglas Fairbanks and Mary Pickford. I was late; my pant legs were wet to the knees. I stood dripping in the entryway, listening to the raindrops. A discreet wooden plaque by the door indicated that I had found the right place, but I wondered if I should keep the appointment. An atmosphere of neglect hung about the place. An outburst of graffiti marred the lovely stonework out front. I felt like the hapless victim in a horror film. "It was a dark and stormy night," I thought to myself, as I knocked on the door.

A bent old man peered out at me from within. He opened the door and instructed me to wait in the front hall while he announced my arrival to Father Chan. As I waited, my dripping clothes and umbrella created a dirty pool of water on the floor. The man reemerged.

"Okay," he said. "Follow me."

I stepped carefully after him, embarrassed by my snail's trail of glistening water and uncertain of what I might find. To my relief, no Dracula waited for me behind the heavy oak door that opened onto the kitchen: just an elderly Chinese man with a receding hairline sitting at a table and reading the paper. He looked up.

"I am Father Chan," he said.

Fluorescent lights cast the room in a sickly glow. A box of corn flakes sat on the table next to a copy of the *New York Times*. A plastic mat protected the table itself. The rest of the items in the room were less comprehensible: a book-sized block of shiny yellow cheese by the priest's elbow; a nutcracker soldier in a red uniform on a chest against the wall; on the wall itself, a photo of tigers in a gold frame; and, in the center of the table, a baby spider plant nestled in a glass bowl, sitting snugly in turn in an amber-colored ashtray. The only thing that made sense to me was the heavy wooden crucifix hanging in the center of the wall above the table.

I looked at Father Chan. He too seemed a jumble of odds and ends. Moles dotted his face as if someone had lightly sprinkled him with a few gigantic poppy seeds. His ears were the size of small coasters, and each looked like one half of a translucent heart. He wore thick, black-framed glasses and a white, short-sleeved shirt with a collar. Loose black trousers struggled to stay on his skinny frame. He had on a pair of flip-flops. His appearance was not quite what I had hoped for. I had come wanting to find a dignified, paternal teacher, someone who could guide me through the past. I had expected him to greet me in a wood-paneled office with a mahogany desk and a richly detailed Oriental rug. Instead, I found myself dripping water all over a green linoleum floor, facing a cartoon character of an old man.

"Sit down," he said.

I asked him about my mother.

"Well," he said, "since you call, I'm trying to remember her. But we had so many students. In the forties, fifties, sixties, I think we have about four thousand Chinese students from different parts of the Orient."

"So," I prompted, "you don't remember my mom?"

"Not really so well," he said, which, coming from a Chinese, meant no. He tried to explain again. "Every year, we give more than one hundred scholarships. We get lots of students from Taiwan, Hong Kong, Macao."

"My mother went to Marymount." I tried to jog his memory.

"Marymount in Virginia," he said. "I don't know. There is a Theresa Sun, a student over there. We had about three, four students at Marymount at the time. Your mother's one of them."

It was an interesting statement. No, he was saying, he did not remember my mother, but yes, he knew she had been a student at Marymount. From then on, my mother existed in his mind as one of his students. He might not remember her, but he could reconstruct her identity and file it away among the 3,999 other students he had brought to the States. She had been magically rehabilitated, like a controversial Soviet politico when a new regime comes into power.

"Why did you send her to a two-year college," I asked, playing along with his game, "and not a four-year?"

"It depends on what's available," he said. "Your mother maybe come in late, so I have that scholarship available. Also it depends on what they want to study. Your mother graduated from Marymount. Later on, did I send her to another college with a junior, senior year?"

I marveled at how easily he switched from helpfully informing me—as if I had not just told him moments before that my mother had graduated from Marymount—to asking where he had sent her next.

"She became a medical technician," I said.

"She was probably studying nursing," Father Chan said. "That was a pretty good outlet. We had many nursing scholar-

ships. In the fifties we gave over one hundred scholarships to
nursing schools."

He had nothing more to offer on the subject of my mother. I
tried Dolores instead.

"Yes," he said brightly, "I remember her. She had a sister who
went to school in Connecticut."

After such a promising start, he ran out of information.

"So many students," he said, waving his hand apologetically.
"So many to remember. Sometimes seventy, eighty of them come
at one time. I went to San Francisco in 1947, 1948 to greet the
students who came by boat. I have to get them this cheap price
for railroad to go to their colleges and universities. Most of them
go to Chicago first. Then from Chicago, you go to Wisconsin, go
to different places. Then another group came to New York.
From New York go to different places."

"Where did they go?" I asked.

"All over," he said. "There were more than three hundred
Catholic colleges at the time. In New York, you have St. John's
University; Fordham; St. Francis College in Brooklyn; Seton Hall
in South Orange, New Jersey; Mount St. Vincent Girls' School;
Manhattan Boys' College. Then you have Marymount in Tarry-
town. All in this area—at least fifteen Catholic colleges, universities. Many more in the rest of the country."

Silence followed. Rainwater splashed noisily into the window
wells outside. I pictured thousands of Chinese students bent like
marionettes over books in school libraries across the country.
The strings attached to their wrists led to Father Chan, but he
was himself a mere wooden doll, controlled by the great puppet
master, Archbishop, later Cardinal, Yu Pin himself. The cardinal
had died years before. Father Chan could not hope to remember
all the students they had once helped. Nor should he have. As it
turned out, my mother and thousands of others never bothered
to remember him.

He sat with me in the kitchen for a long moment, his old eyes
regarding me calmly. In the silence, I could hear the softly an-
noying hum of the fluorescent lights.

"And now?" I asked him. "It's so quiet. Is this the way it
would have been forty years ago?"

"Now?" he repeated. "Now, it's very difficult for us to get scholarships. Five, six, seven scholarships every year if we're lucky. It's not the same."

He sighed, and I shivered a little from my still-damp skin and the sound of the rain drumming against the windows.

"Do you keep in touch with the students?" I asked.

"I'd like to," he replied, "but they don't keep in touch with me. The Chinese say, 'When you cross a bridge, you don't need that bridge anymore.' Who cares if the bridge stays or not? I told them I have a contract with them. I said, 'After you graduate, at least once a year, you get in touch with me.' But forget about it. I have this fund-raising affair sometime. Every year, I send raffle books, ten dollars each. I ask, 'Do you want to help us?' Then I have Double Ten dinner in October, so I ask them to send something to help maintain this place. You know, some of them do, some of them don't. But that is usually how it goes."

He put both his hands on the tabletop and lifted himself up with another tired sigh.

"Come," he said, "I will show you the house."

What followed was a tour of old splendor in new ruin. The heyday of Sino-American Amity had ended years before, victim of the warming Cold War, the secularization of university education, the growing wealth in Asia. Father Chan, who had once provided invaluable assistance to thousands of students, remained nothing more than a living relic. I followed him down a rickety set of steps to the basement. The soles of his flip-flops slapped each stair as he descended. We stood in a large, empty room.

"This was the rec room for the students," he said. "There was a Ping-Pong table there."

Wood paneling would have made the room snug had it not been for the dusty floors and the leaking walls. Small pools of water glistened in the dim light. For the past twenty years, the Catholic Review had rented the space from Sino-American Amity and produced a magazine called *Homiletic and Pastoral Review.* The organization had recently moved on, leaving this mausoleum of a house practically empty. Now the five rambling floors and basement were home only to Father Chan's three-priest operation.

As we walked through the building, glimpses of its old splendor still shone through. A broad staircase wound its way grandly if not gracefully past the various floors. Hand-carved oak paneling hung in the passageways and in almost every room. At the second-floor landing, we paused before a portrait of Cardinal Yu Pin as a smooth-faced youth dressed in red robes. It had been painted when he was still the bishop of Nanking and China was still a republic.

"As you can see," Father Chan said proudly, "he's a wonderful man."

Just beyond the painting lay the rooms that had once been Cardinal Yu Pin's living quarters. They contained a hodgepodge of ornate furniture, filing cabinets, and knickknacks. A minute Nationalist flag—the sort children wave at parades—stood in a plastic holder next to a red lacquer table with gilt trim.

"That table came from the Imperial Palace in Beijing," Father Chan said.

The next floor housed Father Chan's own office, a smaller room, crammed floor-to-ceiling with books. Postcards of the Virgin Mary from all over the world were tacked to the wall. The priest pointed out another picture to me of a fund-raising dinner that had taken place in Boston in 1957. The photo contained a roomful of formally set tables at which were seated scores of elegant people dressed in black tie. Many were Chinese; almost as many were white. They were all celebrating the fortieth anniversary of the founding of the republic.

We walked down the hall to a small chapel past room after room of what had once been offices for other priests. They all stood empty. The chapel itself contained just two seats, two benches, and two hymnal racks.

"Everything's old here," Father Chan said quietly, and turned to lead me up yet more stairs.

We arrived abruptly at the ballroom. Unlike the other floors, the fifth had no landing. When I mounted the steps, I was immediately confronted with a wide expanse of room. Had it been a nice day, the sunlight would have streamed into the long windows and bathed the baby grand piano in warm gold. But it was raining, and the only color in the room came from the ancient yellow curtains hanging from the windows. They were fraying so badly that even though the rain continued to pour, the feeble light from outside still managed to shine through the worn fabric. On the ceiling, a large oval of rotting plaster dripped water onto my head. Off to one side was a room the size of a prison cell. It contained a mattress, a sink, and a single naked bulb that dangled from the ceiling. A priest, long dead, had lived there in the past. The three priests who remained lived one more modest flight up in an area that was kept off-limits by a No Trespassing sign of the sort that one usually sees nailed to a tree in the woods. Another sign said, "Private Quarters." I wondered whom they could possibly be trying to keep away.

Father Chan pointed to the piano at one end of the room.

"Yo-Yo Ma played here when he was six," he said. "His sister was ten. She played the piano. He played six movements of Bach without sheet music. Sixty people came to hear him. There was a cellist in the audience, and later he came up to me. He said, 'This boy's got it.' "

He smiled at the memory and turned as if to ask me to dance.

"We go down now," he said.

In my mind, I saw the ballroom as it was in my mother's student days, with gleaming wood floors and sparkling windows. Every dance the church organized was packed with at least seventy or eighty kids. One time, a record three hundred came in one night. The men wore suits and ties and slicked their hair back in the fashion of the day. The women wore dresses that showed off their narrow waists and flared into full, pleated skirts. They wore stockings and lipstick and tried to curl their hair—all the things they had been taught not to do back home. Together, the couples waltzed, did the fox-trot and, if they felt particularly daring, a jitterbug or two. The room of gliding, handsome pairs could have been mistaken for a gathering of any young Americans. The men leaned out the windows to blow cigarette smoke into the night air. The women powdered their faces in the bathroom. The only difference lay in the music. Anything racier than big band—say, Elvis, for example—was strictly prohibited by Father Chan.

They were the organization's glory days. Back then, the U.S.

viewed Catholics and nonmainland Chinese, particularly those
from Taiwan, as great allies in the Cold War and encouraged
them to study in the States. America itself was enjoying an un-
precedented period of prosperity. Every summer, Father Chan
found jobs for his students, including my mother, at resorts in the
Catskills. He held lectures in the ballroom before they went, introducing them to the Jewish culture they would encounter in the
mountains. He demystified lox, gefilte fish, and matzoh ball
soup, and then he sent them by the hundreds up to such places
as the Concord Hotel. He visited them throughout the summer
to make sure they were all right. When a resort tried to fire one,
Father Chan became a union leader. "If you don't allow this one
to work," he said, "then I take all the students out."

For their pains, the students earned about a thousand dollars
a summer. Never before had the cliché "Gold Mountain" rung
quite so literally true. It was not surprising then that outside of
America, in wartorn, poverty-stricken parts of the world, the
people looked to the country with hope. Everyone wanted to immigrate. Father Chan's students knew that they were the lucky
ones, even if, like my mother, they were living in shabby room-
ing houses in provincial places learning skills in which they had
no interest. When the men looked out into the night from the
fourth-floor ballroom to the lights of the New Jersey suburbs
across the Hudson, they felt themselves on the verge of all that
was new and promising. In a few years, they would find work as
engineers and academics. They would move out to the same suburbs they saw from the window. They would buy houses and
raise children. And they would take the women, who looked so
pretty twirling in their pleated skirts and who spoke their language, with them. Together they would become Americans.

When I left Father Chan at the Sino-American Amity building
that rainy day, he took my address.

"Tell your mother to stay in touch," he told me. "Tell Dolores."

Then he flapped his bony arm in farewell. Two months later, I
received my own invitation to the annual Double Ten celebra-
tion, which celebrates the overthrow of the Qing dynasty and the
founding of the republic. The invitation consisted of a Xeroxed

sheet that urged me to come down to Chinatown for the evening's festivities. Tickets were twenty-five dollars a person. I had no intention of going, but I wanted to send a donation to this kind old man to thank him for all he had done for my mother and for the multitude of other Chinese students he had brought to America. I kept the letter as a reminder. First it served as a pleasant souvenir of our talk and a physical tie to the past I had been trying so hard to find. Then it became a glaring accusation of guilt. I had not gotten around to sending Father Chan any money, and I probably never would. Just like the thousands of students he had also helped, I no longer needed him. When I could no longer stand the sight of it, I threw the invitation in the trash.

In 1959, my mother was riding the train back to Hartford from yet another weekend in New York. As always, the train stopped in New Haven for an hour to switch tracks, but this time my mother struck up a conversation with a pleasant young man in the seat next to her. They talked and talked, and when the train reached Hartford, the man asked for her telephone number.

"I have someone to introduce you to," he said.

The person he introduced her to became my father. He and the young man on the train had gone to college together and were now both working at the same insurance company. My mother was young and alone, without any reason or desire to return to Taiwan but without any sense of what to do in America. Her job as a medical technician simply paid the bills. On her lunch hour, she would walk around a quiet green horseshoe of a street near the hospital, admiring the imposing houses. She imagined living there one day with her own family, something she had not been part of in a long time. A year after they started dating, my parents were married.

It was September 1960. That same fall, Dolores enrolled in a doctoral program at New York University for mathematics. She could continue to live at her mother's familiar apartment in Morningside Heights and, as she had at Hunter, commute to school. Just as she had rejected Marymount four years before, Dolores now rejected marriage. She claimed that in those days, she only went out one evening each year: New Year's Eve. The rest of the time, she studied. Romance could wait. She had other ideas.

In 1953, when Dolores had first come to New York, the el still ran along Third Avenue. Morningside Park, which lay a few yards down the street from Dolores's apartment, was being touted in the *New York Times* as a lovely place to enjoy spring's greenery. The original Pennsylvania Station remained to greet travelers with a majestic dignity. People spoke of living "in" a street, not on it. Hunter College still served tea in the afternoons and had an annual "Sing," a tradition that attempted to echo, if not replicate, the Daisy Chains of Vassar and the Greek Games at Barnard. In the next decade, all that hushed gentility would disappear. In the summer of 1964, Harlem, whose southern end also bordered Morningside Park, would erupt in a riot of Molotov cocktails and broken glass over the killing of a black boy by an off-duty police officer. One-quarter of its population was out of work. They used drugs at a rate eight times higher than that of the rest of the city; they killed each other six hundred times more frequently. Morningside Park became the most dangerous spot in the city. In 1970, the City University of New York system did away with its entrance examinations, throwing open its doors to any graduate of the New York City high-school system. Hunter's glowing reputation, along with that of City College, quickly became a distant memory. Hunter's motto was "Mihi cura futuri"—I care for the future. In New York, it began to seem that no one did.

By then, Dolores and my mother had traveled far down their separate paths. Back in 1960, my mother had chosen Hartford and a husband—or as she would say, those choices had been made for her. Hartford, and the rest of Connecticut, for that matter, were hopelessly provincial. In 1960, there was a total of 388 native Chinese speakers in the entire state. Choosing to live there appeared to be choosing a life of isolation. Dolores, in contrast, had chosen New York and a career. City of immigrants, New York was where Dolores's family and friends lived. If she stayed there, she would never be alone.

The probable does not always become the inevitable. Community ultimately revolves around a much more complicated series of relationships than mere geography. It entails compromise and even surrender of will—time-honored traditions in China, but practices to which Dolores, the first American among her classmates, would never be willing to submit. Isolation, when it came, would befall not my mother but her old friend. It strikes me that ever since Dolores first fled from Nanjing to Taipei as a child, she has lived on an island. Two years before Dolores arrived in her new home city, E. B. White had written, "No one should come to New York to live unless he is willing to be lucky." Dolores had always been lucky; and yet, many years later, after I had met her, I would think not of E. B. White's words but of Henry James's. He had once written memorably about the nineteenth-century inhabitants of NYU's modern-day campus, the very place where, in 1960, Dolores was embarking on the next stage of her life. Of New York, he had said, "The very sign of its energy is that it doesn't believe in itself; it fails to succeed, even at the cost of millions, in persuading you that it does."

People say that the 1960s were a time when America broke free from the conventions of the decade before. Of the four women in this book, this theory holds true only for Dolores. Even as Freedom Riders battled the Ku Klux Klan in the Birmingham bus terminal and thousands of student protesters marched against the Vietnam War, Suzanne, Margaret, and my mother were purposely curtailing their own freedoms. In 1961, in the muggy heat of early September, my mother gave birth to her first child. She had quit work not long before. In 1962, Suzanne married a man whom she did not love. Wedding guests toasted the success of the match at a white wood mansion in the northwest part of Washington, D.C. Three years later, Margaret, who was finishing a doctorate in biochemistry at the University of Maryland, turned down a rare opportunity to work at one of the world's preeminent research laboratories, in Paris, to return to St. Louis and the man she would marry. Only Dolores refused to give up her dreams, even when, after two years of graduate work, she failed out of her Ph.D. program at NYU. She simply switched to Brooklyn Polytech and perhaps to a dawning realization that life would not always turn out as she had planned. In light of the battles being fought in the rest of the country, the classmates' own inner struggles seem unimportant, on too small a scale even to notice; but they would prove to be crucial turning points in their lives, as difficult to reverse as the civil rights movement or the Vietnam War. Just as the rest of the country would have to reap the consequences, good and bad, of its own actions, so too would they.

NEXT TO LOVE

Everything I have," Wallace Stevens once said, "comes from Pennsylvania and Connecticut." I stumbled upon this reference to the poet while doing research in the stacks of Butler Library at Columbia. I had always known that Stevens had spent the last part of his life in Hartford, but I now learned that he had spent the first part in Reading, where Suzanne had also lived for two decades. For years, Stevens's book of collected poems had sat virtually untouched on my bookshelf. I took the volume down, wondering what, if anything, this Pennsylvania Dutch–born, Pulitzer Prize–winning insurance executive, who had died the year my mother came to America, might be able to reveal about her and Suzanne.

In 1965, before I was even born, my parents and my two oldest siblings drove to Indiana to visit my father's sister. On the way, they stopped in Dayton, Ohio, where Suzanne was then living with her husband, Tan. A decade had passed since my mother had last seen Suzanne, the summer that they had graduated from high school. It is typical of my mother's exuberance that she simply invited herself to Suzanne's house for a visit, but Suzanne welcomed her almost as enthusiastically. She and her husband were on the verge of moving to Pennsylvania, where he would enroll in a doctorate program in mathematics. Boxes lined the rooms of their small house, and chaos, in the form of their toddler, Jim, reigned. The place was so small that Suzanne and her husband insisted that my parents sleep in their bedroom while they camped out in the living room.

The visit lasted only one night, but it had a special quality. In later years, it would glow in their memories, transforming the event from something ordinary to something beautiful, like an insect caught in amber. It would speak of an earlier time when the world and their place in it had seemed reassuringly secure. It was a time when, after the uncertainty and instability of their childhood, they had dared to think that they might have at last found a place where the future could only bring happiness.

The rebel and the tomboy had both developed into well-pressed wives and efficient homemakers. Each regarded the other's transformation with some amusement and surprise.

"I was so impressed," my mother recalled. "She's not like the girl I knew in high school—never studies, plays basketball. Now she's a nice mother and a good cook. She never knows how to cook in China, never goes to the kitchen."

Suzanne had even appeared on television to demonstrate her cooking. She also knew how to sew her own clothes. My mother had learned to tuck her shirt in and could herself make a fine pot of *hong xiao*. Both women were married to men with promising futures. My father had just received his law degree. Tan would soon get a Ph.D. In a way, the families mirrored one another, even down to their pasts. My mother and Suzanne had gone to school together. My father and Tan discovered ties of their own.

"Suzanne's husband would have fit into my family perfectly," my father later told me. "In terms of background, he could just as well have been somebody I met in Shanghai going to school."

Tan came from a prominent family of intellectuals and government leaders. His father was a well-known authority on Chinese theater. An aunt was a literary critic. At the time of Tan's marriage, his uncle held the most important cabinet position in the Taiwanese government, that of defense minister. In those days, mainland China loomed large as a threat to tiny Taiwan's security. The 1950s had seen several bombardments of outlying islands that belonged to Nationalist China. Tan's family played a role on the other side of the political fence as well. A cousin of his had risen to power as one of the student leaders of the Communist movement. He had lived with Jiang Qing, the infamous Madame Mao, long before she ever met and married the Chairman. Many years after Tan had fled to Taiwan with his family, an old grade-school classmate who had remained on the mainland wrote him a letter. All communication between the two countries had been cut in the intervening years. The only information the friend had was Tan's name, which he wrote in lieu of an address on the envelope. The family was so well known that the letter arrived, in good time, at the right place.

With his round, full scholar's face, pale skin, and gentle manner, Tan epitomized the physical ideal of the Chinese upper classes. He represented the legions of students who had come to America in droves in the fifties and sixties and who had dispersed like doves released from a cage. What they would make of their lives in this new country remained to be seen. But for four of them on one night in 1965, it seemed as though a little corner of China, now disappeared in China itself, had been recaptured in Ohio.

Even my sister and Suzanne's son suited each other perfectly. Although she was only four years old at the time, Christine still remembered the visit years later. "We were boyfriend and girlfriend," she said. "For a day."

Fate could not have willed a happier confluence of like and like. Perhaps it was fate that had brought them together. My mother and Suzanne cooked dinner in the kitchen. My father and Tan talked politics and Chinese literature in the living room. Christine and Jim played with a set of Legos. Years later, Christine would become an architect and Jim an engineer. They might have built great things together. At the very least, their parents assumed that they would meet again.

Maybe Christine and Jim knew something no one else did. The next morning, while my parents packed the car to leave, the two toddlers clung to each other and cried. They would not meet again for a very long time, and when they did, it would be almost as strangers. I doubt that they will ever meet again.

To understand what happened, it is necessary to return to Wallace Stevens: "Say next to holiness is the will thereto, and next to love is the desire for love." Like so many other immigrants, my mother and Suzanne married their husbands not for love but for the desire for love. At the time, they did not know the difference. They married because they were alone and afraid and because, as Dan Li would later admit to his daughter when she asked why he had married her mother: "There were only so many Chinese around."

The Chinese embassy in Washington, D.C., hosted a reception for Tan and Suzanne with over two hundred guests. The vice-consul's wife picked out Suzanne's dress. It was hardly the sort of wedding other classmates were having around the country. My own mother got married in a nondescript Catholic church in a working-class neighborhood of Hartford. She borrowed her dress from a Marymount friend. Suzanne, kindhearted and generous though she was, could not help being aware of such social distinctions. They pleased her even though she was in love with another man. But he was a struggling pharmaceutical student in California. Their wedding would most likely have involved a quick trip to city hall.

"I was alone," Suzanne told me years later. "Afraid. Don't know how to work. How to live."

In Tan, she saw safety, and even a certain prestige. Her parents encouraged her to marry him, and she did not refuse. As for my mother, I think she was in love with the idea of my father, not the man himself. Because she had no father or mother to tell her anything, she saw everything in extremes, not as the shifting, subtle landscape that life really is. Marriage was good; therefore, her marriage would be good. They did not know it that summer evening in Ohio, but the stems of their marriages were already starting to turn brown. With them, their dreams, like dried leaves, were beginning to curl at the edges.

The Pennsylvania Dutch country where Wallace Stevens grew up and Suzanne spent the better part of her adult life can be a giving place. The region forms a portion of a larger area known in Pennsylvania as the Great Valley. The early settlers of the original thirteen called it the breadbasket of the colonies. Farm wives canned furiously—spring, summer, and fall—to make use of all the bounty given to them. They could even afford extravagance.

Sour cherries, peaches, and strawberries became pies, a dozen of which could be baked in a single sitting in one of the cavernous, cast-iron Dutch ovens that glowered in the corner of every farm kitchen. Bushels of windfalls emerged after long cooking as a few dainty jars of apple butter. Meat, in all its various, glorious forms, was eaten three times a day. A good cook staked her reputation on the "seven sweets and seven sours" expected to appear at her table whenever company did.

With bounty came piety. The Quakers who had founded the colony encouraged a religious tolerance that, in turn, encouraged the settlement of those who would be persecuted elsewhere: Mennonites and Amish, Dunkers and Moravians. They were the Plain People who clung to their plain ways. "What are buttons," goes one Amish saying, "but a place for the devil to catch on." Wearing flat-brimmed hats and long beards, they tilled their lands, raised their barns, and kept insistently to themselves. The tolerance that came out of the Pennsylvania Dutch countryside was nothing like the tolerance of New York City, which arises from the endless jostling and jockeying of its citizens. Rather, the tolerance of Berks and Lancaster counties comes from the insularity of open spaces. The saying "To each his own" should have been coined there if it was not. The Conestoga wagon was invented in Pennsylvania, and one imagines huddled circles of them dotting the Great Plains during the westward expansion— not radical new ways of living but mere extensions of the Great Valley from where they had come.

Each newcomer is expected to adapt to the ways of this land of steady habits. Accordingly, each new community turns inward rather than out. It happened with the Eastern Europeans and the Italians who arrived in the late nineteenth century. It happened with the Southern blacks and the Puerto Ricans who came in search of work after World War II. And it happened with the Chinese. There was one difference. Unlike earlier immigrants, who had come as laborers, the Chinese in Reading came as professionals, drawn by work at local colleges or at nearby Bell Laboratories. They were researchers, engineers, and professors who lived in white suburbs and came into daily contact with the outside world. But in the Reading region, that mingling ended with the workday. The lack of socializing, combined with the often specialized nature of their field, made it easy for others to pigeonhole them. Chinese employees were often already limited by their language skills. They might continue for years at the same position, hoping, but never expecting, to be tapped for upper management, department chair, or dean.

Tan and Suzanne became leaders of this tight-knit community. In 1974, a few years after they moved to the area, they organized a Chinese-language school at a local church. It would be the first of many appearances by Suzanne in the local newspaper, the *Reading Eagle*. Revealing just how little people in the area knew about Asia, the article described her as being born in Nanking, Taiwan. By then, she had become a librarian at the granite mausoleum of a public library on the city's main thoroughfare downtown. Every day, she helped locals with their requests, in her pretty, gentle way; she became known as "that nice Chinese girl at the library." A generic, condescending epithet perhaps, but at least Reading noticed her, which was more than could be said of the other, invisible and anonymous members of the Chinese community.

> *An old man sits*
> *In the shadow of a pine tree*
> *In China.*
> *He sees larkspur,*
> *Blue and white,*
> *At the edge of the shadow,*
> *Move in the wind.*
> *His beard moves in the wind.*
> *The pine tree moves in the wind.*
> *Thus water flows*
> *Over weeds.*

Wallace Stevens meant those lines to convey the beauty of acceptance of one's own insignificance. It is an Eastern philosophy, found "in the shadow of a pine tree in China." For the Chinese in Reading, it had particular resonance. Strangers in an indifferent land, they went about their days quietly, weeds over which flowed water. They viewed life in terms of strategy, not adventure. The object was to survive. As much as anyone else, Suzanne's husband, Tan, subscribed to this philosophy. If he hunkered down, worked diligently, planned for the future, and kept his expectations low, then maybe, just maybe, he could enjoy his last few years free from worry. In this way, Tan fit in with Reading's plain ways, clinging to his own traditions as his Pennsylvania Dutch neighbors did to theirs.

He was not without passion, but it was a passion for principles rather than for living. He had left academia, soon after he received his doctorate, because one semester he had failed all of his students—no makeovers, no compromises, no exceptions. Ideas, not people, mattered to him; but halfway across the world, the Vietnam War was raging, and those who failed out of school quite literally faced death in the form of the draft. The same views of individual life, held so cheaply in the China of Tan's youth, did not hold in America. The school fired him.

Tan recovered. He taught himself about computers, which still were a mysterious new technology, and landed a good job. Then he lost momentum. He had done his duty. He wanted to be free, as the scholars from whom he had descended were in the old days, to study and reflect. For him, this meant holing up in his office and working on his computer. He lived a simple life in a simple home, a modest brick split-level on a quiet street that bordered farmland. His pleasure came in similarly simple moments—playing with his young son or having his Chinese friends over for dinner and conversation. In the community, Tan enjoyed being an elder statesman, a status that was almost automatically conferred upon anyone who arrived before the immigration reforms of 1965. Suzanne, with her grace and mannered sociability, took naturally to the role of hostess. Practically every Chinese gathering occurred in their home, certainly every one of the important annual parties at Christmas and the Chinese New Year. Suzanne, even more than Tan, became the leader of the community; but they remained together in everyone's mind as their village's elders.

"In Reading," one friend of theirs explained to me, "of course, we have some misunderstanding or some disagreement, but there's always one leader, the older couple. They are fair. They solve the problem."

"They were always so happy," she continued. "Always have party."

Tight-knit as the community was, no one knew of the problems with Tan's and Suzanne's marriage. The root may have been mere incompatibility. Even as Tan shrank from America, Suzanne embraced it. Her favorite brother had died in a car crash when he was still in college. She took nothing for granted. Tan's passivity drove her out of the house. He could let life pass him by; she would not. She planted a tree near the pagoda that loomed above the city in the name of Chinese-American friendship. She served as a delegate to the Second Asian Pacific Conference on Publications in Taiwan. She attended the Frankfurt Book Fair. She gave a cooking demonstration for the Women's Club of nearby Shillington. She served as a Pennsylvania delegate to a White House conference on information and library services. She published a cookbook for children called *Cooking the Chinese Way*. Each of these events appeared in the *Reading Eagle*. Whenever Chinese New Year rolled around, the paper asked Suzanne to comment. In 1989, it offered her views on Tiananmen Square.

Every time she appeared in the paper, Tan made the same comment: "What's the big deal?" he would say to his wife. "You think you're great. You're not so great."

The couple never bickered. They simply retreated into their own lives—Tan to his study, Suzanne to wherever she could go. In her spare time, she sat on the boards of the Reading YWCA, the Reading-Berks Human Relations Council, and the Pennsylvania Citizens for Better Libraries. She was a committee member of the Chinese-American Librarians Association and the president of the Reading Chinese Association. She worked as a translator of English-language books into Chinese for a Taipei publishing house. She volunteered to research preschool education for a Taiwanese institute. She wrote for a biweekly Chinese publication, tutored children in English, and acted as an editorial consultant for Lerner Publications, the Minneapolis company that had published her children's cookbook. A publishing house in Jerusalem contracted her to write three adult trade books, the first of which would be a coffee-table volume about the flowers of the world. Suzanne had also operated an import-export business, bringing woodworking equipment from Taiwan into the U.S. She had co-owned a small gift shop that specialized in Chinese artifacts. She traveled as much as she could—back and forth to Taipei, weekends in New York, trips to California and Europe. Throughout these years, she had always held her full-time job at the Reading library.

When I asked her why she had been so active, she shrugged her shoulders.

"I just try," she said with typical understatement, "to get out of the house."

She organized the social lives of her friends with typical fervor. The other Chinese women hated to drive, so on Saturday mornings, she would pile them all into her car for the forty-five-minute trip to the farmers' market. They wandered like children on a school trip, listening to the strange Germanic inflections of the farm wives who sold them such exotica as cup cheese, shmierkase, sause, meringue kisses, and eggs boiled in beet juice. On other Saturdays, they would venture to the town of Ephrata, a onetime popular resort that had originally been founded by Moravian monks as a cloistered community. It now housed the most expensive department store in the area, a place called Donecker's, which was set in a quaint grouping of blue-washed wood farm buildings. The other women contented themselves with window-shopping and lunch in the store's self-billed "continental-style" restaurant. Suzanne combed the sales racks for bargains.

"One time," one woman told me with a mixture of admiration and disbelief, "she buy a thousand dollars' worth."

Suzanne was the only one of their group who had white friends, people she had met through the library or her endless volunteering; but Reading society offered little in the way of sophistication. She met one friend when the woman's daughter came to the library looking for a recipe for fortune cookies. She was directed to Suzanne because, as everyone knew, fortune cookies were what Chinese people ate for dessert. That's why the local chop suey joint served them with the check. Later, the girl's mother, the one who would become Suzanne's friend, would talk to me about the Chinese "alphabet." The irony was that Suzanne, who made friends easily, fit Reading less well than Tan, who simply kept to himself. She had married him for security, but over time, their quiet, low house and the fussy, red-brick architecture of hilly, narrow Reading began to represent captivity instead of safety.

In 1977, Suzanne caught a glimpse of a way to freedom. Her old boyfriend, the pharmaceutical student she had once thought about marrying, reappeared in her life. His name was Richard, and he had been Suzanne's college sweetheart. They had met at her father's house at the New Year in 1954. Because of his position, Suzanne's father oversaw all the overseas students in Taiwan. He often invited some of them over to his house. Richard, who was from Hong Kong, went to a party there with one of his closest friends, a man who was also the son of a friend of Suzanne's father.

A group of them decided to go boating in the river that ran behind Suzanne's house. Suzanne and her sister climbed into one boat with Richard. A second one carried the others. What happened next sounds like a scene in a Restoration comedy. Richard described it charmingly.

"I don't know," he said, "by some arrangement, she fell off the boat."

"By some arrangement?" I asked.

"Yes."

When I asked Suzanne, she giggled.

"He says I fall off on purpose," she said. "It was an accident."

Accident or no, Richard reached down and pulled her out. She was soaking. It was February, a month when even Taiwan can get chilly. Richard gave Suzanne his jacket. Then he walked her back to the house. By the time they reached it, the two were falling in love.

When Suzanne's father found out, he forbade her to see him. Richard was not the sort of boy he wanted his daughter to date. Richard's father was a notorious playboy and a spendthrift. Richard himself was impetuous, loud, not respectful of his elders, almost foolhardy in his risk taking. In other words, he was the direct opposite of Tan. Before he met Suzanne, Richard had been enrolled in a military medical training program in Tainan, in the southern part of the island. He wanted to be a doctor, but he did not want to be in the army. The year he entered the program, the administration changed its rules. People in the medical program now had to undergo military training. Before, overseas students did not have to join the army after they graduated. Now they did—for life. The only way to get out was to fail. But Richard still wanted to study in Taiwan. Back in Hong Kong, an exam was scheduled to be administered to students wishing to go to Tai Da. It came the day after his military exams. During those exams, Richard left every single one of the answers blank, and then he snuck out of the school through a back field, over a fence, and across a river. He went to the house of a local fisherman whom he had paid to keep a set of civilian clothes for him. He changed, sauntered back out onto the main road that led past the soldiers guarding the front gates of the school and into town. There he hired a taxi to drive him all the way back to Taipei. In Taipei, he caught a flight for Hong Kong and arrived in time for the next day's examination. Understandably frazzled, he missed getting into medical school at Tai Da by a few points. He settled for the almost equally competitive pharmaceutical school there instead.

When Suzanne's father checked Richard's file, he saw only that the boy had failed out of military school. It was yet another mark against him. Then there was the issue of Richard's close friend, the son of Suzanne's father's friend. Suzanne's father believed him to be Suzanne's boyfriend. Not only was Richard a failure with suspect family ties, but also he was stealing his best friend's girl.

"Do not see this boy," Suzanne's father warned her.

At the time, Suzanne was going to school in the Taichung, in the middle of the island. Richard was studying at Tai Da in Taipei. Their lives developed into a romantic movie. They wrote constantly. Richard had wanted to be a writer in high school, and he penned long love missives to her instead of learning his chemistry. While the rest of his classmates studied into the night,

Richard cut school to go visit Suzanne. When she came back up from Taichung, they would meet clandestinely at the train station. They arranged dates by meeting at the homes of mutual friends. It was a heady affair, forbidden, intensely passionate, that contained echoes of the great romances of the West: Romeo and Juliet, Héloïse and Abelard, Tristan and Isolde.

But it was not the West. It was the East. Real life intruded. Richard contracted tuberculosis and went home to Hong Kong. The flame flickered. A misunderstanding developed. They emigrated to the United States separately. By then, Suzanne had already met Tan. He asked her to marry him. A year later, Richard married a Chinese-American.

Maybe if Suzanne's father had never raised any objections, maybe if Richard had not come down with tuberculosis, maybe if the relationship had simply run its course, what happened three decades later might not have. But the memory of the romance and the excitement, the sort that they had never known before and would not know again for many years, lingered in their minds. They both started their new lives with new spouses, asking themselves the same question: "What if . . . ?"

In 1975, after twelve years of working in the pharmaceutical industry, Richard decided to go to medical school. He was thirty-nine years old and the father of three school-age children. When I found out years later, I, who had known nothing about his previous life, was amazed by his daring.

"You did what?" I asked him.

"Yes, yes," he said in his brisk Cantonese accent. "So it was a gamble.

"This is a unique medical school," he continued. "You can go through from scratch, but all candidates have to have a Ph.D. in science-related field. You finish in two years. It's only one school in the country, one school in the world where you can do this, because, you see, the basic science, we compress it to nine months, but you cannot skip too much the clinical parts, so you go to clinics. But essentially, you compress two years into nine months. Every week, there's a midterm, final, final, midterm. That was worse pressure than there was in Tai Da. This is the highest pressure than anything else."

Something about his manner was slightly off-putting. Perhaps that is too strong a description, but at the very least, I was not used to seeing such a combination of arrogance, conceit, and self-confidence in a Chinese of his generation. It both fascinated and annoyed me.

Richard finished his account of his fortitude and resilience with a triumphant flourish.

"At that time I applied," he said with no pretense of modesty, "there's about fifteen hundred applicants—Ph.D.'s—and they took in thirty-six. They can take just about anyone. They took me. Actually, it turns out I was the oldest one on the record."

This arrogance also appealed. Richard took risks. He fulfilled his dreams. He did not live vicariously through the blue glow of a television screen or a computer monitor. Around the same time he went back to medical school, he taught himself how to ski. I came to skiing myself when I was already eighteen years old. The confidence and fearlessness of those who started much earlier will always elude me. I cannot even imagine picking up the sport at thirty-nine. Hurtling increasingly brittle bones or ever weakening knees down an icy slope, an action that mirrors no movement one's body has ever made before, seems madness at an age when one's mortality looms. It is also inspiring.

In 1977, Richard graduated from medical school. He had done what everyone else had thought impossible. America had taught him not to believe in dead ends. For a long time, his marriage had felt like one. He had become a doctor in spite of the odds; he knew he could find Suzanne too. He heard that she was living in Pennsylvania. He went to the library and looked in vain for her name in every phone book for the state. Finally, he tracked Suzanne down through a mutual friend, the one who had brought Richard to Suzanne's house in Taipei so long ago. Suzanne agreed to meet him. He told her his plans. He was going to California for his residency. His wife and children had already moved there. He just needed to drive the rest of his belongings out from the East Coast.

"I want you to come with me," Richard told her.

Suzanne told Tan that she had a business trip. She spent a week driving with Richard to the West Coast. When they reached San Francisco, Suzanne flew home. She had a husband, a son just starting high school, friends, and a job. She could not think of divorce.

"After my trip," she told me years later, "I fly back to Reading, and I never got back in touch with him. I thought, at that time, I just close that chapter."

I believed everything Suzanne told me. I already knew about her affair. There was nothing left to hide. I see now that the truth is neither completely objective nor completely subjective. Rather, it is like light reflecting off glass: turn the glass and the pattern changes, but that's not to say the first pattern was not just as real as the second. Both contain the appearance of truth—brilliant, hard, ephemeral. The way I understand it, either three events occurred in 1977, or only one.

The second would have happened later in the year on a rainy weekend, probably in summer. Suzanne told her husband she was going to New York to attend a trade show for her gift shop. That Saturday, the co-owner of the shop picked her up in the car. They cheerily waved goodbye. A few hours later, Tan received a phone call. It came from the Reading airport.

"We wanted to let you know, sir," the voice on the other end said, "your wife's plane to California has been delayed."

A few days later, Tan received a postcard from New York, which said, "The trade show is great. Will tell you about it when I get home."

When Suzanne did come home, the couple had an argument that their son, Jim, who was fourteen years old at the time, still remembers. Years of silence crumbled into fighting. In the end, Suzanne agreed that she had done wrong.

"All right," Tan said, "let's call the doctor and tell him this."

When they reached Richard, Tan explained why he was calling.

"It's not right," he said, "for you to see another man's wife like this. If you want to be friends with Suzanne, we can all be friends. We can all see each other together."

Richard laughed with the assurance of someone used to getting his way.

"There's nothing wrong with it," he said. "You're old-fashioned."

Even so, Suzanne complied with her husband's wishes: she would not see the doctor again.

Later that year, Tan's father died in Taiwan. He and his sisters decided to bring their mother to the States to live. Someone would have to go pick her up. Suzanne volunteered. Coming back to America, they flew in to Los Angeles, where both Suzanne's sister and Tan's sister lived. The four women were supposed to meet at the airport, but Suzanne had disappeared. Tan's sister took their mother home with her. Three days later, Suzanne reappeared in Reading.

"I went to see Richard," she admitted to her husband. "When I was in Taipei, I saw a fortune-teller. She told me that I have something difficult . . . that I can even die. I wanted to see Richard before I die."

"Okay," Tan said. He did not believe in fortune-tellers and predictions of gloom, but he humored his wife. "Okay, so you want to see your boyfriend before you die. But this is the last time."

Suzanne told him that the fortune-teller had instructed her to put a cabbage under her bed to ward off the problem, but she never did. Instead, she continued to consume her days in a frenzy of desperate energy in an attempt to stave off the boundaries closing in around her. In 1979, the worst nuclear power plant accident in United States history occurred at Three Mile Island, just downriver from nearby Harrisburg. Half of the two hundred Chinese in the Reading area left, engineers who could no longer find work constructing plants. In 1981, Jim graduated salutatorian of his high-school class and left home for MIT. The house grew even more quiet. As hard as she worked, as often as she stayed away, Suzanne could not stop the silence from crowding in on her whenever she returned. It reminded her of her lonely girlhood in Taipei. She and Tan had stopped sharing the same bedroom years before. The next time Richard called for her, she did not know what to say.

Many years after Suzanne had left, I drove to Reading. The road into town had split from the thruway as far back as Allentown, meandering in its four-lane way past green farmland and under blue skies. This was hometown America—birthplace of Dixie cups, Hershey bars, and Heinz ketchup. Hand-lettered signs by the side of the road advertised shoo-fly pie and sweet corn. Fading hex signs decorated weathered barn doors. John Updike, who had grown up in Shillington, had written of Pennsylvania's "mild, misty, doughy middleness." Tan—pot belly, shuffling slippers, shrunken shoulders—belonged here in a way that Suzanne never could. For those who longed for peace, Reading offered heaven. For those who did not, it seemed a sort of mind-numbing hell. Wallace Stevens, who left Reading as a young man, was inspired by a trip back home to write the following in his journal: "Reading looked like the acme of dullness and I was glad to get back to this electric town which I adore." That electric town was New York, and just as Stevens had once hoped to find his future there, Suzanne would find hers.

For Stevens, in fact, the future belonged not to New York but to Hartford, city of my mother's adulthood, where she, like him, would live longer than she would anywhere else. Many other similarities existed. My mother raised her own family a scant quarter-mile down the road from where Stevens had once lived with his wife and daughter. On weekends, we rambled through the same Elizabeth Park that had once given the poet so much pleasure. The Reading native rose through the ranks of Hartford's insurance industry to become a high-level executive, as did my father. Stevens even used to insist on walking to work, a route that would have daily taken him past the entrances to our street, but the similarities ended there.

"I want," said Stevens once about his adopted city, "to keep everybody at arm's length in Hartford where I want nothing but the office and home as home."

Stevens had his Reading boyhood and his New York electricity to remember. My mother had only a series of way stations. To paraphrase a Stevens biographer about the accidents of fate that landed the poet in Hartford, my mother did not choose Hartford; Hartford chose her. But, unlike Stevens, she tried to make the entire city and its surrounding suburbs—not just the four walls around her family—home.

It was both easier and more difficult than assimilating into Reading life. In Reading, the act of living apart was a sort of assimilation in and of itself. In Hartford, conformity was the only option. The town had been founded in 1636 by Puritans as a deliberately exclusive community, an escape from their more wayward brethren to the northeast. These Puritans, who regarded worldly success as a sign of God's favor, made commerce in Hartford thrive. By the middle of the nineteenth century, Hartford's merchants and captains were being called the "river gods" because of the myriad sloops and schooners that plied their valuable wares, mostly from the West Indies, up the Connecticut River; but rich as they became, the locals still hewed to their puritanical ways. They frowned on ostentation and believed deeply in charity. It was a mix of values which could only produce a contradictory ethos. Wealth was admired, but not the display of it; exclusivity reigned, but caring for others opened the door to heaven. For outsiders like my family, life in Hartford boiled down to two options: live apart and be ignored, or ape those around you and be grudgingly tolerated. My mother chose the latter, not realizing that tolerance would never equal acceptance.

As soon as they could afford to, my parents bought a house on the same quiet street where my mother used to spend her lunch hour, walking and dreaming. It was not in West Hartford, a more socially prominent town; but for those who knew it, Woodside Circle had a mystique all its own. A small horseshoe of a neighborhood off a busy main road, it contained only seventeen houses, built in the 1920s on the grounds of an old apple orchard that had belonged to the Goodwins, one of the city's leading families. When my family first moved in, my father received a phone call from a woman who had read about the real-estate transaction in the newspaper.

"Is your name Chang?" the stranger asked him. "And are you Chinese?"

My baffled father responded yes to both questions.

"And you bought a house on Woodside Circle?"

Again, he answered in the affirmative.

"Well," the woman sniffed, "that street certainly has gone downhill."

With that, she slammed down the phone, leaving my father sputtering and helpless on the other end.

The atmosphere of the neighborhood reminds me now of an

Edith Wharton novel. Most whites—including, no doubt, the woman on the phone—had fled to the suburbs in general and to West Hartford in particular. But the old guard remained rooted on the Circle in the same way that Wharton's ancient Dutch families had stubbornly continued to cluster around Washington Square. Mr. Hooker, who lived just around the curve of the horseshoe, was a direct descendant of Hartford's founder. Mrs. Parsons down the street presided over the area's chapter of the Daughters of the American Revolution. She was the sister of Ellsworth Bunker, the nation's one-time ambassador to Vietnam. Mrs. Goodwin herself lived in an imposing Georgian colonial across the way from us. Her house had an elevator and a ballroom. Her gardener lived in a cottage next door. When my family first moved in, before I was even born, Mrs. Goodwin came to call on my mother one day. She must have been very old already by then, but she marched, without the slightest stoop to her spine, up our front walk and rang the bell. When my mother answered the door with a baby in her arms and two more children clinging to her legs, Mrs. Goodwin handed her an engraved card. Nothing, not even her etiquette lessons at Marymount, had prepared my mother for such an occasion.

As welcoming as the people on the street were, my mother, more than anyone else, made the place our home. She brought steamers of dumplings to new neighbors. She offered to drive the neighborhood kids to and from school every day. Unlike many of her high-school classmates, she never let fear or intimidation get in her way. She spoke her imperfect English with such gusto that her white friends picked up her newly minted slang: "Wassip" for "WASP," "junks" for "junk," and so on. She befriended all sorts. There was the elderly Russian woman who lived alone on our street behind a high iron gate in a house guarded by a snarling Doberman pinscher. The shades were always drawn, as if the occupants were permanently asleep, but they opened for my mother, who felt at home among the antique chess pieces and silver samovars. They reminded her of the piano lessons she had taken so long ago. Later, when she was working as a real-estate agent, she found a house with a singularly low down payment for our carpenter. She then arranged a special mortgage. She also located an affordable house for a working-class single mother in a town an hour and a half away—so far that it practically bordered Massachusetts. Such cases were akin to pro bono work for a lawyer. She made commissions on them, but they were so small, they did not begin to compensate her for her hours of work.

Shortly after I was born in 1970, the insurance company where my father worked made him their first Chinese vice-president. In those days, Chinese of my parents' type were engineers, academics, and occasionally doctors. They did not work in staid, WASP-ruled professions, much less move up the corporate ladder within them. Almost by definition, there is no more conservative an industry than insurance. My father's boss encouraged him to join a club. The world still worked that way back then. Business was brokered over the golf links, alliances made in tennis doubles. My family joined the Hartford Golf Club.

There are three major country clubs in West Hartford. Tumble Brook was for Jews, Wampanoag for Catholics. The Hartford Golf Club, the most exclusive of them all, was the province of WASPs. One couple I spoke to remembered being among the very first Catholics to join. The year was 1968. Over time, several more Catholics would be granted entry, and even some Jews would join, but my family were the first—and for the entire time we were members, the only—people of color at the club who were not wait staff, caddies, gardeners, or maintenance men. I remember once inviting a white neighborhood playmate to come swimming in the club's pool.

"My mother won't let me," she replied.

"Why?" I asked.

"Because," she said, as if I ought to have known better, "they don't let black people swim there." The irony of the situation escaped me at the time.

My friend belonged to one of the many young families who were moving back into the West End, the neighborhood where we lived. They did so because they wanted to make a commitment to the city, to integrated schools, to racial harmony, to the ideals of the late 1960s and early 1970s. Never mind that most of them ended up sending their children to private schools by the time said offspring reached the seventh grade.

"We were," my sister, Christine, the oldest of the four children in our family, recently commented, "in the middle of champagne socialism."

Our fellow West Enders enthusiastically embraced a Chinese family as one more stripe in a glorious multicultural rainbow. The welcome might have stemmed from too much liberal tokenism and not enough real insight, but it was a welcome nonetheless. This was not the case at the club. I remember only one incident in my personal experience of overt unfriendliness, but I was a child, unused to tuning in to the subtleties of a dismissive greeting or a snub. I do believe, though, that our presence at the club must have dismayed some members down to the straw soles of their espadrilles.

But my mother, as always, led the charge. She and a neighbor taught themselves tennis in the course of one summer. Every morning they would wake up early and hit the courts with the dogged determination that possesses my mother when she decides to accomplish something. An old friend of hers told me about another summer, before I was born, when my family was still living in the first house they ever bought, in Bloomfield. The house needed a new coat of paint. My mother decided to paint it herself, and she did, with two small children underfoot and not a single person to help her. When I heard the story, I called her to see if it was true. I wondered if she would even remember; she had had such a difficult time piecing together her past for me before.

"Oh yes," she said, allowing herself a small measure of satisfaction. "I remember."

The smile quickly turned to regret: "But I never finish the garage. There's just one part I can't reach."

Not surprisingly, my mother soon found a circle of friends at the club—women she played tennis with in the summer and paddle tennis in the winter. They formed a cooking group and met at each other's houses. My mother made Peking duck using her secret recipe. The others pronounced it delicious. Gradually, the rest of us made friends, took tennis lessons, lounged by the pool. My brothers joined the swim team. One summer, my mother even became the chair of the swimming pool committee. Not everyone wanted to be friendly, but my mother always managed to find those who did.

I have heard the stories of many of my mother's classmates, and I have visited their homes. I can say with certainty that my mother managed far more successfully than any other of them to assimilate into the white mainstream. My father gave her the tools with his law degree, his job at one of Hartford's most important companies, his nearly flawless English; but a lesser woman would have shrunk from the expectations that his position placed on her. My mother did not even have a college degree. She had no career. She spoke English with a heavy accent. But none of that mattered in the face of her forceful personality. She did not just assimilate; she was a one-woman melting pot in which every ingredient was given new life. She had no parents, and so she adopted grandparents for us—not just one, but two sets: an Australian pair and a Jewish one. Her Catholic schooling ensured that we ate corned beef and cabbage on St. Patrick's Day. She understood the finer points of that favorite WASP pastime euphemistically described as coupon clipping, and when invited for dinner at a Yankee home, she knew to expect anemic roast beef, goldfish crackers, and stiff highballs.

As effortless as my mother made assimilation seem, it was not. For both my parents, home became a place to release the pressures that came with their paradoxical positions as outsiders and role models both. A better-suited couple might have found strength in each other. My parents found only dissension. No one wanted to be the adult in their relationship. My mother simply slammed doors when the shouting started. She was incapable of introspection. My analytical father used his skills only to delineate the wrongs done against him. He spent his time bitterly bad-mouthing my mother in between puffs on an ever-present cigarette. After she started selling real estate in the mid-seventies, he derided her business success, hurt that it had taken precedence in her mind over his own. Their marriage had always been founded on the ephemeral hopefulness of which Wallace Stevens had written: "Next to love is the desire for love." My parents had married not because they complemented each other but because they felt that they ought to.

In retrospect, a more unlikely pair would be difficult to find. My mother lives in extremes, manic one day, depressive the next—the type of person who does not bother to look up the listing in the paper but simply shows up at the movie theater to see if something good is showing. She has essentially two modes of operation: action or sleep. The pleasure of sitting alone with a cup of tea or even a book for company appears to her like a punishment. She must always be doing. My father, on the other hand, epitomizes caution. Our family used to take trips into New York once or twice a year, and while my impatient mother hustled the children around in a frenzy of shopping and sightseeing, my father liked nothing better than to sit in the living room of our hotel suite, happily reading the newspaper, while the cleaning people vacuumed around him. He used to save every *Wall Street Journal* he ever bought, "just in case." My mother never thought about "just in case." Her life was already a series of worst cases. Her experience had given her a disregard for convention and planning that, to this day, remains inconceivable to my father, who had watched his proud parents devolve into a pair of elderly, anonymous immigrants, clinging to the remnants of their past.

My mother wanted nothing to do with such bittersweet nostalgia. Instead, she toughened us up in imitation of the way life had toughened her. She saw the family as one entity. She was hard, so we had to be hard. She criticized herself, so she criticized us. It was a paradoxical situation. She showered her clients with presents, dinners, and attention, but she forgot my fifteenth birthday. We got presents only if we bought them ourselves and asked for reimbursement. When I was eight, my mother handed me back the day calendar I had given her for Christmas, saying that she did not need it. She had already gotten a perfectly good appointment book through her office. That was the lesson she had learned growing up alone in Taipei: don't be wasteful. She never understood the point of name brands, frivolous toys, and silly amusements. She dressed my oldest brother in a clip-on tie for his first day at a school with a jacket-and-tie dress code. He has yet to recover from the resulting trauma; she still cannot comprehend what she did wrong. The sheer exuberant excess of

Americans mystified her. When she was a young housewife living in Bloomfield, she befriended a newlywed whose father-in-law had given her a convertible for a wedding present. "The car had air conditioning too," my mother said, still astonished years later as she remembered the incident. "It's a convertible. What do you need air conditioning for?"

Another time, my mother and her friend Terry drove Derek, the younger of my two older brothers, up to his first day of boarding school. The trio arrived at a bare, grim, concrete bunker of a dorm, twin to the one that Tim, my oldest brother, had vacated just a year and a half before. And as she had with her first son, my mother moved her second one in with a desk lamp, an assortment of heavy plastic milk crates stolen from our local supermarket, and little else. Terry looked about with horror. Her house practically bulged outward with the combined volume of her many chintz slipcovers, chenille throws, needlework pillows, golden retrievers, and towheaded boys. My brother's dorm room made her shudder. Gray concrete blocks formed the walls. Linoleum lined the floors. The furniture consisted of a narrow, lumpy mattress on a squeaky metal frame, a scarred wooden desk, a plastic chair, and a built-in wardrobe.

"Oh, Mary," Terry said, "he can't live like this!"

My brother left to attend some orientation activities. The two women went to buy him supplies. While my mother was choosing a fan and some ramen noodles, Terry was picking out a throw rug for the floor, a cozy spread for the bed, a blotter for the desk—anything to make the place seem more like home. Her home, not ours.

When my mother saw Terry's shopping cart, she snorted. "He doesn't need that stuff," she said.

"Come on, Mary," Terry pleaded. "What about just getting the rug?"

"No," my mother said. "It'll make him soft."

She turned on her heel and walked toward the cash registers, clutching one small basket of necessities, which she would later unceremoniously hand to her fourteen-year-old son. The shopping cart, with its multitude of colorful treasures, stood abandoned in the aisle.

During his years in Hartford, Wallace Stevens was hailed as America's greatest living poet, yet he remained discontent and adrift in the place he called home, a feeling he reflected in his poetry. He could have been writing about my mother. In her own small way, she had conquered Hartford—successful real-estate agent, member of the exclusive Hartford Golf Club, wife of a respectable insurance executive, mother of four healthy children—but, like Suzanne, she spent her days trying to consume time rather than live it. The granite-shouldered, tight-lipped city, where her four children attended school with the descendants of General Gage and Cotton Mather, refused to take her in, yet demanded that she keep knocking. Her American offspring did not appreciate her sacrifices. Her resentful husband preferred home-cooked meals and a more respectful attitude.

As similar as my father and Tan were, they had turned out to be as dissimilar to their wives. Like Tan, my father had harbored the same sort of condescension towards those around him, particularly towards his wife. I had grown up listening to him dismiss my mother's efforts in almost every arena, from cooking ("too careless"), to working ("never sees the big picture"), and, most hurtful of all, to child raising ("undisciplined, inconsistent, never around"). To my knowledge, nothing she has ever done has ever garnered unmitigated praise from my father, just as nothing Suzanne ever did could satisfy Tan. They were raised, privileged boys in privileged households in one of the world's most patriarchal societies, to be cosseted and praised. In America, it seemed that no one, least of all their wives and children, even wanted to know who they were.

In the same way that Suzanne never belonged to Reading, my mother never belonged to Hartford. When she finally left it, she did so with a broken heart—not because she was leaving her home or her friends but because everything that she had worked so hard for appeared to amount to nothing. She had given thirty years to an indifferent city and a faltering marriage. Her children seemed poised to forget her. I, her youngest, had already left for boarding school and was about to enter that last transition to independence, college. She now inhabited a mindscape that came hued with regret and shaped by unfulfilled dreams. But neither

Hartford, my father, nor we children could take all the blame. Within her lay her grief and her history. They ensured that, no matter how hard she or we might try, she would never really belong to any of us. When my parents moved, barely speaking, only screaming, to New York, I felt the weight of their failure and took it for my own. Years later, when I came across Wallace Stevens in my old school library, I hoped that the poet could teach me more about my mother and Suzanne. I soon realized that he wrote not just of them, but of me as well: "I cannot bring a world quite round, Although I patch it as I can."

I think of these middle years as the war years, a period when the classmates struggled with countless problems: the strictures of their upbringing, the expectations of their husbands, the demands of their children, the stereotypes of their neighbors. During these years, they hunkered grimly down, like soldiers in the trenches, waging a battle of attrition, which was one part frenzied activity and one part mind-numbing routine. Dolores eventually got her doctorate, married, and had a son. She and her family settled in Brooklyn, a short train ride from her job as a mathematics professor at a local university in the city. Margaret also received her doctorate, married, and had two children, one a girl my own age. She lived in the Los Angeles area, obediently doing her duty at her research laboratory and in the classroom. Suzanne and my mother had their myriad activities. Alone, in different parts of the country, the four classmates lived eerily parallel lives, toiling away in unthinking obscurity as they separately fumbled toward the same blinding moment of truth.

TO GAIN AMERICA

Around the same time that my mother started working, Margaret stopped—not literally, but, rather, mentally. She continued to wake up in the mornings and hit the Los Angeles freeway with the other bleary-eyed commuters. She continued to study the metabolism of RNA and teach students such courses as physiology, genetics, and molecular biology. Every day, she did approximately the same things she had been doing ever since she had entered the field; but where before she had tackled projects with enthusiasm, or at least a sense of responsibility, now she had stopped wanting to.

The obvious explanation behind Margaret's change in attitude was that she had lost the grant that funded her research professorship at UCLA. The obvious explanation is not always the right one. As is also often the case in science, cause and result do not separate themselves neatly here. The loss of her grant may have been the reason for Margaret's lack of interest in her work, but it may have been—in fact, was probably—just a symptom.

"The scientist," wrote French mathematician and physicist Henri Poincaré, "does not study nature because it is useful to do so. He studies it because he takes pleasure in it, and he takes pleasure in it because it is beautiful."

In truth, there exist plenty of scientists who do study nature because it is useful. Perhaps Poincaré should have qualified his statement to read, "The *successful* scientist does not study nature because it is useful to do so." Stereotypes suggest that scientists are tediously careful, painstakingly methodical, pedantically exacting. They are, but not for the reasons that others assume—that they are stuffy or unimaginative. Rather, their extreme precision serves actually to balance their extreme passion. At heart, a devoted scientist is as romantic as any poet, and even more rebellious. The scientist seeks the truth, often at the expense of the status quo, sometimes at the expense of his own liberty. Galileo lived out his life under house arrest for daring to suggest that the earth moves around the sun. Darwin published his radical theories on evolution in spite of the controversy he knew and dreaded they would cause in Victorian England. Simply to postulate such heresy, a scientist must be a renegade and a nonconformist, willing to listen only to the laws of nature, not those of man.

Well into the twentieth century, this ideal of the visionary purist dominated the field of science, such as it was. In those days, science was less of a profession than a calling, almost akin to the devout being called upon to serve God. Few were chosen. The ones who were, more often than not, came from the upper classes, where the material means to devote oneself to years of study abounded. In fact, tradition dictated that scientists, ought to be working for the good of humanity, rather than for a living. "If our discovery has a commercial future," said Marie Curie of her technique for purifying radium, "that is an accident by which we must not profit."

By World War II, science had already changed. Both world wars had created work for legions of new scientists, from the advent of chemical warfare to the development of the hydrogen bomb. The profit from explosives had even funded the field's most prestigious and lucrative honor, the Nobel Prize. The old taboos against making money began to lift. Suddenly, scientists became the new celebrities, almost divine in the public's perception of their power. When Jonas Salk introduced a vaccine against polio in 1954, the resulting praise was so great that Congress debated minting a dime in the scientist's image. James Watson and Francis Crick showed the world the very shape of life.

There was talk of landing a man on the moon. Science made the impossible seem within reach, and the United States government, flush with money in the aftermath of the war and anxious to establish itself as the new world leader, began funding research on a giant scale. The institutionalization of science was well underway, and in the process, science itself had ceased to become a calling to become a profession instead.

"Be a doctor or a scientist," Margaret's refugee father told all of his daughters. "You have a special skill then. No matter where you end up, you can still use your special skill."

Five of them obeyed. The sixth, the product of an American high school, defied him to become a lawyer. Margaret, the middle child, had always readily adapted to other people's expectations of her. She became a scientist—not for the sheer love of learning, like the monk Gregor Mendel laboring in obscurity over his pea pods, or like Albert Einstein, the anonymous patent officer who studied theoretical physics in his spare time—but because her father advised her to. She became a scientist for the most practical of reasons: to get a job. If cooking had offered the same sort of security, status, and perquisites, perhaps she would have gone to culinary school instead. From the start, then, Margaret, who was practical, not romantic, a realist rather than a dreamer, found herself at odds with her chosen profession.

Neither the painstaking laboratory work nor the teaching appealed particularly to Margaret's impatient mind. She told me once that she enjoyed research more than teaching, but when I asked her why, she had no definitive answer. In fact, she sounded almost begrudging, as though she was at a loss to choose one or the other.

"I think," she said, "I like research better, but research is very tough. First, you have to get money, and you have to have a good, original idea. And you have to work very hard, and you have to be lucky."

The very first step stymied her. Doing research required getting grant money, which, in turn, required writing a seemingly endless series of applications. For a non–native English speaker, it could be the most frustrating aspect of the entire procedure. Another Beiyinyu graduate, a highly regarded endocrinologist, told me how relieved she was when she began to make enough money to pay people to edit her grant applications for her. Margaret, who had a natural gift for languages, spoke English more fluently than most of her peers from Taiwan, but even so, the grant application posed just one obstacle to success among many—difficult enough to overcome when one enjoys the work, nearly impossible when one does not.

As for the actual thinking and research, Margaret admitted to me that it did not come naturally—an ironic statement, considering that her work involved genetics. As she learned how RNA and DNA worked, producing people with all their different shapes and personalities, she was also learning how her own genes were specifically not encoded to make for a good scientist.

"Because my nature," she told me candidly, "I'm not that good, born scientist. Some people are so good. They think of good ideas. They stick to it. In science, you have to be really very good. I don't think I'm that careful. I tend to be a little sloppy sometimes."

Teaching posed different problems. As good as her English was, it made her uncomfortable to stand up in front of a class and give a lecture. She was so self-conscious that when someone coughed in the back row, she worried that it was because she had made a mistake. Margaret, who had always been at ease in new situations, moving from mainland China to Hong Kong to Taiwan without a problem, now found herself questioning everything she did. America was a different place entirely, incomprehensible in so many ways, from the bean chili she found disgusting as a student in South Dakota to the abrupt way in which students simply spoke up in class. As different as Taiwan, Hong Kong, and the mainland were from one another, they had all adhered to a certain Chinese system. In America, when she applied for a new job and a misunderstanding arose about the amount of her compensation, Margaret said nothing, even though the sum was much less than what she was expecting. Her employer had made an honest mistake, one easily rectifiable, but Margaret could not bring herself to tell him.

"I was scared to death to face authority," she said years later, when recounting the story. "Not to know how to fight for what's yours."

In America, it became her responsibility to look out for herself. In China, someone else—her parents, the teachers at school, the system itself—always had done that for her. Margaret knew how to pass the right exams and get into the right schools. That was easy for her. She had done what was asked of her all her life. Only when she had to make her own decisions did she falter. The problem was not that she had become a scientist against her will. It was that she did not know her will, which is why, nearly two decades after she came to America to study biochemistry, Margaret found herself living in the Los Angeles suburbs with two children, a husband, and no job.

The moment could have been an important turning point. Margaret did not lack money. Her husband was a doctor with a family inheritance. The couple owned a comfortable place built on a hillside on the upscale Palos Verdes peninsula. The house had the prerequisite characteristics of upper-middle-class southern California living, with a sunken living room at the front and a swimming pool out back. From the bedroom windows on the top floor, one could see the blue expanse of ocean below and, on a clear day, Catalina Island in the distance.

Ironically, the very fact that she did not have to work made her life more difficult in some ways. Margaret, who had never had any choices before, now had too many. She liked music and painting. She was good at languages. She thought about becoming a social worker. She had been elected the first woman president of a local organization for Chinese scientists and engineers. She and some other women had formed an activist group in the mid-1970s to protest Japanese attempts to annex the Taoyutai Islands. She flirted with the idea of running for city council. No matter what the ultimate decision might be, it was hers to make.

Margaret scanned the newspaper for job listings and took the first position she was offered: teaching at a small women's college in Brentwood. She scrounged up more grant money to fund a minuscule project on gene sequencing at UCLA. The undertaking was designed more to teach students how to become researchers than to accomplish any groundbreaking work. Margaret had finally come to a crossroads and, instead of turning, had gone straight ahead, stepping on the brakes to decrease the speed, but never wavering from the same direction.

I accompanied Margaret to work one day. We stopped first at her laboratory at UCLA to check in.

"I usually go two times a week," she explained as we walked past the blocky, rose-colored buildings that dotted the campus. "But sometimes I work out or I go have breakfast with friends instead."

A few students lolled about in the small lab room. Even to my unpracticed eyes, they looked aimless. A young woman poked her head in to borrow some equipment. One of the students nodded. No one was using it.

Margaret introduced me to an older man. "Meet my boss," she said.

"Collaborator," the man said, smiling. "Not boss."

They talked for fifteen minutes, and then Margaret motioned to me.

"Okay," she said, "we can go, don't have to stick around."

Recently, she had spent a sabbatical volunteering at a large laboratory at Stanford. "Just to keep up to date," she had told me. That lab had hummed with activity. It was not so much a room as a series of rooms: industrial-size coolers in one, centrifuges in another. Earnest postdocs wearing white lab coats had measured, spun, calculated, and taken notes. There were ten of them, and they were each being paid $25,000 a year. The lab at UCLA could not begin to compare. The students were undergraduate volunteers. They wandered in and out at will. They had no research experience.

"It's really small potatoes," Margaret apologized later as we walked to the car. "You can't run a lab like that."

We drove next to the small women's college in Brentwood where Margaret taught biology to undergraduates. On the way there, she explained that she had decided to teach full-time after the children were born because the hours were less demanding.

"But," she said, "I feel inadequate, because only people who aren't talented enough to do research teach full-time."

We passed the fraternity houses of Westwood and then giant mansions half-hidden by iron gates and high hedges. Ahead of us, on a mountaintop, loomed the sprawling new Getty Museum, which was still under construction. We turned onto O. J. Simpson's street and then started to climb up past Normandy chateaux, English Tudors, Mediterranean villas, and New England farmhouses complete with picket fences. At last, we reached the entrance of the school, a Catholic women's college, which was still run by nuns. It had the same genteel atmosphere that Marymount, my mother's school, once had, although the style was more California press-baron estate than East Coast country club. Tile roofs, stucco walls, and a formal garden existed harmoniously together. A long covered walkway with arches completed the picture. The one jarring element consisted of the students themselves.

"Dat's what I be sayin,' " said one girl to a friend as they passed us. They were both loudly chewing gum.

Margaret had one class that day, a lab from three o'clock to four-thirty.

"Is that it?" I asked, and she looked slightly embarrassed.

The day's exercises consisted of testing for exo-enzymes, enzymes bacteria produce outside the body to break down nutrients for digestion. The point was to see how different bacteria reacted to different substances.

"What does fermentation mean to you?" Margaret asked the class.

No one replied. A student in front rested her head against her arm. She leaned across the lab counter and tapped a water faucet with her pen.

"How," Margaret persisted, "do you make wine or vinegar?"

Again, no response.

"You have to let it sit," she explained finally. "You have to do what?" She answered her own question. "Stomp on the grapes."

Everyone laughed.

"What does that produce?" She answered her own question again. "Glucose. It's a sequence of chemical steps that start out mostly with sugar, and sugar goes through a bunch of biochemical steps that changes it into something else. Okay?"

The students looked at her blankly.

"So," she said, "we're testing to see, can bacteria take glucose and change it to lactic acid? Or take lactose and change it to something else?"

The students began their experiments and Margaret wandered around answering their questions. They called her Dr. Li. As they worked, they talked about other things.

"If you don't eat," one student warned her lab partner, who had started a new diet, "your body will turn everything you eat into fat."

A blond girl with an upper lip that curled practically into her nose asked me what I was doing.

"I'm observing," I said.

"Okay," she said in a Valley voice. "Whatever."

The lab ended, and the students began to clean up. They filed out, group by group. Two girls remained behind for help. Margaret sat down with them and opened the textbook.

"When you read your book," she said, "pay attention to pictures, photographs, and the summary. That helps you a lot. Sometimes the questions are too hard, scare you half to death. You think you don't know anything."

All traces of Margaret's trademark impatience had disappeared. One of the students stared intently at the page as if she intended to hunt it down and kill it. The other's beeper went off. Margaret did not even roll her eyes. She looked as if she were in line at the post office. By four-thirteen, everyone had left.

As we drove home, she told me about her students. Most of them were studying to be nurses and physical therapists. Many came from poor neighborhoods. They had large ambitions but few skills.

"I think they are too pampered in high school," Margaret said. "The teacher just passes them no matter what. They come to college and they aren't prepared. They think they can just read the title of the chapter and that's it." It was an attitude towards learning wholly unlike her own.

She described the two-year students in even more disparaging tones. "They're really stupid," she said bluntly. "They get out in two years and become nurses' aides. One of them is going to kill a patient one of these days, they're so stupid. They don't know how to figure out 10 percent of sixty-five or how to dilute a solution in the proper proportion. It's the most basic thing, and they think it's high science."

I asked Margaret if her experience teaching at the school had taught her anything.

"I've become more tolerant," she said.

In truth, she had just become more apathetic. The patience I had seen on display in the lab came not from a desire to encourage the students but a desire simply to get through the day.

At first glance, Margaret exudes self-confidence. Her face wears an expression of stern bemusement, as though she were looking down from above, slightly annoyed but very entertained by the antics of those below her. She favors solid, neutral colors in expensive fabrics. Usually, her only jewelry consists of a large, perfectly luminous pearl ring. It is difficult to understand how this capable-seeming person could not take charge of her own life; she seems so ready to take charge of everyone else's. Indeed she is, but only in very specific circumstances, only within the protected confines of her own community.

Communities define Los Angeles. Each one is sharply distinct and distant from the next. Many even have gates, forbidding entry to those who do not belong. In other places, the freeway effectively cuts off undesirable neighborhoods from their more affluent neighbors. Symbolic barriers stand just as impenetrable. By tacit understanding, only locals are allowed to surf the clean, smooth waves that roll into Lunada Bay off the Palos Verdes coastline. People in Los Angeles do not feel an affinity for the city as a whole. It covers far too much ground, physical and psychological, for such unity. Instead, the area's inhabitants prefer to identify with their own insular communities, an identity that comes as much from whom they keep out as whom they let in. Many of the suburbs that ring the city proper, including Palos Verdes, are direct results of this attitude. Once part of the city itself, they incorporated themselves during the postwar era to avoid Los Angeles taxes and to institute their own local, homeowner-friendly governments. Los Angeles's worst critics claim that the only spirit of civic duty that permeates the area is the desire to maintain real-estate values. It is a world of Us versus Them, the Us becoming ever and ever smaller. Even within Palos Verdes, distinctions are drawn. The horsey set, which rides along the bridle path set in the lushly landscaped median of the long, shady boulevard that leads to Malaga Cove, has nothing to do with the arrivistes whose giant mansions cling to ridiculously small parcels of cliffside land. The most exclusive area on the peninsula, Rolling Hills, has only two entrances to the outside world, both of them manned by guards.

Wealth presents one divide; race, another. "Oh no," Margaret's daughter, Wei, said once, when I asked her if the different races socialized on the peninsula. "The worlds don't mix. The white community belongs to country clubs. Then, all these Chinese—they're completely separate. They never intersect."

The Chinese in Palos Verdes represent a community within a community. They may live next door to white neighbors and send their children to the same schools, but in their own way they are as isolated from the mainstream as any Chinatown on the East Coast. These days, they might even conduct their business—import-export, clothing manufacturing, real-estate development—only with other Chinese in Hong Kong, Taipei, Shanghai, or nearby Monterey Park. Their isolation differs in one important way from the ghettos in Boston and New York. The Chinese of Palos Verdes have achieved all the trappings of the American dream. At one small gathering at Margaret's house, the cars parked outside resembled a vehicular summary of upper-middle-class suburbia: two Jaguars, a Mercedes, a Lexus, and a more discreet, but no less iconic, Volvo. While it is true that their white neighbors may shun them, the feeling is mutual. Unlike my mother, who had almost no choice but to assimilate or be lonely in Hartford, Margaret is surrounded by other Chinese where she lives. According to the 1990 census, Asians made up about 18 percent of the population of Palos Verdes. Of those, about ten thousand were Chinese, the largest minority group on the peninsula, with a large enough population and enough money to constitute its own self-sufficient, independent community.

Around the time that Margaret began working at the women's college, in the early 1980s, these numbers had exploded. As early as 1982, the *Los Angeles Times* was quoting Margaret and Dan in an article about the rapid increase in Asians on the peninsula, from 1 percent of the population in 1970 to 8 percent in 1980.

"The Chinese traditionally care about their land," Margaret told the newspaper in her deadpan way. "They would eat hamburger every day, but they wouldn't mind paying for a good piece of property."

Already, she was being considered an elder stateswoman, as so many of her fellow Beiyinyu graduates, early arrivals to America, were expected to be in their own respective communities. Just as Suzanne had been asked for her opinions on Tiananmen Square by the *Reading Eagle,* and my mother was shown feeding my brother and me dumplings in the *Hartford Courant,* so too was Margaret being asked to filter the experiences and opinions of her community for a mainstream readership. With her dry humor and straightforward attitude, she seemed a natural to marshal the forces of the expanding Chinese population in her area. Instead, she used the safety of their numbers to slip back into anonymity. Being a leader in her own community came easily. Being a spokesperson on their behalf to the outside world did not.

"It's hard," said Dan Li in the same article, "for a person like me with a strange accent to speak at the City Council meeting."

He might as well have been speaking for Margaret. She was not willing to expose herself to the embarrassment and pitfalls that attend those in public life. She was not willing to take the risks required to change professions. During one of my visits with her, we were waiting at a bus stop for a shuttle, whose schedule we did not know. After a few minutes, I spied a courtesy phone and dialed the operator.

"When's the shuttle coming?" I asked.

When I hung up, Margaret looked at me expectantly.

"Five minutes," I said.

"See," she said, slightly embarrassed by her own timidity. "I would never call. I just wait. If the shuttle comes, then it comes."

What a contrast from her behavior at the reunion. The difference startled me: the crowds of women applauding her entry, the hearty laughter she provoked with a sly comment or funny story, the gruff impatience with which she dealt with annoyances. One morning in Maui, we sat waiting on a van that would take us on a tour of the island. By some accident, the trip had been over-subscribed. Two people were left without seats. Margaret strode aboard. She was wearing linen pants the color of sage and a simple cashmere sweater. She looked like a Chinese Lauren Bacall: commanding and well dressed. She stared disapprovingly at us from over the rims of her glasses.

"Two people," she said, "did not reserve ahead. You will have to squeeze into the seats."

She made the statement calmly, unaware of the consternation it was producing among her classmates. If two people were not going to volunteer to leave, Margaret was not about to force them. She had no time for this nonsense anyway. Her sea-kayaking lesson started in twenty minutes. A woman rose from one of the back seats and made her way up front. She had volunteered to help organize the reunion, and her fumbling efforts had caused Margaret no small measure of annoyance. Now Margaret rolled her eyeballs at the sight of her self-appointed helper coming down the aisle.

"Okay, okay," Margaret said, "don't get excited."

She waved her hand at the woman, shooing her back to the seat. The would-be helper slunk meekly away. Margaret stood for another moment or two to see if anyone would volunteer to give up their seats or if the latecomers would confess to their crime. No one came forward. She shrugged her shoulders. The helper stood up again to say something. This time, Margaret looked at her, shook her head in disgust, and walked off the bus.

In America, Margaret had become a classic fish out of water. Among her own kind, she was bold and self-confident, comfortable with established rules and old ways. In a different environment, she became shy and demure, unable even to inquire about a bus schedule. For better or worse, the substantial Chinese population in Palos Verdes had allowed her never to have to assimilate. She and her friends lived in a gilded ghetto, a psychological place rather than a physical one. The most regular contact they had with outsiders probably came in the form of the Latin American laborers who mowed their lawns, cleaned their houses, and clipped their hedges. White people, even their children's friends, simply did not interest them.

"When Wei was dating Chinese boys," Margaret once told me, "then I get interested. 'Do I know his parents? What province is he from? Is he Cantonese?' When she told me about her white boyfriend, and I say, 'Oh.' There's nothing else I can say. I don't know if he's Jewish or Irish."

The women in Margaret's circle wore designer clothes and flew to Banff to celebrate their birthdays. They donned leather driving gloves to tool around in their Mercedeses. In 1990, when they decided to make a show of their power and affluence, they chose, of all things, to hold a debutante ball, a tradition redolent of the Old South. Twenty-one girls, mostly from Palos Verdes and Orange County, came out at the Winter Blossom Ball, the first Chinese-American cotillion in the city's history. Wei was one of them. She wore an off-the-shoulder dress with a ruffle along the neckline and a pained expression. The other girls smiled happily. Sequins glittered on some. Lace made others look like wedding-cake figurines. All of the debutantes wore elbow-length gloves and carried red roses. Their dresses were the color of skim milk. They had spent months before taking dance lessons and learning about etiquette. Jane Pauley covered the event for a segment on her *Real People* show and said she was "presenting the daughters of the American dream." Wei infuriated all of her mother's friends when she told a *Los Angeles Times* reporter that she had not been allowed to invite her white boyfriend. One of the presenters called it "a history-making event" that was "receiving worldwide attention." But after the hubbub had died down, the cotillion had not changed anything. These days, the Winter Blossom Ball has subsided into quiet oblivion. Some years it is held; some years no one bothers.

The ball had been the idea of a group just coming into its own. Like participants at a masquerade ball, they had been playing dress-up, trying on first one identity and then another. Back in 1990, the committee had toyed with tradition because the custom meant little to them aside from an opportunity to wear black tie, have a party, and raise some money for charity. The girls at the first cotillion had ranged in age from high-school seniors to a woman who had graduated from college. The outside world had also paid scant attention. As if to underscore this fact, Jane Pauley had persistently mispronounced the last name of one of the families. One father summed up his attitude toward the proceeding matter-of-factly.

"If she's happy about it," he told the interviewer, "and I don't spend too much money, then I'm happy."

He shrugged, and the rest of the world shrugged with him. L.A. was the land of self-invention, after all. If Margaret and her friends tired of debutantes, they quickly found another project with which to amuse themselves. Dan had ballroom-dancing classes four nights a week. He took singing classes on Wednesday nights. He even happily had a go at Chinese opera. Margaret had aerobics, painting lessons, and art history lectures. She had once served as the president of the area's Beiyinyu alumnae association, a group that, in Los Angeles, consisted of some three hundred members. She ate breakfast with a close circle of friends twice a week. On the weekends, the couple biked along the coast. Their lives were rich with family and friends.

The opposite was true of my mother, stuck in Hartford with a scant handful of other Chinese families. In Palos Verdes, the Chinese community was large and vibrant, a safe haven of parties, laughter, and money. Margaret found sanctuary there from the frustrations of work and the inadequacies that she felt among whites. In Hartford, the Chinese community was so small that it was claustrophobic, so small that it was always painfully aware of the rest of the world around it, who were likely to have one of two reactions: judging the Chinese or ignoring them. To feel part of something larger, one had to reach outside. My mother, who had always struggled to fill the empty spaces in her life, did not want to be known simply as our mother or as my father's wife or as the funny little Chinese lady who chaired the swimming committee at the club. A lifetime of uncertainty made her long for independence. She tried to escape by running to work, rather than, like Margaret, from it.

In 1976, after I, the youngest of her four children had started school, she began selling real estate, a task she plunged into with her usual fervor. She had not worked in fifteen years, since the birth of her first child, my sister. Looking back, I am reminded of Suzanne's own desperate fever of activity, but my mother was not trying to escape her home, just herself. The irony was that in the process of abandoning her old self, she left us behind too.

Work became an all-or-nothing proposition. Evenings, weekends, even holidays, if a client needed her, my mother was there. I felt as though I no longer existed for her. My family had always loved to argue, but now home life disintegrated into an ongoing war. By this time, my sister and oldest brother had both gone away to school. The sides drew up sharply, distinctly. My mother was the enemy. My father, my other brother, and I waged battle against her. At one Chinese gathering at our house, my brother followed her around from room to room, cursing and screaming at her, while my parents' guests looked on in astonishment. The other Chinese families gossiped about us behind our backs. When my mother showed up to potluck suppers with cartons of takeout, the rest of the wives clicked their tongues disapprovingly.

"We feel so sorry for your father," they told me years later. "And for you kids."

I resented their pity then and now. I sensed too that it was tinged with jealousy.

"Everyone in Hartford knew your mother," an old neighbor once said to me. "Everyone."

She went where no one could follow her, not the other Chinese families in our community, not her husband, not her own children. As the years passed, my brother, Derek, disappeared too, into a sanctuary of friends, much like my mother once had so many years before in Taipei. I remained behind and alone, longing for my mother's presence even as I dreaded the fighting that erupted between my parents the moment she returned home.

The suburban-housewife-turned-realtor has long been a fixture on the landscape of upper-middle-class America. She is almost a joke, going to the office two or three days out of the week, writing off her new BMW and her ladies' lunches as business expenditures. But my mother was never the typical suburban housewife. The work never came easily. Even though she plied her trade in West Hartford, she actually lived in déclassé

Hartford. She dressed in jeans and wore sweaters with holes in the elbows. For years she drove a manual-transmission Volkswagen Rabbit that hurtled itself over bumpy back roads so recklessly that her clients would clutch the door handles from fear. Most importantly, my mother was a Chinese woman working in a town whiter than a Colgate smile. In 1980, there were 160 Chinese people living in Hartford. There could only have been fewer in sleepy West Hartford. The head of West Hartford's most prestigious real-estate firm used to negotiate deals over the back nine at the golf club. Dressed in bright madras pants and an alligator shirt, he ran what one ex-employee termed a stable of blond fillies. The people in his office used to refer to my mother, the competition, as Mary Mao and Ching Chang Ying Yang.

I asked another realtor who still works at the same place about her employer.

"He's prejudiced," she shrugged. "An anti-Semite. Everyone knows that."

About my mother, whom she knew casually from having worked in the same field, she stopped to think. I could tell she was weighing her words carefully, not wanting to offend me.

"You couldn't read her face," the woman finally said. "You couldn't tell what she was thinking."

Then she hit upon the description she was looking for: "She was inscrutable."

In this environment, my mother had a mission to prove herself every day. Whenever she held an open house, she called every person who had signed the guest book. One time, she reached a local man who said that he had been tagging along with a friend from California who was thinking about relocating. She called the friend in California. He told her that he had been considering taking on a job heading Kaiser Permanente in Hartford but had decided against it.

"Well," my mother asked, without wasting another second, "who did take the job?"

Sure enough, she sold the new head of Kaiser a house.

Another time, my mother's friend Terry, who often co-brokered deals with her, came to our house to take her to the airport to meet a client. It was late at night, and my mother had no doubt been fighting with one or all of us. She emerged from the house dressed in a pair of maroon sweat pants and a matching sweatshirt. On her head sat a navy-blue knit ski cap, which she had pulled down over her ears. Terry, who was dressed in the uniform of the early-eighties career woman—navy suit, silk shirt, floppy tie—turned to her.

"For Christ's sake, Mary," she said. "You look like a refugee."

"Shut up," my mother said, and folded her arms. "I look fine."

They drove out to the airport without speaking. When they arrived, my mother said that she would go in so Terry would not have to park the car.

"Well," Terry said, handing her a hairbrush, "at least comb your hair."

My mother threw the brush at her and stalked off. Terry waited in the car, but when my mother did not come out, she grew worried. She went into the airport herself and found the client but no Mary. Rather than keep the client waiting, she decided to drive him to his hotel. My mother, who had been waiting in the wrong area of the airport, could take a cab home, which she did. She shared it with a businessman who just happened to be the CEO of a local company and who just happened to be in the market for a new house. Dressed in her midnight burglar outfit, ratty hair and all, my mother somehow convinced him to become her client. Soon after, she sold him a house for $600,000 at a time when homes in the area almost never went for more than five.

"Only your mother," Terry said years later, laughing as she told me the story. "Do you believe her?"

"But," she added, turning serious, "she worked her ass off."

Month after month, my mother would consistently win the award for most real-estate sales even as West Hartford doyennes blackballed her from prestigious listings. If she could not get access to the mansions that lined the streets off of Mountain Road, my mother settled for listing two-family houses in Hartford. If she needed to show a house on Christmas Day, she did. The prizes she won were known as champagne awards because the realtor could choose either a bottle of champagne or a plaque to commemorate her success. My mother always chose the plaque. I can picture them still—modest wood rectangles with blue metal plates that listed her name, her agency, and the month. It was the one example I can remember of my mother choosing sentiment over pragmatism. She may not have had a taste for champagne, but she could have always given the bottles away as presents. Instead, she collected plaque upon plaque, which she never even displayed. She stacked them, like so many dusty bricks, in the makeshift bookshelf that lined the long back hallway to my parents' bedroom.

I think it is telling that the summer before she returned to work, my mother decided to organize the first Beiyinyu reunion, twenty years after she had graduated from the school. The stagnant life of Hartford was beginning to weigh on her. Across America, Tupperware parties and school carpools were no longer satisfying women's expectations. But there was something more to my mother's own frustration, which those around her could not understand. In spite of all the new friends she had made, she felt alone. When I asked my mother what had inspired her to hold the reunion, she could only shrug.

"I don't know," she said. "Maybe I was longing for old friends."

My mother did not know who would show up at the reunion. It had been difficult to find people. She simply told her friends to pass the word. She arranged for housing at a nearby women's college and paid the fee out of her own pocket. Then she waited for people to arrive. One by one, the cars rolled up the driveway of our home. Over a dozen women came to that first reunion. Almost all of them brought their husbands. Many had children. They came from all over the Northeast, most from the tri-state area. One woman had even packed a husband and five kids into the family station wagon and driven all the way up from Maryland for an event that lasted just over twenty-four hours. Surprises greeted my mother with every ring of the doorbell. The smartest girl in their section appeared without warning. My mother had sat several rows behind her. They had not been friends in school and had never spoken in the intervening years. My mother had certainly not expected her to drive all the way from western Pennsylvania to come. But they recognized each other immediately. The woman looked as young as she had in high school, still wearing white tennis shoes and a shy, sweet smile. But another woman, a tomboy like my mother, had altered completely. She wore blue eye shadow and tight bell-bottom jeans. She had married a white man. Others kept arriving.

"Lao Niu!" my mother cried in delight when she saw one. "Old Cow!"

Other nicknames reverberated in the afternoon air. Teasing but affectionate, many of them had been coined by my mother. "Lao Niu" was a pun on its recipient's last name, Liu. "Old Hen" was so dubbed because she took forever to finish a chore. "An hour to wash vegetables," my mother tsked loudly. "Skinny Bones" had looked like a chopstick in high school, long and narrow. That she had since given birth to a son and filled out a bit in the hips did not stop her friends from using her old nickname.

It felt like a beginning, but something had ended, the first phase of the classmates' lives as Americans. They owned homes and were raising children who spoke perfect English. Some, myself included, did not even know how to speak Chinese. A few years before, mainland China had welcomed Nixon. A few years later, Taiwan would lose its seat in the United Nations and develop into a major East Asian economy. These events seemed almost beside the point to the classmates. They were busy with marriages, children, and work. They might eat Chinese, speak Chinese, even read Chinese, but they no longer thought Chinese. I once read something a critic had written in a review of a book by a famous Chinese-American author. "It takes one generation to lose China," the reviewer had reflected. "How many does it take to gain America?" My mother and her friends had already almost lost China in just two decades. Their children certainly had. But it remained to be seen whether or not they would gain America.

Together, that weekend, the classmates sat around the round table in our bright orange kitchen and made dumplings, the same way they once had to bid farewell to Dolores, to my mother, to each of the girls who had left, one by one, to go to America. In Taiwan, they had first had to make skins out of a simple dough of flour and water, which they rolled out into circles the size of large cookies and the thickness of fruit leather. Now they used too-thick wonton skins from the freezer section in the supermarket. For the filling, they mixed ground pork, salted cabbage, Chinese scallions, rice vinegar, sesame oil, and soy sauce. The idea behind the process of forming dumplings was easy enough to grasp, but the execution required practice and dexterity. To make sure the wrapper stuck together around the filling, each classmate dipped her fingers into a bowl of water, then ran the wet tips along the outer rim of the skin. By the end of the dumpling-making session, the bowls of water had grown cloudy with flour and errant pieces of filling. Having made the edges of the wrapper sufficiently adhesive, the cook would crimp the edges together to form a crescent with a scalloped border. This was *jiao zi*. The *jiao zi* then went into the boiling water. When the dumplings rose to the surface, the classmates poured cold water into the pot and waited for the *jiao zi* to rise again. The second rising signified that the dumplings were cooked, ready to be dipped into the mix of soy sauce, vinegar, and hot pepper oil that someone had stirred up, and, at long last, consumed. But while eating was the inevitable result of dumpling making, it did not actually serve as its purpose. Socializing was the real purpose. Dumplings provided the excuse. That they emerged as a consequence of an afternoon of talking and laughing made their appearance that much more marvelous.

My mother is a good cook but a careless one. She cooks to feed her family, and on special occasions, to give them pleasure, which, in turn, gives her pleasure. But the act itself holds little joy for her at all. When I eat dumplings, I think of my mother laboring at the kitchen table, rolling out the dough for the skins with a special pin which bulged in the middle, resembling a boa constrictor digesting a meal, and tapered into points like a spindle. I see her filling, folding, puckering. And I see her all alone.

It was tedious labor and required great patience, not one of her strong points, but my mother persevered even though she would rather have been doing something, maybe anything, else. My sister says she cannot ever remember my mother hugging or kissing her when she was little. Maybe not. But my mother comes from a culture in which parents did not show affection to their children. Instead they called them names like Little Ghost and sang songs about hitting them for being naughty. Showing love was foolish. It tempted fate. So my mother fed us instead. *Jiao zi, shao mai*—each delicious morsel an expression of her love. I wonder now what she used to think about as she turned out dumpling after dumpling with quick, practiced fingers and only me and my clumsy hands for help and company. Perhaps she was remembering a kitchen full of friends whose own fingers flew with speed and deftness as they talked and joked the afternoon away.

Perhaps this simple act suffices to explain what drew the classmates to stifling, landlocked Hartford, a place not known for its tourist attractions or its natural beauty. Something, after all, had compelled them to simmer pots of chicken in soy sauce and fry egg rolls in hot oil in the middle of a muggy summer. Something had convinced them to forget about how exhausting it would be to sandwich a reunion between Friday and Monday, to pack up a car full of screaming children and drive all the way to our house only to turn around the next day. Try as I might, I could not get them to reveal, years later, what that something was. I doubt whether they themselves knew. My mother's original explanation provided the only answer I could find: "I was longing for old friends."

Less than a year later, my mother was laboriously crafting her own real-estate ads in her imperfect English and puzzling out long legal contracts. One phase of her life had indeed ended; another begun. Alone again, she was trying to gain America even as, on the other side of the country, Margaret and her friends were redefining it. Their journeys had taken them to two very different places—austere New England, where lineage counted more than wealth and even the rich drove ten-year-old cars, and showy Los Angeles, where people flocked to reinvent themselves on the world's brightest, gaudiest stage. The differences had shaped them accordingly. In Hartford, the Chinese defined themselves through the white community. Success meant fitting in. If that meant pandering to white tastes—serving duck sauce with egg rolls, serving egg rolls to begin with—then so be it. In Palos

Verdes, the pressure to conform came strictly from within. Chinese families used other Chinese families to measure their own successes. The white world existed in a parallel but alternate universe that did not interfere with their own.

As different as they were, something did connect Margaret and my mother. Neither my mother's hectic work schedule nor Margaret's whirlwind social life could disguise a void at the center of their lives. Some ten years after she first started working, my mother would quit and move to New York. Her champagne awards would not survive the journey. Not much did. Margaret, still at the same job, lapsed into a deeper and deeper indifference. They both felt that their lives had amounted to little, if anything. It was around this time, at yet another Beiyinyu reunion, that they would meet again for the first time since graduation and realize just how much they had in common—more, perhaps, even than when they had been at school together.

"Curiosity, obsession, and dogged endurance," Albert Einstein once declared, "combined with self-criticism have brought me to my ideas."

Einstein was a towering figure in the Western world, one of science's greatest heroes, the kind of person Margaret had perhaps once dreamed of becoming. My mother had dreamed of nothing. She had simply become. But Einstein's quote held relevance for them both. They too had been shaped by the dogged endurance and, above all, the self-criticism of which he had spoken. These were Chinese characteristics, bred from birth out of hardship. Curiosity and obsession were what remained foreign and indecipherable, self-indulgent sparks from a more leisurely life. They would leave those for their daughters to discover.

Almost without realizing it, the classmates had arrived at the end of midlife, bewildered guests of honor at a badly timed surprise party. Instead of feeling contented, they became more anxious than ever, perhaps because, for the first time in their lives, they were, for better or worse, making all of their own choices. As the children grew up, and they began to contemplate retirement, the unfamiliar shadow of introspection started to break down the carefully constructed barriers in their minds. During this latest phase in their lives, the circle would turn unto itself. Events, like ghosts, would bring the women into renewed contact with the past. In 1987, when my mother moved to New York, she had not seen Suzanne in more than five years, Dolores in nearly a decade, Margaret in more than thirty years. Over the next five years, she would encounter them again, refugees still, who had briefly stopped at the same way station on their very different journeys in life.

BEHIND THE CLOSED DOOR

For years my mother, aware as she was of the value of friend-ship, had tried to keep in touch with Dolores. She and an-other of Dolores's classmates and close friends, a woman named Judy, had left numerous messages for her at her office. They had even telephoned Dolores's sister, who told them only, "I'll tell her that you called." Dolores never got back to them.

Then in the summer of 1993, my mother, through ways I no longer try to understand, discovered that Dolores's mother was very sick. She and Judy finally reached their old friend. They wanted to visit her mother. Dolores put them off. For weeks she postponed visits and canceled others, until one day she finally agreed to let them visit. Her mother was about to die. Together, Judy and my mother made the trip to St. Luke's Hospital, which was across Amsterdam Avenue from Columbia University, not far from the old apartment on 120th Street. Dolores's mother had held on to the place all these years, even after both her daughters had married and moved away. It was a familiar path that Judy and my mother traveled that day to see the woman who had in many ways adopted them when they were alone and parentless in a new country.

Dolores was waiting for them when they arrived. The three old friends walked into the room together. Four decades earlier, my mother had sat at the deathbed of her own mother in a very different hospital room, far removed from the modern, bustling confines of this one. The time had come for her to say goodbye to yet another link to that long-ago past.

Dolores's mother was ninety and frail, a wizened doll of a woman, not the plump, elegantly groomed senator the girls remembered. Life had treated her roughly, and she had met its every challenge. She had survived two wars, three divorces, breast cancer, a goiter operation, and immigration to America. Old age remained the only foe she could not beat. Even so, she remained lucid to the end.

When the women entered the room, her eyes were closed. Her breath came in short, rattling gasps. My mother and Judy stood by her bed and spoke gently to her in Chinese.

"It's us," they said, and gave their names. "We came to see you."

The breathing continued laboriously. The eyes remained closed.

"Do you know us?" they asked.

The old woman opened her eyes and stared at them. In that moment, the years unrolled in the distance between them. Behind Dolores's mother lay the past—the days of revolution, the early years of optimism—all the hope that my mother's generation had never known. Beyond my mother and her friends lay the future, what the old woman would not live to see. Dolores's mother nodded. She knew them.

She died the next day.

At the funeral, my mother asked Dolores if there was anything she could do. "No," she responded. "I'm doing all right."

Unbeknownst to my mother at the time, Dolores had quit her job two years before and had already nearly depleted her savings. Her husband had been laid off around the same time. Their sole source of income came from her modest pension. For nearly a year, Dolores and her family had been staying in her mother's apartment and taking care of the old woman. They planned to stay there after her death. Her mother had lived in the same rent-stabilized place for nearly forty years. The rent hovered, good-fairy-like, around the six-hundred-dollar mark. Dolores had everything under control. She was playing the commodities market, and she knew she would win. The family could take shelter in her old home until her strategy paid off.

A year later, Dolores called my mother. The landlord had raised the rent in her mother's old apartment to one thousand dollars. Dolores had gone to court to contest the increase, saying that she had established tenancy in the apartment and should still be charged the same rent that her mother had been paying. She had lost the case and was now living in Queens. At the time, my mother had two apartments in New York, one on top of the other. She offered one of them to Dolores. Dolores declined.

"I can't do that," she told my mother. "First of all, the apartment's too expensive. Second of all, sometimes I don't pay my rent. You're my friend. I don't want to do that to you."

Instead, my mother loaned her a few thousand dollars. Dolores promptly lost the cash in the commodities market.

"When I was in need," my mother shrugged off the loss to me, "Dolores's mother open her house to me whenever I come to New York. I was paying my debt."

She also felt a certain sympathy towards Dolores's dreams. By that time, my mother too had started investing in the market. She had spent the previous few years in a lackluster fog of indifference. She had gone back to school to improve her English but quickly tired of the humdrum environment. Next, she had attempted to sell life insurance. This pursuit involved making money, so it had kept her interest a little longer. She had even gone so far as to ask her friends in Hartford to clip out birth announcements so that she could sell policies to responsible new parents. After a while, the novelty wore off. Selling insurance lacked the excitement that she craved.

During those years, I could always find her at home. When I was still in college, she used to make the long trek up to Columbia from her apartment just to bring me my mail in the hope that we could spend some time together. I tried to resist, relishing my independence. After I graduated, she took to stopping by my office for unwanted visits. She called at least once a day. She wanted me to come over for dinner, to go to the movies, to run some hopeless errand with her that ate up entire clock revolutions of my time. Then the calls tapered off. At first I welcomed the respite, but as I stopped hearing from her, I grew alarmed. She disappeared for whole days at a time. She would walk down to Wall Street and vanish within the dungeons of the discount brokerage houses, reemerging only when the market had closed. Instead of going home, she next would head to one of the Barnes and Noble superstores that were sprouting like dandelions all over the meadow of the city. She treated them like her own personal library, settling into a cozy nook and devouring the most recent copies of *Fortune, Forbes, Money, Smart Money, BusinessWeek,* and other money bibles devoted to helping people get rich quick. Now when I arrived for dinner, she ignored me. Two televisions blared simultaneously. One showed CNBC shows she had taped during the day while she was downtown. The other ran the current programming. She wandered from one to the other, writing notes in a hardback Mead composition book, the kind I used to use in grammar school. The television never shut off unless my parents had company. I obviously did not count as such. Instead, my mother would slap a hunk of broiled salmon on top of a bed of rice down in front of me.

"Here," she would say, as though I were a customer at the local greasy spoon and she the waitress.

The stock market had become my mother's obsession. She, better than anyone else, could understand Dolores's fixation with the sport of buying and selling shares. But one important distinction existed between the two women. My mother played the stock market not for the money but for the entertainment. It filled the void in her life once occupied by real estate. It even bolstered her shaky sense of self-esteem.

"You know so much," she told me, explaining why she loved trading stocks. "When you talk to people, they respect you now. Before, all the women always talk about theater, books, reviews at cocktail parties. I don't like to read books, so now I can talk to them about stocks—not just stocks, companies—and the guys always raise their eyebrows; how come I know so much?"

"Yeah," she concluded with satisfaction. "I like that."

In contrast, Dolores had left a career that she enjoyed in order simply to make money. Unlike my mother, she was depending on the commodities market for her livelihood. My father, a corporate executive, brought home a yearly salary and a bonus. My parents owned a house in Westchester. They had savings. True immigrants, they lived frugally, and now that their children were out of school, they had almost no expenses. My mother played the stock market, not the commodities market like Dolores did. It was an important distinction. Commodities are far riskier than stocks. The pay-off can be greater but, so too, can the losses, losses that Dolores could not really afford. After twenty years and getting tenure at the university where she taught, Dolores had only a small pension to show for all her work. She and her husband did not own their own home. She had plowed all of their savings into the market.

If my mother had been in Dolores's position, she would not have continued. But my mother would never have let herself get into Dolores's position in the first place. Money tantalized her, not because she was status-conscious or power-hungry, but because she longed for the security she had never known. When we were growing up, my family rarely took vacations. We drove the same cars until their rust-corroded sides began flaking off in the streets. My mother never redecorated the house on whim the way her friends did. When she finally did paint the walls, sand the floors, and put up new wallpaper in the kitchen, it was because she was trying to sell the place. We never had luxuries simply for the sake of having them. My parents viewed everything as an investment—the membership at the golf club that would further my father's career, the enrollment at private schools that would give us children the best education, the bestowal of expensive presents on my mother's clients in the name of creating good business. To this day, taking a taxi instead of the subway can ruin my mother's entire evening. When I was growing up, I had thought my family bordered uncomfortably close to poverty, so earnestly did we all try to save money.

Dolores had never faced the uncertainty that my mother had. Her own powerful mother had brought her to America and put her through school. She was the cosseted younger child with an older sister to pave the way. Dolores had spent more of her high-school years in America than she had in Taiwan. The lessons she had learned differed drastically from those that my mother, scrambling to find a way to come to the States, was learning in Taipei. When Dolores found herself in debt after her mother's death, she automatically looked for a magic pill, rather than a realistic solution. That is not to say that she was frivolous. She had gotten a doctorate in mathematics, after all. It was just that some part of Dolores still believed in the fantasy of America that Hollywood had spun for her when she was a girl in China. No one had ever called her practical.

When her mother had first fallen ill, Dolores quit her job to spend more time with her even though her husband had been laid off. At the time, they were renting an apartment in Brooklyn. Their son, Mark, was in college. But Dolores's mother had a bank account that contained around $300,000. Dolores had also inherited some money from her father and had her own savings. She decided that the entire family could live on the combined amount. Instead of trying to save money, she rented a house on Long Island because her mother had always wanted to live in a house. While the apartment on the Upper West Side lay empty, the family lived extravagantly in the suburbs. They hired a live-in nurse to look after Dolores's mother. Mark owned his own car. On the weekends, there were surprise trips to Las Vegas or, once, a luxury cruise. The family flew to Hawaii twice and to Taiwan, first class each time. They stayed in suites in five-star hotels. They ordered room service. They gambled at various casinos. In about a year, the money was gone. The nurse left. The family moved back to the apartment in Morningside Heights. Mark dropped out of school. Even now, a glint of pride, coupled with an utter lack of self-awareness, revealed itself in Dolores's account of those heady times.

"My sister hinted I just squandered away my mother's money," Dolores told me indignantly. "I squandered it on her. We traveled first class all the way. Not just one ticket, four tickets, because there's Mark, my husband, and me also."

The rent increase in her mother's old apartment was typical of Dolores's lack of planning. Under New York's rent-control laws, she only had to live with her mother for a year to establish her tenancy, but the family fell just shy of the mark. On some level, perhaps, she had thought her fantasy life would never end and so she never worried about the hard times that the future would bring. Even when they came, she clung to her daydreams as the rest of her family struggled to keep afloat.

Mark had quit school, and started working to help out. Dolores's husband made spasmodic attempts to conjure up employment. Only Dolores herself refused to consider the thought. After her mother's death, the bills mounted. In my family, the natural recourse would have been to find a job and patiently grind away, for years if necessary, until every one of those debts had been paid. Almost everyone at her school, from the staff to the students, had liked Dolores. Her old job might still have been waiting for her. Certainly, opportunities existed there for teaching positions, if not for tenured professorships. Dolores turned them all down. She was going to make a fortune in the stock market with a mysterious strategy that she refused to divulge. She would erase all her debts with one triumphant trade. She would return to the house in the suburbs. In actuality, what she did was sit in her cramped study in Queens, staring at a computer screen all day. She owned a contraption that continually flashed the changing prices in the market at her throughout the day. She read them. She talked to her broker. All day long, she sat in the dark room papered oddly with scenes from antebellum Southern life—Mississippi riverboats, Greek-revival plantation homes, graceful magnolia trees. She emerged only to go to the bathroom or to quickly down a meal.

"Because of my training," she told me proudly, "I could sit for eight hours without moving to study or try to solve a problem."

Somehow I did not think it was to this end that her math professors had instilled such disciplined work habits in her. Her behavior dismayed me. Perhaps if I had had a better understanding of her passion, I might have had more empathy, but my mind and finance act like two magnets when they meet: that is to say, they do not attract, they resist. No matter how hard I press the two together, a stubborn distance remains. I enjoy money as much as any daughter of capitalism, but, much to my parents' everlasting disappointment, it is the spending of it that gives me pleasure, not the making.

I asked my mother to take me with her the next time she went downtown. Perhaps in the very cradle of American finance I could better understand its sometimes fatal attraction. We made the round of my mother's various brokers. They were all discount outfits, crack houses for stock-market junkies. The best was the first. It had a real office. We rode a newly paneled elevator to the eighteenth floor, where two young women desultorily manned the desks. A garish imitation of that already garish daub known as *The Bears and the Bulls at Market* hung over the receptionist's desk.

My mother approached one of the young women. Cute, bored, and in her early twenties, the woman wore a brown A-line skirt and a vacant expression.

"Hi, Maureen," my mother said cheerfully. "This is my daughter."

"It's actually Tara," Tara said in a monotone that hinted of the outer boroughs. "Maureen's my cousin who used to work here."

My mother shrugged, cheer undiminished, and settled her account. As she examined her invoice and wrote out her checks, she maintained a steady patter of conversation with Tara. By the time she rose to leave, she was giving the young woman career advice.

"You don't like customer service," my mother said. It was an observation.

"Not really," Tara admitted, and sighed, interest lighting her eyes for the first time since we had entered the room.

She lolled against her desk. Finally, a customer existed who understood her travails, who could imagine what it was like for her, Tara, to sit day after day in the recycled air of the office under an icky painting of wild animals and livestock.

My mother nodded sagely. "You should get out," she said. "Your heart's not in it."

As we walked towards the elevator, my mother called over her shoulder one last time: "Bye, Maureen."

She stopped walking a beat later and said, "Oops, I mean Tara."

This time Tara smiled and waved. "It's all right," she said.

At the next place, a front office did not even exist. We walked straight into a room of anxious-looking brokers, bit players on

Wall Street riding their computers like jockeys. One woman had long, bleached-blond hair and Jessica Rabbit's figure. A black leather cap perched on another one's head. A cheap pinstripe suit covered her too ample behind. One pod of computers appeared to be reserved for smokers. It was centered in the middle of a room with no partitions. Through the haze, I heard a voice calling my mother's name. My mother pushed me forward.

"These are my buddies," my mother said, introducing me to two men. "Ken and Gary."

Ken exuded a ruddy air of health that did very little to counteract the effect of his greased-back hair and the thin gold chain that dangled from his hairy wrist. At least he did not appear tubercular, which was more than I could say for drooping, dissolute Gary, who looked like the villain who ties the heroine to the train tracks. He wore a turtleneck and black pants, which hung from his thin frame.

Ken gestured to my mother: "Over here."

They conspired by his desk, and she bought some puts. Then she showed him her newest toy, a hand-held device called a Quotron machine, which supposedly allowed her to obtain up-to-the-minute stock prices. The problem was that it did not. It had a time delay of about fifteen minutes. My mother refused to believe her own eyes. She walked out of the office with the machine held before her like a divining rod. Its antenna threatened to stab various passersby. She did not notice. Her eyes focused on the screen only. As she crossed the street, a car almost hit her.

"You're going to get killed," I said, "unless you pay attention."

She mumbled something and looked down at the screen. Only when it started to rain did she put the machine protectively away in her backpack.

We stopped in a coffee shop on the way to the last brokerage house. The counter person, a young Latina, turned to my mother. Without even exchanging a greeting, my mother turned both her thumbs down and started pumping them furiously.

"Mexico's going down," she hissed.

"Really?" the woman asked.

Her lips were painted scarlet, and when she spoke, I could see lipstick on one of her front teeth.

"Down," my mother whispered furtively, and leaned forward as if she were offering the woman drugs.

The woman leaned in too, listening raptly.

"Excuse me," a customer interrupted with a whine. "Could I have my order?"

The customer was a young woman also, but white, and dressed in a dull, dark suit. Irritation and impatience made her words brittle. She tapped her foot. The counter person turned toward her.

"Oh sure, honey," she said sweetly. "What did you have again?"

"Roast beef," the woman snapped, heaving a loud sigh.

The customer had to get back to important business. The counter person existed to serve her, not to have conversations on the job. My mother turned to leave. Her friend, thoughts still full of Mexico, called after her.

"Mary," she said, "you want a tea?"

My mother shook her head no. The customer shook her head too.

It turned out the first two places we had stopped had been mere training for the last. Here, in the bowels of one of Wall Street's grand old stone ladies, a gaggle of the desperate convened. The company's employees worked behind a glass partition as if to shield them from the loonies beyond. The loonies themselves hung around a room bright with fluorescent light that revealed every scuff mark and stain on the peach walls. A sign in the corner sternly instructed: Please No Eating, No Smoking, No Food or Drink. It might as well have said, Don't Feed the Animals.

There were four terminals and eight people on this rainy day. Most of them were older. "Retired," my mother told me. They were all men. They wore khakis and collared shirts. Some had donned jackets, others sweaters. It looked like Saturday afternoon at the men's grill of a country club, save for the slightly seedy, desperate air that permeated the place.

"Hey, Mary," they called out to her, and she introduced me around.

Then she headed for a terminal and immediately began calling up information on her stocks. Others tapped away around her. One balding man sat watching the TV—showing the ubiquitous CNBC—with an air of absolute concentration. Another man blustered to his friend: "I'm not going to buy a stock some snot-nosed kid put in his grandfather's ear."

And then the snot-nosed kids started arriving. It was lunchtime, and they nipped around the corner from their jobs at nearby financial firms to check on their own portfolios. They wore suits and ties if they were men, pumps and pearls if they were women. Today, it was raining, and they wore trench coats. The loonies wore windbreakers.

Later, on the street, my mother would give me the lowdown on the regulars. Her favorite, Tom, had a red face, a jovial manner, and severe depression. He had lost his job at a brokerage firm after he had suffered a nervous breakdown.

"He doesn't want to take antidepressants," my mother said, "so he eats candy all the time."

Inside, Tom nudged my mother with an elbow.

"I'm no in-and-out trader like you, Mary," he kidded her. My mother was famous for selling the moment a stock showed a profit. "You got to think long-term," he added.

Recently, Tom had netted ten thousand dollars on a trade. My mother expressed her admiration and envy. "Next time you do that," she said urgently, "tell me."

Tom shook his head. "Oh, you don't want to trade with me," he said. "You want to trade with Pete. He put in two thousand dollars, got sixteen back. Pure profit. He wasn't adding cash. That's who you want to trade with."

It was my mother's turn to shake her head.

"You want to fly with Pete, Mary?" Tom asked, laughing. "Fly with Pete?"

Later, my mother revealed that Pete took too many risks. She called him a mess. He lost too much money.

"Everyone," she said, as though I were some boob from the backwoods, "knows that."

As my mother punched up her stocks, she tried to teach me about their movements, telling me why she had bought them and at what price. I nodded dumbly. Try as I might to learn, the process bored me. The numbers scrolling down the screen meant nothing to me. All I could hope to retain for more than a few minutes were the names of the different companies. Even that proved to be a stretch.

"Oh," someone said when he saw our two heads bent together over a terminal. "Are you teaching her how to trade?"

"She has no interest," my mother said, pursing her lips. Her eyes did not move from the screen. "No interest."

It was true. Coming here had not given me any more insight into Dolores's obsession. It only made me realize there were plenty of others like her. They were all gamblers, addicted to the elusive dream of hitting it big. Unlike Dolores, though, they still craved the sense of community that they had previously gotten from their offices or their neighborhoods, a place to which they could belong. Living on the fringes of the world had not made them stop wanting to be part of it.

In this, Dolores had become as different from my mother, who loved being around other people, as anyone could be. Give my mother five minutes with a stranger and she will make a new friend. She does not even have to speak the same language. Dolores presented a mystery. She was likable and seemed to want to be liked, but the better I got to know her, the more she seemed to shy away. I could not decide if she was deliberately shutting the door or simply reacting to the feeling that the door was shutting on her.

She lived in Queens, just a subway ride away from my parents' apartment in Manhattan, but it was well after I had started working on the book that I learned of her existence. She did not join the gaggle of women who briefly formed an investment club with my mother. Whenever a classmate came in from out of town, anywhere in the country, tradition and hospitality dictated that the locals take her out to dinner. Dolores never showed up for these events. I doubt that she was even invited. On the list that my mother had given me of classmates in the tri-state area, a writer who had denounced all her classmates for their political apathy and a class star who had suffered a nervous breakdown and become something of a recluse in the States had both been mentioned. Dolores had not.

When I did finally hear of her, I forced my mother to arrange
a visit, which she did only with great reluctance. It was with even
greater reluctance that she agreed to accompany me.

Dolores lived in a residential neighborhood at the edge of Forest Hills. Her house sat on a side street off a busy avenue, anonymous in a row of almost identical houses. They were cozy,
two-story buildings with faint touches of Tudor. I noticed, with
delight, that a small window on her upper floor had mullions.
Then I realized, with far less pleasure, that many of the houses in
the row had the same charming feature.

The door flung open to reveal a plump woman wearing blue
eye shadow and pink lipstick. Energy radiated from her. Non-
plussed, I stepped back slightly in an attempt to absorb the sight
before me. She wore her hair in a style favored by adolescent
boys in the outer boroughs and members of the band Journey: it
consisted of bangs on top, was cropped to outline the shape of
the head, and ended in a cascade of stringy hair to the shoulders.
I had recently read a disparaging article on the same style in the
Beastie Boys fanzine *Grand Royal*. The writer had called it a
"mullet," once worn by the likes of Michael Bolton, Roger Clinton, and Andre Agassi. The women's version was, according to
the same writer, technically known as a "femullet." However unlikely I might have thought such an occurrence would be, the
proof stood before me. A classmate of my mother's had a femullet.

She greeted my mother and me and, without taking a breath,
craned her neck around to face the stairway behind her.

"Mark!" she called. "Come down here!"

"I want Mark to meet you," she said. "That's my son. Mark!"

"Coming," a voice reluctantly called from above.

"Someone I want you to meet," she told him, and then turned
to us. "Come in. Come in."

We stood in the hallway, waiting for Mark to emerge. Dolores
yelled his name another five times before he descended. He was
not slow. She simply called for him every thirty seconds. She
spoke the best English of all the classmates I had met thus far.
Her voice contained a faint touch of the foreign, just enough to
charm. While we were waiting for her son, she entertained us

with a running monologue about her cats. One of them had already brushed against my ankles.

"That's Muffy," Dolores said. "She's the mom. We have five cats." She picked the animal up and scratched between its ears. Muffy stretched languorously in her arms and purred.

"Poor Muffy," Dolores cooed. "We found her. She was a stray. A tiny thing."

At that moment, Mark came down the stairs. His appearance surprised me. From the way he had answered his mother, I had been expecting a shy, gawky boy of about twenty. But Mark was older than I was, and tall. He had his mother's full face. He smiled and shook our hands and then, without complaint, went outside with my mother to make sure that our car was all right where we had parked it.

Dolores and I went into the living room. By this point I had visited many of my mother's friends. Their houses varied greatly. Some could be called mansions. Others were modest ranch houses. The rest—contemporaries, colonials, town houses—fell somewhere in between. But none of them were as humble as the one I was standing in. The living room contained two mustard-brown sofas which faced each other. Set into a wall of mirrors was a fireplace. A large television dominated one corner of the room. Beyond it was a small dining room, from which another cat appeared. I began to feel like sneezing.

"Do you want to watch some television?" Dolores asked. "Do you want something to eat? Do you want some Coke?"

I shook my head.

"Nothing?" she persisted. "How about orange juice?"

"I'll have some tea," I finally said.

"Tea?" she said with surprise. "You drink tea?"

She went into the kitchen and reappeared with a large bowl of potato chips and a cup of tea.

"Let me give you Coke," she tried again. "I'm sure you like it better."

I managed to resist one more time, and she sat down. An uncomfortable silence settled over the room. She looked at me and beamed. Her body practically vibrated with the effort to keep still. Dolores was different from all the other classmates I had interviewed thus far. The vague intimation of failure that hung about the house gave her a dark edge that contrasted sharply with her forceful exuberance. She shone at a higher wattage than most. I felt that anything she attempted would yield spectacular results, of either dizzying success or dumbfounding ruin. I remembered what my mother had told me when I asked her why she never spent time with Dolores even though she lived so close by.

"She owes me money," my mother said. "So I don't want to call her. I don't want her to think I'm always after her to pay me back. Understand?"

When she returned to the house, my mother seemed not to remember the delicate nature of their relationship. Instead, she barged in and almost immediately demanded to see Dolores's quote machine.

Dolores demurred. No one was allowed in her office except the cats. My mother insisted. "You two stay down here and talk," she said. "I'll go upstairs."

"No, no, Mary," Dolores said. "Stay here with us."

I sat amazed, watching this exchange: the one woman throwing aside all courtesy to insist that she be allowed to use the other's equipment, the other, equally shockingly, refusing to let her do so. I also knew how my mother felt about Dolores's straitened circumstances. I could not believe that she now insisted on forcefully drawing her friend's attention back to the machine that had been the source of her downfall. Not to mention that it was Sunday. The market was closed. For once, Dolores did not want to touch her quote machine, or at the very least, she did not want my mother to touch it.

In the end, the two women compromised. We trooped upstairs past Mark's room, the door of which hung slightly ajar. Later on, he would tell me why. He occupied the master bedroom. It was mid-January, and the sound of a postseason football game emanated from the crack of space that led to his room. Next to it lay a small, plainly furnished room with two narrow twin beds. This is where Dolores and her husband slept. Its most striking characteristic were the walls, which had been painted a violent shade of pink. The third bedroom served as Dolores's office. The door was firmly closed. Once inside, I felt as though I were standing in a large walk-in closet. The three of us clumped together made me feel claustrophobic. To make matters worse, Dolores immediately pulled down the shades, even though the sun had started to fall and barely shone into the room. I looked around. Stacks of newspapers leaned against a bookshelf. Next to them sat a pair of battered blue suitcases that looked as if they had not been on a trip in a long time. The only pieces of furniture were a desk and a chair. In the center of the desk was the machine in which my mother had taken such a great interest. It looked like an ordinary computer and had a label on it that read, "Data Transmission Network Corporation."

My mother sat down and was immediately transfixed by the numbers scrolling past her on the screen. She was so eager to start using it, her hands trembled. But just as my mother began to type, Dolores turned off the machine. The deal had been struck. She had shown my mother her office. That was as much as she would allow.

"Okay," Dolores said. "Now we'll go downstairs."

On the landing, she poked her head into Mark's bedroom. He was lying on a queen-size bed watching a television even bigger than the one downstairs. The Cowboys and the Packers were dueling it out on the football field.

"Come down and talk to us," she said.

"I'm busy," he replied without turning his head.

Downstairs, we flipped through Dolores's old photo albums, which contained picture after picture of her Beiyinyu days.

"That's Suzanne," my mother said, pointing at one. She turned to another picture. "This, we were in somebody's house. See, Dolores is leaving, so we all meet there every night to say goodbye to her. She's coming to America."

The picture showed three rows of well-scrubbed girls smiling at the camera. They wore cardigans, blouses, and pleated skirts. Their hair, which fell just below their ears, was held in place with barrettes.

"You're the perfect person to talk to," I told Dolores. "You know everyone."

She looked at the picture of all her old friends gathered to wish her farewell.

"But," she said, "the thing is, your mom has kept in touch with them, and I haven't." I wondered why she had bothered to keep their pictures then. She had many more photo albums than my mother.

I asked about her high-school days, and memories came tumbling forth like warm clothes from a dryer. As she talked, I noticed, her English worsened. Before, she had spoken like someone who thought in English—fluently, directly, and without hesitating. Now, it was as if she were translating her memories from Chinese.

"I don't know if you were in the group one weekend," she said, looking at my mother, "we had to study for the exams. We go to the school to our classroom. We pile up all the desks. Were you there that time?"

My mother started chuckling in a low undertone. I recognized the sound. It was the noise she makes when she has been caught doing something naughty.

"Made a fort," she said. "Right?"

"Yes, made a fort," Dolores said eagerly in a torrent of reminiscence. "We piled up all the desks layer by layer. We climb on top, and we're sitting right at the ceiling. We were studying there all day right at the top. It was really funny. And we also shoot paper balls. There's one teacher—she wore glasses, she always wears a bun. She teaches geometry and trigonometry, and very boring, so we used to use a rubber band and firing off the paper balls and then we would shoot towards her, and she would turn, and everybody just sit like this."

Dolores's face assumed an innocent, wide-eyed expression. She turned to my mother again.

"I know you know that," she accused her, "because you did it too.

"We went on outings," she continued, "mountain climbing, bicycle riding. Your mom only came a few times, because she has her other friends, and the other friends are a little more mature, because they go dancing."

"Not really dancing," my mother protested.

They began to talk about the social structure of the class. This surprised me. No one before had admitted that cliques existed or

that some people were more popular than others. Other classmates had painted a benign picture of their classrooms as a har-
monious place in which fifty-five adolescent girls got along
famously and were all friends. This never rang true to me, but I
could never get anyone to admit that it was not so. Until now.
But even while Dolores debunked the myth of unity, my mother
continued to cling to it.

I asked them what factors contributed to schisms at school.

"I think money is important," Dolores said.

"I didn't think it was all that important," my mother responded.

"See," Dolores explained, "your mom attract all those girls
with money and boyfriends."

"Who did?" my mother demanded.

"You!"

"I did not."

I listened, amused, as their dialogue reverted to the cadences of
adolescence. What amazed me even more was the earnestness
with which they tackled the subject at hand. High school was not
a remote event that had taken place some forty years before but,
rather, an experience they still thought about. And of all the
women who might take such a fervent interest in the issue, these
two seemed among the most unlikely—Dolores because she had
long ago turned her back on the very classmates whom she now
discussed with such enthusiasm, my mother because she lacked
all notions of sentimentality and introspection. In any other situation, my mother would have conceded to her friend long ago,
out of boredom if nothing else. But instead she persisted.

"Ohh," she breathed. "I think you are wrong. I don't feel that
way. I was just friendly whoever wants to be friendly with me.
Whoever wants me I go to their house."

"But you always have cliques," Dolores said. "There's always
little groups. I'm sure there's some jealousy."

"Nobody ever jealous of me," my mother said, "because I
wasn't good student. They always worship the good students."

"Yes," Dolores affirmed. It was the first thing they had agreed
on so far.

"Because," Dolores continued, "anyone who get into that high school are the top of their peers. The girls' school we went to, it's equivalent—how do I compare?—it's equivalent to Harvard. It's like Ivy League of the high schools."

My mother nodded her head. Regardless of their differing opinions about day-to-day life at Beiyinyu, they agreed on its purpose: to serve as a door to the outside world.

"Did everyone talk about going to Tai Da or America?" I asked.

"That's all they talk about," my mother said.

"It's always the ones who come out top of their class who have a better chance of coming out to the United States and be accepted in U.S. universities," Dolores said. "That's why everybody studies so hard. They want to be top of their class. They want to go to the best school, which is Tai Da. This way they are accepted in U.S. universities, and they have a better chance of coming here."

"I don't know how to explain," my mother said simply. "Everybody wants to come here."

"So you were lucky," I said to Dolores. "You were the first in the class to come to the U.S."

"Everybody was very envy of her," my mother said. "We don't know what's our future. We didn't know when we would get to there, but she's there."

Dolores was describing her first experiences in America when she mentioned the Chinese in Chinatown. It had come as a startling discovery to me when I was young to realize that my parents did not speak the same language as the shopkeepers in Chinatown. Since then, Chinatown has changed somewhat, crowded with immigrants from all parts of East and Southeast Asia, not just China, many of whom had been professionals in their home countries. But in my childhood, Chinatown, the ghetto, had existed as the prevailing image the rest of the country had of the Chinese. For my part, I had drawn careful distinctions between its inhabitants and me, as anxious as any bigot to reassure myself of my own superiority. They lived in tiny apartments crammed with people. They used too much grease when they cooked. They had missing teeth and flat faces. They were uniformly short. In my mind, I called them "the nut people," because their brown, wrinkled faces reminded me of nothing so much as shelled pecans.

"What do you think of the people in Chinatown?" I asked Dolores.

Her answer surprised me, not for what she said but for the way she said it.

"I think we're different," she answered, "but I respect the Chinese in Chinatown because they have a difficult struggle, and they have to go through a difficult life also, so even though we may be a little different in terms of background, I respect people from Chinatown. I don't look down on them."

Her voice wavered at the end. I noticed with surprise that she had tears in her eyes.

"I don't judge people anymore by their education," she said. Her voice continued to wobble. "This is awful. I'm going to cry. I don't think that anymore. You know why?"

I waited, silently encouraging her to continue. She seemed to be summoning up the courage to deliver a stunning revelation. Eventually, she did begin to cry.

"This is so hard," she whispered, and then unleashed a torrent of Chinese.

I could not follow much of what she was saying, but I managed to catch the last part, which, it turned out, contained the crucial information.

"*Wo er-zi mei you de* B.A.," Dolores said.

My mother nodded sympathetically.

"It's okay," she said.

I must have looked confused, because my mother translated for me. She thought I had not understood.

"She says that Mark doesn't have his B.A."

But I had understood. The translation did not clarify the situation. Dolores's son had not graduated from college. I knew that, and I still did not understand what the problem was. But Dolores acted as though it were the worst tragedy imaginable.

My mother seemed to think it was very significant too. She kept patting Dolores on the back and telling her not to worry. She handed Dolores a tissue. Dolores blew her nose. Then Dolores looked at me.

"So I don't judge people anymore by their degrees," she said. "Twenty years ago, I was very shallow and would. I'd probably look down on people who never graduated from college. I'd probably think they weren't good citizens. But now people on the street I see, people just handling garbage—you know, my garbage handler?—I say hello to them. I come out and talk to them, and I thank them. I thank them as though they're doing me a favor.

"I do that," she said, leaning forward and looking earnestly into my eyes, "because anybody who does honest job, earn a honest living deserve our respect."

"But," my mother explained, "this is not the thinking we had in Taiwan. In Taiwan everybody think you got to go to school. You got to do this and that."

"Exactly," Dolores said. "Exactly."

I saw then the full force of the peer pressure to which my mother and her classmates had been subjected. Dolores had isolated herself from her classmates from a combination of guilt and embarrassment. She lived so much more humbly than they. Her husband did not have a successful career. She was spending her time and money on investment strategies that had failed to produce any success thus far. Her son did not have a college degree. Above all, she wanted to protect her family from the hurtful gossip that she remembered all too well from her days at school. In most ways, Dolores was more American than any of the other classmates, but here lay proof that, in spite of her seeming aloofness, she would always remain attached to them.

I needed to readjust the focus of the lens through which I was viewing Dolores's world. I was looking through my own glass, not through hers. Questions I had about my identity, my place in American society did not trouble her. She knew who she was and from where she had come. For her, self-doubt began not when she failed to measure up to mainstream America or to fit in somehow, but when she failed to measure up against the people with whom she had shared a classroom forty years before. Their influence still held sway in spite of the distance and the lessons she claimed to have learned.

Dolores stood apart. Whatever else America had done to her,

it had given her a perspective shared by few, if any, of her class-mates. She dared to take risks. What surprised me was that in-stead of admiring her, I pitied her. Instinctively, almost against my will, I found myself siding with my mother and her friends. I wondered, with a growing sense of impatience and indignation, how Dolores could have stumbled so badly, how she could con-tinue to be so blind in the face of reality. I wanted to shake her into consciousness, the way I am sure many a Chinese parent has wanted to shake a rebellious child who refuses to follow the path so carefully laid out by the generation before.

We went out to eat later that night. Before we left the house, Dolores called out to Mark. "We're going for dinner," she said. "Do you want to come?"

"No." The answer floated down the stairs. "I'm going out later."

"He's always going out," she grumbled. "I never know who he goes out with or where he goes."

He's twenty-eight years old, I felt like saying. You're not sup-posed to know.

The restaurant surprised me. I usually only ate Chinese food in Chinatown and Flushing or in California. In all of those places, the clientele was predominantly Asian. Here, the majority of the diners were white. I thought I could feel their stares as we walked in. They probably had not even noticed us. My reaction was re-flexive, a throwback to my childhood in Hartford when I dreaded walking into any Chinese restaurant because the patrons did stop and stare.

"How cute," I used to imagine them all saying, "the Chinese family is going out for Chinese food."

The food was a throwback too. Dolores took charge of the or-dering.

"Orange beef," she said, "pork chops. All the young kids like that. Not your mom and me. We're not used to big chunks of meat, but these American kids—that's all they want to eat."

I grimaced. "Not me," I said. "No, really. I'd be happy with some vegetables and maybe some tofu."

She waved her hand at me. "You don't like tofu," she said de-cisively. "Mark doesn't like it either."

At the end of dinner, my mother and Dolores fought over the check. Fighting over the check is the only appropriate way to end a Chinese meal unless one man is dining with a group of women. In that instance, the man is expected to pay. In all other cases, not to fight over the check indicates a lack of breeding. In spite of Dolores's isolation and her poverty, she had not relinquished all her ties to the past.

"*Gai wo*," she demanded when the waiter appeared with the check. "Give it to me."

"*Bu dwei*," my mother said. "That's not right. *Gai wo*."

The waiter stood between them, a look of boredom on his face. He had probably seen many meals end the exact same way. The older couple across the way from us were not so blasé. The wife, who had a head of dignified-looking gray hair, kept craning her neck around to stare at us. The exchange dragged on through a few more rounds of "*Gai wo*" and "*Bu dwei, gai wo*" when my mother suddenly changed tack.

"Ah," she said and pointed to me. "*Gai ta.*"

She managed to startle the waiter out of his indifference.

"*Gai ta?!*" he demanded. He shook his head indignantly, no.

"*Dwei*," I said, and reached for the check.

"*Bu gai ta*," he said firmly. "No."

He spoke to my mother. In his eyes, I was still too young to be addressed directly in the presence of elders, much less to be responsible for paying the bill. While he was admonishing my mother, Dolores took advantage of the distraction and grabbed the check out of his hand. My mother, thinking equally fast, stole Dolores's pocketbook off her lap and threw it across the table at me. When Dolores reached for the bag, waving her hands frantically in the air, my mother expertly plucked the check out of her fingers. She handed it to me.

"Go pay," she said.

I nodded back, unable to speak. I was in the presence of a master. Dolores, indignant but laughing, gave in. For a moment, the two women giggled, heads together. But on the ride home, when we pulled up to the intersection of her street, Dolores quickly reached for the door handle.

"Just drop me off here," she said.

"On the corner?" my mother said. "Are you sure?"

"Oh yes," she responded.

She opened the door in the middle of the street without even waiting for me to pull over.

"Bye," she called out, and slammed the door.

My mother quickly looked at the backseat.

"I knew it," she said. "She didn't take the leftovers."

The light was changing from red to green. My mother grabbed the leftovers and ran down the street after Dolores. I saw her catch up to the tightly bundled figure and thrust the plastic bag into her arms. Cars were honking for me to move when my mother returned to the car in triumph.

"She took them," she said happily, oblivious to what she had done.

I stared at Dolores's retreating figure. She had almost reached her walkway. Her head was bowed, and her shoulders were hunched as though tightly clutching something to her chest.

Back at the restaurant, before the fight for the check began, the waiter had served us wan orange slices and fortune cookies. Dolores opened hers, and a smile spread across her face.

"This is very nice," she said to my mother. "And true."

Dolores read it out loud: " 'There is a true and sincere friendship between you both.' "

My mother opened hers.

"I can't read it," she complained. "It's too light."

She handed it to me.

" 'The time is right,' " I read, " 'to make new friends.' "

The silence between Suzanne and my mother was also broken by the ringing of the telephone. Nearly a decade had passed since the two women had seen each other last, when Suzanne and Tan had stopped at our house in Hartford on their way to drop Jim's things off at college. On that visit, so unlike the one in Ohio so many years before, the two couples had faced each other as familiar strangers, each mired in a similarly deep, but different, unhappiness, made that much worse by the happy memories they

had shared. To reach out to one another would have been impossible. Living in the middle of their own private suffering, they
had only had their illusions to protect them; but by the time
Suzanne called, not even their illusions were enough.

Suzanne could no longer bear the doughy, dying silence of her
marriage. My parents' marriage was dying too. When I first
learned of my father's affairs, I was not at all surprised or even
particularly angry. At sixteen, I already had an ancient, jaded,
unattractive soul. Some part of me had always recognized his
selfishness: I had it too. In our family, it sometimes proved a
necessary trait for survival. What shook me was not my father's
behavior but my mother's. On a trip out west to visit colleges,
she abruptly drove our rental car onto the shoulder of the freeway between Palo Alto and San Francisco and dissolved into a
fury of tears and curses. I still remember watching the sunlight
glint off the water while my mother curled her pliant hands into
tight little fists that she banged so hard against the steering
wheel the entire car shook. She did not know how to recover
from this latest betrayal, one of a long series that had haunted
her life. Adrift in a new city, she focused all her energy on hating my father instead of healing. Ironically, my mother had
come to New York to keep a watchful eye on her husband while
Suzanne had come to get away from the watchful eye of her
own. When she finally called my mother looking for help, it was
unclear who needed it more.

The request, after all those years, must have come as something of a surprise.

"Can I come stay with you?" Suzanne asked.

The words tumbled out quickly. If she did not say them all at
once, she would not say them at all.

My mother did not hesitate. "Of course," she said. "Any-
time."

She demanded no explanation. She asked no questions. Their
shared past led them to a mutual understanding. My mother, for
all her pragmatism, had her own strict moral code. An old friend
could always count on her for help.

When I asked Suzanne, many years later, why she had picked
my mother to contact out of all the classmates who lived in the

area, she answered simply: "I never even question it. I know she would take me in."

When Suzanne arrived at our home, she was locked out. No one was there, and my mother had mistakenly given her the wrong set of keys. She waited in the hall until my father arrived from work. His eyes widened when he saw her standing with her luggage. She had asked to stay for just a few days, but it looked as though she were moving in. Three suitcases, a garment bag or two, and several totes surrounded her. She flashed him the embarrassed smile of someone caught in a shameful predicament. It was a smile both of my parents recognized. It was the smile of a refugee.

That night, after dinner, Suzanne and my mother went outside. They found a park bench under the skinny branches of a leafless tree. It was November, and even though the wind whipped across the open plaza where they sat, they remained for hours talking. Suzanne's story slowly emerged. The Taiwanese government had started a library in New York. They had offered her the job of head librarian. She had never dreamed of having so much responsibility before. The position essentially meant building a collection from scratch. It intimidated and exhilarated her. In the end, she decided to try. That was why she had come to New York.

My mother waited patiently. Suzanne continued. She revealed the whole of her unhappy marriage. Her husband, the other Chinese in the community, the entire town, in fact—they were the sort of people who let life pass them by, much as the new interstate had passed Reading by many years before. She had always aspired to greater things. This new job proved that she was more than the sum of the tiresome parts from where she came. And . . . she hesitated. There was something else.

"That is," she said, "there's someone else."

Richard had returned. He had separated from his wife and filed for divorce. He and Suzanne talked almost every night.

"What are you going to do?" my mother asked.

"I don't know," her old friend answered, and asked her again for help. "I need some time. I'm buying time."

My mother did not just help Suzanne. Suzanne helped my

mother. My mother gave Suzanne a place to sleep and a warm dinner every night. Suzanne gave my mother a project. When my mother had first moved to New York, her anger had sustained her. She spent countless hours poring over old credit-card bills and telephone records, determined to catch my father in another lie, but by the time Suzanne came to her, my mother had lapsed into a melancholy that frightened me so much I refused to acknowledge that it existed. I had never seen her in such a state before. Deprived of her job and her vast network of friends in Connecticut, she faltered. She watched movies all the time, at a loss for what else to do. She called either my sister or me constantly and begged us to meet her for lunch or to go shopping. My sister told me recently that she still hates to hear our mother's voice on her answering machine. The memory of those pleading, wheedling messages closes in on her like an asthma attack. But my sister always agreed, at the very least, to talk to her. I tried to put her off as much as possible. After years of desperately wanting her company, I found myself in the strange position of pushing her away.

But Suzanne never did. She stayed at my parents' place from November until March, almost five months. I wonder still that no tension ever arose between the two. My mother was famous for her generosity, but she also dreaded being taken advantage of. Sooner or later, every one of the people who passed through our house felt the brunt of her wrath if they stayed long enough to provoke it—her father-in-law, her two sisters, her half-brother, various Chinese students. She welcomed them out of a genuine desire to help. She arranged visas for people to come to this country. She found jobs for them once they arrived. Things always went smoothly at first, but as weeks turned into months and, on occasion, years, their presence would begin to grate on her nerves. Part of the problem lay in the fact that she expected them to act with unremitting gratitude towards her. It was the way she would have acted, had acted in the past when she had found herself in their position. She held impossibly high standards, but because she could live up to them, she demanded that everyone else do so as well. The minute a long-term guest forgot to offer to help cook dinner or clean up afterward, resentment began to grow within my mother. From that point on, she regarded the person with suspicion. Inevitably, hard feelings would follow.

Suzanne never crossed that line. I think too that my mother's loneliness made her more tolerant. She had always been working and raising children in the past. Other people in the house, unless they could anticipate her every wish, only served to annoy. Now, she welcomed companionship, and she could find none more giving than Suzanne—none who had ever understood so well as my mother did just what her obligations were. At the time, my parents were living in a simple two-bedroom apartment with one of my brothers, who had just started working in the city. Suzanne slept on the foldout couch in the living room. Every morning, she woke up before anyone else and quickly showered and dressed. She carefully folded the bed back into the couch, making sure to make as little noise as possible. Then she put away all evidence that a person had been sleeping there. Blankets were folded and stored in the linen closet along with pillows. Her own suitcases stood in an orderly row beneath the windows. Not so much as a shirt corner peeped out from their firmly zippered sides. By the time the family had woken and wandered into the living room, Suzanne had already retrieved the newspaper from the front door and started the coffee.

My mother responded in kind. Every night when Suzanne came home from work, my mother offered her a glass of wine. And even though Suzanne did not like to drink, she always accepted it. They made an unlikely pair: Suzanne so tall, thin, and angular, my mother short, soft, and cozy. Suzanne wore lipstick every day. She waved her hair. My mother did not even blow-dry hers. She walked around in tennis shoes, khakis, and old T-shirts that my brother had won at crew meets. Suzanne wore silk dresses, pumps, and stockings. The state of my parents' rumpled, lived-in apartment must have horrified her, she who kept her own house as clean as a hotel. My mother whipped dishes up in the kitchen out of necessity. Suzanne chopped with careful precision. If a dish called for soaking an ingredient overnight, she did. My mother would not bother to make such a tiresome meal to begin with. Nevertheless, the friendship deepened. The two women went shopping together. They took aerobics classes. They saw the Christmas show at Radio City. More importantly, they relied on each other as they did on no one else.

Jim came to visit his mother. The long-awaited reunion between him and my sister finally occurred. Of course, Christine was married by then, and Jim had a serious girlfriend. But the two families had dinner together like they had so many years before. The only person missing was Tan. Jim called my mother "Auntie." Christine enjoyed talking with the girlfriend, who was living in the city and studying medicine at Cornell. Jim would be visiting her often. There seemed to be no reason why they would not get together again and become better friends—except one that was unforeseen by everyone that night, except perhaps Suzanne. My mother and my sister have not seen Jim since that long-ago evening. I doubt that they will ever see him again.

Practically every night, Suzanne and Richard would talk on the phone. She would huddle under the puffy duvet that covered the foldout bed and speak quietly into a cordless phone. Richard came all the way from California to visit her two or three times that winter. Tan never did. At that time, Suzanne had still not made up her mind what to do—find an apartment and stay in New York, go to Richard, or return to Reading. She waited for her husband to give her some sort of sign.

"I was hoping he would come and visit me," Suzanne said later of Tan. "Just be friends. But he never did."

For the first time in her life, Suzanne had absolute control of her own decisions. No one else could make them for her. She would not rush into anything. Instead, on the weekends, she would go dutifully home to Reading. She would travel down to Chinatown early Saturday morning and stock up on groceries— cans of bamboo shoots and lotus leaves, packages of dumplings and steamed buns, dried plums, green vegetables, and other delicacies that were difficult or impossible to find in Reading. Then she would go to Penn Station and board a bus, which spent three hours lumbering past the smoke stacks on the other side of the Hudson, into the green heart of New Jersey, and through the tired coal and iron towns of Pennsylvania. Tan always met her at the bus depot. They would drive home, practically in silence, to the modest white-brick split-level they had lived in since the early 1970s. There, Tan would return to his newspaper or his computer while Suzanne began to clean the house. She would throw open the drapes that Tan always kept closed. She would wash the dishes piling up in the sink and tidy the clutter that had accumulated. She would cook him meals—pots of chicken in soy sauce, fried rice, oxtail soup, simple dishes that he could reheat throughout the week. On Sunday, he would drive her silently back to the depot, and she would board the bus to New York. As the months passed, each trip home helped cement the decision that was slowly forming in her mind. Each time she went back to New York, she carried a little more luggage with her.

"At first," a friend of hers told me, "she came home every weekend. Then every other weekend. Then she stopped coming at all."

One of those weekends, she came with my mother. They drove out in my family's yellow Volvo, following the same route that Suzanne had taken by bus so many times before. They stayed for one night. Suzanne slept in the master bedroom. My mother slept in the guest bedroom. And Tan, as he had for the last seventeen years, slept in yet a third bedroom. In the morning, Suzanne began to pack. The two women loaded the back of the station wagon with suitcases. It was February, and their warm breath steamed in the freezing winter air. It was time to go. Tan came out of the house without a coat on. He stood silently, looking at the jumble of luggage crammed into the back of the car.

"He knows," my mother told me, remembering that afternoon, "something's going on. He knows, but he doesn't say anything."

Instead, he gave his wife a baleful stare, turned, and slowly shuffled back into the house.

A few weeks later, my mother and Suzanne flew to Taiwan. Suzanne's father was in the hospital. His family worried that he might die. A car and driver met the women at the airport and drove them directly to the hospital. Suzanne held her father's weak hand gently and uttered not a word about her personal life. Her father recovered. The family held a press conference. Suzanne stood smiling and blinking in a row with her siblings as the flashbulbs popped. A spell that had started on a warm day in 1962 had finally been broken. Back then, a cheerful crowd of well-dressed wedding guests had gossiped among themselves: "Now, three of the country's cabinet members belong to the same family." They had meant Suzanne's father and two of Tan's uncles. It was a modern-day fairy tale, but Suzanne had felt like someone else, not herself, was getting married that day. Later, she would not even be able to describe her wedding dress to me.

"I don't know," she said. "It was white, pretty fancy."

Someone else had picked it out for her, just as, in a way, someone else had picked out her husband, not in so many words but in every lesson she had ever learned as a child: appearance means everything. Now, she was back in Taiwan, watching the most powerful man in her life lie, sick and old, in a hospital bed. He would not die then, but he would die soon.

The two friends flew back to the United States. This time, Suzanne stopped in California to visit Richard.

"We are not young people anymore," Richard told her. "How long do you want to wait?"

Suzanne thought about her dying father and her own stale life.

"I went back to Reading," she later told me. "See all these people like me. The only difference is, they don't have the courage to break it or have the ability to have an independent life. I'm lucky, find someone I love and someone to love me. I just needed some courage."

On that trip back, she gathered the rest of her belongings. She entered the house while her husband was at work and ended a twenty-nine-year marriage by writing him a note. She had new-found courage, but not quite that much.

Suzanne returned to Richard and the apartment they had rented. For a year, she saw practically no one. She read books in the library and walked around, reveling in her freedom to simply be happy. She told no one save my mother where she had gone. For weeks, my mother fended off telephone calls from Tan, from Suzanne's sisters, from Jim, from Jim's girlfriend even. But as difficult as it was for her not to tell Jim, my mother refused to divulge Suzanne's whereabouts. She could not understand that about Suzanne, that she would want to be in hiding from her own child. But she not only humored her friend, she had played a key role in helping her make her escape. She could have done no less. Suzanne had made a daring leap into another life, an adventure my mother had often dreamed of but on which she had never dared embark.

Suzanne's independence came at a cost. Her divorce raged like a wildfire for over three years, destroying everything that had been. By the end, two of Suzanne's sisters refused to see her. She and Jim had stopped talking to each other. Suzanne brought next to nothing from her old life, not even a photo album of her family. Some part of her felt that this was the price she must pay for happiness. In California, she bloomed like the golden poppies that lined the freeway. She no longer hunted through the sales racks at department stores. She did not spend every waking moment trying to leave her home but, instead, passed long hours lovingly tending to the flowers in her garden. Ironically, she who had spent her adult life trying to escape being a housewife now found that she actually enjoyed it. Not all was well, though, and Suzanne made a painful decision. If she could not have a new life and her son both, then she would sacrifice her son.

"I don't want to make him choose," Suzanne told me, explaining her estrangement from her only child. "This way he can be with his father."

As American as her escape to freedom had been, the traditional, guilt-bound ways of China still clung to her. It never occurred to her that Jim might not have had to choose, that he could remain friendly with both of his parents. In China, sides were always sharply drawn, as sharp as the sound of Dolores closing the front door on her father and his sad peace offering of fruit. The only thing, in fact, that Suzanne salvaged from her recent past was her friendship with my mother. At Richard's and Suzanne's long-awaited wedding, my mother was one of the handful of guests.

When I asked Suzanne to define their relationship, she groped for an adequate explanation. "My emotion toward your mother is deeper than to my sisters," she finally said. "My most difficult time in my life, she's there for me. Everybody's walking away from me, and she gave me that support."

All those long years, when they had been apart, their lives had been so similar. Now that they were close again, their lives differed dramatically. Suzanne had done the one thing that my mother did not dare to do—with her sense of loyalty, would never really even think of doing. But in spite of their differences, something—perhaps it is the recognition that their friendship once saved them both—continues to bind them together. It is as if Suzanne, having discarded so much of her old life, was reclaiming an even earlier past. Back in Reading, she had avoided the Beiyinyu reunions and deliberately lost touch with her old classmates. Now she often joins their large number in the Bay Area for dinner and other events, particularly when my mother is in town. Since moving in with Richard, Suzanne has even gone to the past two reunions. I am not sure how much of this participation is voluntary and how much is at my mother's urging. I do know that in the years since Suzanne moved to California, my mother has visited her at least once and sometimes twice or three times a year. She will stop by for a weekend or for two weeks and, very much like a family member, offers little in the way of advance warning before she arrives. The two friends see each other more often now that they live thousands of miles apart than they ever did when they were only a few hours away. When they get together, they gossip and giggle, like the carefree schoolgirls neither of them ever really was.

As for my parents' own relationship, it lapsed over time into a sort of begrudging stalemate that was not without a certain comforting familiarity. It was as if they had both undergone so many radical changes in the past that neither could bear to confront another. Over time, they have mellowed even further, finding a sort of companionship in one another that, if not perfect, at least surpasses being alone.

One weekend summer, after she had been living in California for some time, Suzanne organized a trip to a friend's condominium in Tahoe. My parents, Richard, Suzanne, and I drove up from Richard and Suzanne's home in the Silicon Valley. When we arrived in Tahoe, I complained that the altitude was making me dizzy. Soon, my mother and Suzanne began complaining too. Richard waved off our concerns.

"You'll be fine," he said.

When we arrived at the condo, the smoke alarm had been beeping. It did so again, a sign that the battery was dead. Richard stood on a chair to pull the battery out. Getting down, he stumbled and hit his shin. He was rubbing it when Suzanne playfully poked him.

"Maybe you're dizzy too," she teased him.

He looked up at her from where he was sitting, still rubbing his shin and smiling.

"I get dizzy," he said, "whenever I look at you."

Later, we drove to Nevada to spend the afternoon visiting casinos and old mining towns. In Virginia City, my mother ran excitedly down the wooden sidewalks, looking for a set of swinging saloon doors that she could kick in. "Like John Wayne," she said.

There weren't any. The saloons had all been transformed into tourist traps, guarded by flashing rows of one-armed bandits. The much-vaunted "Suicide Table," the advertisements for which had shown it luridly dripping with blood, turned out to be just an ordinary piece of furniture.

On the ride to Reno, my father gazed out at the dusty mountains, which were covered with wiry scrub and tumbleweed.

"Hmm," he said. "I bet land out here is really cheap."

My mother snorted. "So?"

"So," he said, "we could buy some for an investment."

She laughed and then said, "*Ai-you,* that is so stupid. So typical."

In Reno, we looked in at a casino. Suzanne fingered one of the slot machines.

"The last time," she said, "I just put in a quarter and all this money came out."

She reached into her pocket and pulled out another quarter, which she stuck in the machine. Pieces of fruit flashed by in their little windows and came to a stop as the distinct clatter of coins falling began. The money continued to come crashing down, the sound cleverly amplified by the casino operator to produce as much of a racket as possible.

Catching sight of the gleaming torrent of silver, my mother clapped her hands and turned happily to Suzanne: "It's your lucky day."

Margaret and my mother met again, appropriately enough, at a reunion. They had not seen each other since graduation and had never been more than acquaintances, but when they saw each other again, something clicked. They both had a quality that many of their other classmates lacked, a certain no-nonsense ability to cut through the superfluous debris that makes up most of social life. They viewed other people as they viewed themselves, without ever compromising their opinions. At the same time, people loved them. They shared a sense for the dead-on quip, honest enough to be funny but funny enough to avoid being malicious. Many of their classmates had been raised to shirk from attention. Among them, Margaret and my mother stood out in their own ways. In a good mood, my mother is rumpled and loudly appealing, always willing to try new things and to ask questions.

I remember traveling with her through Nova Scotia and pointing out a beautiful yellow church from the road. "Mmm," she had said, "pretty." But when she noticed the people milling around on the grounds outside, she sat up. The church was holding a fair. "Let's go in," she said.

I pulled the car into the lot, and we walked into the crowded basement, where the area's farming and fishing families had gathered to celebrate the end of summer. It was strictly a local affair. People stopped to stare as we walked past. They were polite but bewildered by our presence. My mother paid them no notice except to smile and point at each new thing that caught her eye.

"Oh," she said, spying a chafing dish that oozed a sticky foodstuff, white and unidentifiable, that was selling for three dollars a plate. "That's different, is it?"

I cringed at her bluntness, but the woman ladling the substance out looked up and grinned broadly.

"This is our food," she said. "Do you want to try some?"

Without even asking what was in it, my mother nodded eagerly. The woman gave us a free plate and watched as we tasted it. I never did learn what it was called, but it had the consistency of paste and tasted of salt and little else. My mother made a face, handed the plate back, and gestured no with her hand. Instead of being offended, the people around us laughed. Her good nature was that infectious.

My mother tried to include everyone in her exuberance. Chinese New Year usually found her surrounded by friends and family, people whom she had sought out. I remember a dinner in Flushing one year that included Wei, her boyfriend, and a couple of other stray children of my mother's friends.

Wei arrived bearing a wooden box of mandarin oranges.

"*Gong xi fa cai,*" she greeted my mother, with the traditional New Year's wish for good fortune.

My mother beamed and took the oranges. Later, she told me, "That's very proper."

Margaret had instilled a strict sense of etiquette and a respect for Chinese tradition in her children. I, on the other hand, was eighteen before I even learned about *hong bao,* the famous red envelopes stuffed with money that Chinese children receive at the New Year.

At the end of the meal, my mother surprised me by pulling out a fistful of *hong bao.* Five seconds before, the waiters had all been yawning with dramatically open mouths as they waited for us to leave so they could begin their own celebrations. Now every single one of them was looking our way. The small, bright red envelopes printed with gold designs served as a beacon to the curious. *Hong bao* has that effect. The waiters, understandably enough, wanted to know how much we were getting.

My mother handed around the envelopes, and we each took one. Wei opened hers first and started to laugh.

"What?" I asked, looking over.

She was holding a small card covered with bold yellow bursts and purple lettering.

"They're scratch-and-win tickets," she said.

The waiters all smirked and looked away. Scratch-and-win tickets held no interest for their jaded eyes.

"I bought them at the store across the street," my mother said proudly. "Do you like them?"

We were all too busy scratching away to answer her. She knew her idea had been a success. My mother has a knack for creating just such moments—different, slightly goofy, always fun. I aspire to do the same, but where I labor long and hard to achieve spontaneity, she gives rise to it simply by doing. And when she does, she is at her finest. She charms without intimidating. She gives pleasure in her complete lack of pretension. In her joy, she creates joy.

Margaret's charm was of a different variety, definitely not the enthusiastic sort that marches into crowded country fairs in rural Canada. Her kind blended a mixture of engaging diffidence and dry wit, the type that is admired at cocktail parties and elegant dinners. Her reserve had a paradoxical effect on people. Instead of being put off by it, they wanted to please her. At the same time, she had an undertone of self-deprecation that made her seem, if not exactly humble, then suitably self-aware. When she was in a good mood, she dispensed droll anecdotes like so many amusing party favors for her audience.

At one dinner, when the conversation turned to the Chinese and their love of food, Margaret told a story about seeing some seals with her uncle.

"The first thing he said," she said, "was 'I wonder what they taste like.' Not 'Oh, how interesting. Where do they live? Where do they come from?' but 'Can you eat them?' That's typical Chinese."

Every typical Chinese at the table had thrown her head back and roared.

As different as Margaret's and my mother's abilities to charm were, they came from the same source, one that would have surprised anyone who knew either of them—a deep-rooted insecurity. My mother approached people eagerly like the orphan that she was, a stray dog at the pound, wagging its tail and licking the fingers that managed to find a way through the wire mesh of its cage. It was almost as if she hoped to protect herself, by accumulating as many friends as possible, from the loneliness and abandonment that she had known as a girl. This is why she plunged into the life of Hartford in spite of the many barriers that came between her and the locals. In her way, she managed to surmount most of them—except, perhaps, the most important one, her own sense of inadequacy.

Margaret, in contrast, preferred to stand back, coolly assessing strange situations before joining in. When she did participate, she never simply plunged in the way that my mother did. Perpetual new girl that she was, she learned all the rules before she set out to play. She needed to make sure she could win before she even tried. If the rules eluded her, then she hung back and pretended that the game was beneath her notice. It happened when her career in science stalled, and it happened with the white people of Palos Verdes. What Margaret and my mother shared was not what they possessed but what they lacked: self-confidence.

When they met again at the reunion, they felt an affinity that might have surprised them. Back in Taiwan, they had headed down very different tracks. Margaret, the good student, was one of the country's great hopes, trained at Tai Da and sent to America to become a scientist. My mother, who had done poorly in school, was given the remains of the country's resources. She gratefully took what was offered to her. What neither of them realized at the time but would come to see in their new country was that their lives had remained the same in one important aspect. To both, rather than by both, their futures had been dictated, not chosen. In America, they became more alike than they might have thought possible.

One time, Margaret recounted a telephone conversation she had recently had with my mother.

"I thought," she told me about a comment my mother had made, " 'Oh, that's exactly what I would say.' "

"What did she say?" I asked.

"I just ask, 'How are you?' " Margaret remembered. "She said something that give me the impression she's not completely satisfied with her life, but she doesn't know what to do. Says that life is passing her by, and she hasn't done anything."

Margaret spent her days thinking the same thing. Aside from work, life for her had turned into a series of pleasant social activities: meeting friends for breakfast, taking aerobics classes, going out to dinner. This way of life satisfied most of her set, the wives of newly rich Taiwanese businessmen, but it left her, the daughter of intellectuals, feeling not just discontented but also embarrassed by the way that she was spending her time. She tried to rectify the situation by taking painting lessons. A landscape that she had painted hung in her cramped office at school. She sat in on lectures on art history and classical music. She read novels by Somerset Maugham and listened to tapes on Buddhism. Ironically, the one thing that truly differentiated her from her more self-indulgent friends was the very job that she loathed. The small sense of self-worth it gave her was perhaps one of the most compelling reasons that she had kept it all these years.

"I guess," she admitted to me, "it makes me feel superior to them."

I remembered a conversation that we had had over dinner one night. Margaret was telling us about the last time that she had gone to a casino. She had won three hundred dollars.

"I was going to buy a Chanel bag," she remembered. "Then I saw how expensive they were. I said, 'Forget it.' "

"Wei could probably get you one cheap," I told her, laughing, "on Canal Street."

"What's that?" Dan asked.

"It's where they sell knockoffs."

Margaret had brushed the idea of an imitation Chanel off with a wave of her hand.

"Oh, these ladies," she had said, referring to her friends in Palos Verdes, "they could tell. Some of them are so mean. They say, 'Hmm! She has a Chanel bag? How could she afford it?' "

She told me about one friend of hers whose son, a student at Berkeley, had hurt his leg playing basketball. The injury was debilitating but not overly serious, yet the woman had immediately flown to San Francisco to nurse the boy back to health. This included hiring a car and driver to shepherd her precious offspring daily across the Bay Bridge to the best specialist in the area, an orthopedic surgeon at UC San Francisco.

"Oh," Margaret said, "you should see this woman. She wears all Armani. Everything is always perfect—jewelry, makeup, everything. The people in Berkeley did not know what to think. After two weeks, she decides she better fit in more. So she stops wearing suits and starts wearing designer T-shirts instead."

She told the story in a playful tone—classic Margaret, meant to amuse rather than ridicule—but I detected an unmistakable note of scorn below the surface. Wei had already briefed me on life in Palos Verdes among her parents' friends, rich businessmen from Hong Kong and Taiwan. While the husbands earned millions, the wives shopped and lunched. They wandered from hair-dressing appointments to dance lessons. They flew to Paris to buy new clothes. It was a world as wholly unfamiliar to me— Connecticut Yankee that I was, in upbringing if not ethnicity—as the squalor of Chinatown. Wei's descriptions had intrigued me, but she spoke from her position as a younger skeptic. I wondered what her parents thought. Her father, I guessed, with his fasci-nation with luxury hotels and penchant for stylish clothes, fit right in. He had grown up in a similar environment. His grand-father had been a laborer who had made a fortune in Borneo. His father's generation had never had to work. They had lived in Hong Kong off the earnings from an empire of rubber planta-tions, timber mills, and railroads. That money had paid for Dan to come to the States and study medicine at a time when his counterparts in Taiwan could only hope to get scholarships.

Margaret came from a very different family. In the Chinese way, which Americans never can understand, her family, al-though poor, came from a higher social class than Dan's. In a sense, they could not even be compared. Dan's family simply made money. Margaret's family formed part of China's political and social elite, many of whose members were also wealthy, but whose money was always a result of their honored status, not a cause. Even though her parents had advised her to do something useful and practical, Margaret's chosen career still lay within the realm of the intellectual rather than the material. Her family cared about art, politics, literature, and social issues. Her father had studied at Oxford and the London School of Economics. That in itself catapulted him above any indolent son of a mer-chant, no matter how prosperous. Ostentation and vulgar dis-plays of wealth were all anathema to a family of education. After Margaret's father made a fortune in real estate, he had chosen to donate most of his property to Berkeley rather than leave it to his daughters. But usually when such people came to the United States, they either withdrew, like Tan, Suzanne's first husband, or they adapted to their new country and its ways. The Chinese who have flooded into California over the last twenty years were not, for the most part, like the people with whom Margaret had grown up. But they were a great deal more fun. Margaret found herself caught between wanting to completely surrender to their playful, thoughtless ways and feeling guilty pangs of conscience, reminders of her more duty-bound upbringing.

In her more reflective moods, she felt some disgust at her mode of life. Margaret had once marched in protest of the verdict in the trial of Vincent Chin's killers and had served as the first female president of a professional organization of Chinese scientists and engineers. She had thought about entering politics or going into social work. Instead, she had stayed at the same unfulfilling job because it was easier than trying something new. She had encouraged her daughter to be a debutante. The history of the professional organization that Margaret had once led paralleled the trajectory, in many ways, of her own life. As the numbers of Chinese had grown in southern California, so too had their sense of self-satisfaction. Prosperity had made them lazy. Activism lost its appeal when compared to the luxury of having one's own swimming pool. Gradually, over the years, the society had simply disbanded, a victim of its own success. Still, a thought continued to nag at the back of Margaret's mind, a lingering sense of self-doubt that did not seem to plague many, if any, of her friends.

My mother's self-doubt had been shaped by the opposite force of the one that had molded Margaret's. It was not her upbringing that made her feel inadequate but her lack of one. She had drifted through adolescence and early adulthood never feeling a sense of accomplishment. No one had ever taken an interest in her or encouraged her to succeed, so she never realized just how magnificently she had. In her insecurity, she and Margaret could have been twins.

I do not know whether or not the two of them recognized this common bond when they met again at the reunion. They did like each other enough to exchange telephone numbers and addresses. When Wei decided to move to New York after graduation, Margaret called my mother. Their daughters, it would transpire, would forge a second link between them.

I first met Wei reluctantly. When she moved to New York, my mother kept asking me to dinner to introduce the two of us.

"She's the daughter of one of Mommy's classmates," my mother told me. "Doesn't know many people here. Come meet her."

Months passed before I finally agreed. I had already written Wei off in my mind as another one of my mother's charity cases. There had been many in the past: random children of random friends entering and leaving my life without making so much as a scratch on the armor of my reserve. When I was little in Hartford, they were always social outcasts, misguided souls who wore their pants two inches too high and were friends only with their own siblings. As I grew older, it was a shock when they began arriving from other cities, more successful and better adjusted than I. Neither variety held much appeal for me. They both proved embarrassing, the ones from my childhood because they branded me, in their own solitude, with the same outsider status; the ones later on because they made me feel inadequate. They inevitably attended better schools and got better grades. Valedictorians, Presidential Scholars, math-competition champions, promising pianists, regionally ranked tennis players from California. They became the usual set of doctors, lawyers, and engineers. One went on to write speeches for President Clinton at the tender age of twenty-three. Another was a catastrophic combination of naked ambition and tiresome pomposity—the sort of person who pronounces the word "France" as the French do. After college, he joined an investment bank where my oldest brother had made a minor splash a few years before. He promptly introduced himself to everyone as our cousin, a fib whose risks far outweighed any possible advantages. But he was the exception. In general, it was not that the children of my mother's classmates were so terrible. It was that they were so good. I knew before I even met them that I would not like them, and so I never did.

The night I was to meet Margaret's daughter, my mother had rounded up a few other stray children of her friends—a banker, an engineer, an accountant. In that company, I did have the sense

to recognize that Wei was different. She had come to New York
to dance. Even publishing, which was where I was working in
those days, lay far outside the realm of my parents' experience.
And Wei was a modern dancer, not a ballerina or a crowd-pleas-
ing hoofer. If she had told some of her parents' friends that she
planned to eat dirt for a living, they could not have regarded her
chosen profession with more suspicion. Whenever one of her
aunts saw her, she always asked if Wei had made it to Broadway
yet. I admired Wei's courage, but I still did not intend to like her.
Then, at the end of the evening, after the rest of the young people had scurried back to the safety of their apartments on the
Upper West Side, my boyfriend, Wei, and I walked downtown,
where our own homes lay.

I was angry at my mother for some small infraction; I can no
longer remember what. "I can't believe her," I complained to my
boyfriend as we walked down the street. "She always does that."

He murmured something soothing but noncommittal. He had
long since learned the danger of airing his opinions in such matters.

"Oh," I continued, "she drives me crazy!"

With that, Wei turned to me.

"Really?" she said pointedly. "Well, I think she's nice."

I resisted the impulse to stare at her. She was unlike any other
of my mother's friends' children I had ever met before. But different did not mean better. Her impudence settled the issue once
and for all. I had had no intention of becoming friends with her
before the dinner, and I certainly was not going to start now. She
could take her pert little attitude and dance right back out of my
life.

Yet the more time I spent with her, the more she began to fas-
cinate me. Talking to her carried the same discordant, eerie feeling of recognition that suddenly catching sight of your own
reflection does. She was so different from me and, at the same
time, so familiar. Her experiences appeared as distorted echoes of
my own: same general outline, different shape. We became
friends after all, and in so doing, I made my first voluntary step
back towards a world that I had, consciously and subcon-
sciously, always been trying to flee.

It was appropriate that Wei be my guide for this journey. In her own way, she had also been trying to escape. We both resented the expectations that others had for us. Hers came more from within her community and mine from the outside world, but that difference did not matter. The end result amounted to nearly the same thing. In Connecticut, people automatically tried to set me up with Asian boys whom they knew for no other reason than that we shared the same race. In California, Margaret's circle gossiped about their children's romances.

"I know," Wei once told me about the complications involved in dating her white boyfriend, "if we got married, all my mother's friends would be whispering, 'Oh, she married a white person.' "

Academically, we were supposed to have the same specific interests. All the other Chinese children I knew excelled in math and science. I felt abnormal because I preferred English and history. Wei's grandfather sternly took her aside her senior year in college to say that since her degree in comparative literature was not going to get her into medical school, then she should, at the very least, go into law. Yet, somehow, in spite of all the pressure to do otherwise, Wei came to New York to become a dancer and I to try to write.

For this, I credit our mothers. My mother because she dared to flout convention: she alone among the Chinese wives who made up our community refused to pigeonhole herself or to be pigeonholed by others. She never shrank back in the face of monolithically white Hartford. My mother declined to cater to anyone else's stereotype, and she taught her children to do the same. Margaret, though not as personally daring, was in her own way no less unconventional. When Wei announced that she wanted to go to New York and dance, Margaret told her that she would give her the money. No one had ever given her the chance to have a dream. She would not let her daughter's die without even a try. Eventually, Wei gave up dancing, but when she did, it was on her own terms. She and no one else had governed her own fate. Margaret, for her part, took a certain pleasure in Wei's individualism. Her friends' children acted like robots, dutifully becoming engineers, bankers, doctors, and lawyers, as unthinking in their own way as she had once been in hers.

I have only seen my mother and Margaret together twice, once at the reunion in Hawaii and once, appropriately enough, in New York. Wei was giving what would turn out to be one of her final dance performances, a matinee, with a company headed by a choreographer from Taiwan. She had complained bitterly in the past about his vision, not least of which was his insistence that she grow her hair long. Still, the performance marked a bittersweet passage in her life. Freedom from the director and his constraints loomed around the corner, but so too did the end of her dancing career. Wei had just received a master's in performance art. She would be going full-time for her Ph.D. in the fall. Everyone would be at this last dance: her parents; her younger brother, Peter; and many of the Beiyinyu alumnae in the area. My mother had called them all up. Afterwards, we would go out to dinner.

We entered the air-conditioned theater and found our seats, which were high and to the right. I leafed through the program, thankful to be in a cool, dark place. By my side, my mother was waving frantically at someone. I looked up. Two women sitting front-row center turned towards us. They smiled and waved back, gesturing to the seat next to them. My mother vigorously shook her head no and pointed at us. She shrugged apologetically.

"It's okay, Mom," I said. "You can sit with your friends."

"I can?" she asked, her eyes round with pleasure. "Are you sure?"

"Yes," I said. I felt like the parent of a teenager who is ashamed to be seen with her elders in public.

She gathered her things without another word and hurried down the steps to her old classmates.

I saw the Lis across the way. They sat quietly in a row, Wei's boyfriend at the end like a tall, blond exclamation point. Margaret, I noticed, had not chosen to join her classmates in the front. She remained firmly in place, intently studying her program.

The theater was two-thirds full. Around us sat clusters of older white people. A balding man in glasses rested his liver-spotted hands on a cane. His wife peered at the program through bifocals. One man in front of me had a yarmulke pinned to his curly hair. To my left were a black couple. He wore a dark suit; she wore a pink jacket and demure gold-knot earrings. I could not even begin to guess what had drawn these different people here. Season tickets, perhaps? Dance enthusiasts? Sinophiles? The only people I could place were the Asians, who arrived in large, noisy groups, like wave after crashing wave on a beach. Friends and relatives who knew nothing about dance. I recognized the type. I was one of them.

The lights went up on a piece called *Double Happiness, One Hundred Sorrows.* Set in 1940s Shanghai, it purported to speak of domestic issues—marriage and its role in Asian culture—but the significance of the setting did not escape me. The dancers were trying to re-create the turbulent China of the classmates' childhood. And in fact, Shanghai was one of the last cities my mother stopped in before fleeing to Taiwan.

A row of curtains appeared on stage. They fluttered and dipped, revealing dancers dressed in long skirts with slits up to the thigh. The dancers flirted with the audience, waving their silk banners like matadors daring us to charge. Then they pulled away. They regrouped and began stepping lightly across the stage in time with the music's plucking notes. They looked like a youth brigade in chic clothing.

Wei darted in and out of these billowing waves of cloth, her two long braids bouncing off her back. She hid behind her fan and pouted prettily. Then the dancers flitted off stage, streamers fluttering behind them, to reappear as soigné denizens of the night. The men swaggered before the audience dressed in white shirts and gray pants. But they served only as a backdrop to the women, who drifted on stage in ones and twos, wearing *qi pao.* Each sheath was a different, beautiful color—scarlet red, pale blue, canary yellow, grass green, pink, lavender—with flowers winding up the sides. I had seen dresses like that before in a trunk that belonged to my mother.

The women began to dance with the men, elegant variations on Western styles—the rumba, the tango, the waltz. The mood was sophisticated but lighthearted. The only tension was sexual. The men flirted with the women. The women flirted with each other. A man stood in the corner, his arms coolly wrapped

around his partner's waist. Two women leaned against one another. A man and a woman wavered on the verge of an embrace.

Then Wei entered wearing a gray *qi pao*. She took center stage
and shimmied with a woman in black. In the background, the
other dancers struck languid poses. A Chinese love song came
lilting over the sound system.

The mood changed again as the dancers shifted position and
took up their streamers. Wei appeared and ran between the
sheets of cloth like a hunted animal. The banners rose up, trap-
ping her in their waves, wrapping themselves around her feet and
hands. The other dancers bore her aloft. They stopped before the
woman in black, who now held a red banner. They lowered Wei
to the stage, and she bowed down before the woman.

Her bindings changed from white to red. She wore a scarlet
flower in her hair. She danced with a man, and they vanished behind a curtain. When they reemerged, they looked broken and
spiritless. The vivid red from the previous scene had disappeared.
In the dark, I put my hand on my boyfriend's arm. He flexed his
muscle, turned, and smiled at me. It was a goofy smile full of
strong teeth, bleached white by years of drinking his native Wisconsin milk. His apple cheeks framed the sides of his mouth. On
stage, Wei came to a halt. She sat straight as a knitting needle on
her partner's bended knee. His dark eyes stared sternly above the
ledge of his high-planed cheekbones. Her body heaved silently up
and down with the effort of what she had just done. They remained there in front of a white curtain until the audience began
to clap.

At intermission, my mother stood up and was immediately
surrounded by people. She led them, Pied Piper–like, over to me.

"Meet Pamela," she said, introducing me to the daughter of
one of her friends. Pamela had recently graduated from the Columbia Business School. She wore a black suit and had long red
fingernails. My mother asked her where she had done her un-
dergraduate work.

"USC," she responded.

I met Pamela's parents, who had homes in Taiwan, China, and
California.

"*Ni hao.*" Her father smiled at me and extended a hand.

"*Ni hao,*" I responded uncertainly. It was the tone of voice I always use when speaking Chinese, no matter how simple the exchange.

Wei's parents wandered over, and I turned in relief to her father. Dan is Cantonese and prefers speaking English to Mandarin. We talked about their trip to New York. The conversation around us rose and fell in the four tones I can still barely distinguish. Sometimes I had no idea. "*Wo gai ta dian hua,*" I overheard someone say. "I called her." Now was that third, second, first, third, fourth? Or third, first, fourth, second, fourth? I had no idea. Most likely, it was not either combination.

Another of my mother's friends, whom I had met before, wandered over. "Oh, Leslie," she said. "Hello." She wore a lurid blue shirt-and-skirt ensemble printed with pink and white flowers. Her hair curled unnaturally. She leaned in. Instinctively, I backed away.

"I can't wait for your wedding," she confided.

I looked at her, thinking I had misunderstood. I had just recently become engaged. I did not know how she could know. My mother must have already spread the news. More importantly, I had no intention of inviting this woman to the wedding. My brain searched frantically for something to say. A hundred replies came to mind, all of them unsuitable.

"So excited," she said.

It was true. She had just invited herself to my wedding. I hesitated. Finally, I managed a weak smile. I seethed with anger, furious at my mother for telling this woman about my engagement. And although no one else blatantly asked for an invitation, they all began to congratulate me. Happy wishes buzzed around me like a horde of gnats. The attention pleased and embarrassed me. I wished my mother had not told anyone, but then I realized I would have been equally bothered if she had not.

After the performance, we drove in a convoy to a restaurant in Flushing. I took the "children" in my parents' car. The older generation still called us that even though the youngest, Peter, was already twenty-one.

I parked the car and walked into the restaurant. Two large tables full of people greeted me. My mother and her friends sat at one. Husbands and children sat at the other. I took a seat next to

Peter. A husband I did not know nodded at me from across the way. Two-liter containers of Pepsi, bottles of Heineken, and wine from a Long Island vineyard revolved on the lazy Susans. I counted seven women at the other table, but there were places set for more. They began to arrive. Two had taken the bus in from the suburbs. Two others had come from other boroughs. Dolores, who lived closest of all of them to the restaurant in this, her home borough of Queens, did not show. I wondered if she had even been invited.

Among the women were two nurses, a midwife, a Barnard professor, three housewives, two research scientists, a pharmacist, and an art teacher. They lived in southern California and Manhattan. Taipei and Long Island. New Jersey, Brooklyn, and Staten Island. They had not all been close in school; and because their class was divided into sections, some had not even met before. But the noise level from that end of the room started out loud and grew even louder as the evening progressed.

My table neatly divided itself in two: husbands on one side, children on the other. With the exception of Wei's boyfriend and the man to his right, the two generations did not mix. We barely even talked amongst ourselves. Instead we watched, stunned, as dish after dish made its appearance. I felt like a goose being primed for its liver. At the other table, the old classmates proceeded to get drunk. Occasionally I would glance over and see a blur of red faces talking and laughing. The women who had entered the room with their different styles and jobs and interests began to meld into one indistinguishable mass. One classmate, bathed in flashy jewels and hairspray, leaned over to a plain-faced one wearing a red turtleneck. Another sporting loud colors and an Airedale's curls talked to a classmate clad in understated tones of beige. I understood next to nothing of their conversation—just occasional snatches of English and the most basic, familiar Chinese—just enough to confuse me. I heard the word "Marxism" followed by a brief spate of indecipherable Mandarin followed by the phrase *"chi dong-xi,"* which means "eat things." I could not even begin to imagine to what they were referring.

From time to time, they threw us scraps of their attention. First they rose to toast Wei on her dance performance. The woman who invited herself to my wedding presented Wei with a lush bouquet of tree peonies from her own garden. They were startling colors—deep, glossy purples and magentas—and they dripped with scent. She placed them in the center of our table, but her husband made a brushing motion with his hand. He was allergic. He was also allergic to cats. The woman owned two. Wei diplomatically took a deep, appreciative whiff of the flowers, admired their beauty aloud, then placed them discreetly on the floor behind her.

Next, the woman toasted my boyfriend and me. "To my favorite couple," she said, raising her glass. She had known my boyfriend for about an hour and a half. But still she swayed before the room, determined to congratulate us. Her bright blue skirt hung limply. Its pink flower pattern fluttered a little with her rocking. She clutched her wineglass and blinked. "You're so . . ." she said, shaking her permed hair, "so . . ." She smiled and sat down.

The owner of the restaurant was a Chinese born in Korea. The meal started with kim-chee. One of the first courses was a noodle dish with slivers of vegetable and meat on the side. The waitress explained to us that Koreans mix the whole thing together along with vinegar and a wasabi-based sauce.

"It's hot," she warned, then looked at us. "Do you want me to mix it?"

Husbands and children looked at each other. We shrugged our assent. "Sure."

"You like that zing," she commented, and poured the sauce on the noodles. Truth was, we just did not care. At the next table, she delivered the same speech with the same warning. There were no indifferent shrugs here. A voluble discussion ensued. My mother pointed to one side of the dish, then the other. She turned an inquisitive face to the waitress. Another woman talked animatedly to her neighbor, making gestures to her mouth. The waitress, who wore a tight skirt and had cascading hair, leaned back on one high heel. She had seen this before.

My boyfriend turned to me and pretended to be one of the diners at the other table. "Okay, so we'd like this third with vinegar, no wasabi. This third with wasabi, no vinegar. This third with wasabi and vinegar. This third—oh, wait. Okay, scratch that. We want . . ."

It might as well have been the truth. The discussion raged on. The waitress folded her arms and pursed her scarlet lips. Finally, the classmates reached a consensus. No wasabi. No vinegar. No mixing. Everyone beamed happily. I tasted my portion. It had only the faintest tinge of heat, barely approaching that of a medium-hot salsa.

In the end, there were twelve courses, featuring a dizzying array of plant and animal life. Gelatinous sea cucumber and crispy pork. Lobster and chicken. Mushrooms, bok choy, tofu. Whole shrimp—heads, eyes, and shell. Chopped cabbage. Jellyfish. Egg rolls stuffed with peanuts. Soup. A nest of crispy noodles holding an entire sea of food—squid, scallops, more sea cucumber, more shrimp. An entire steamed bass per table.

Wei and I talked around Peter, who spent a great deal of time with his head in his hands. He was dividing his summer between two high-powered internships, one at a world-renowned biology lab on Long Island and another in public policy at Princeton's Woodrow Wilson School of International Affairs. He looked wan and listless, wondering only when he could go back to bed.

The next weekend Wei was going to be a bridesmaid in the wedding of an old friend from junior high school, a friend with whom she shared a long history but not much more in common.

"She's doing everything by the book," Wei's boyfriend commented about the bride.

Wei rolled her eyes, transforming her face for a moment into that of her mother. "Everything."

"She went to Duke," she added, "and her maid of honor was one of her sorority sisters. I mean, I didn't know about any of this stuff, but this woman does. Like you're supposed to save all the ribbons from the shower and make them into a bouquet for the rehearsal. Did you know that? Also, there's that rhyme, 'Something old, something new, something borrowed, something blue.' So my friend was telling me that she had to get a blue garter. And I said, 'What for?' I had no idea. Then it goes, 'And a ha'penny for your shoe.' "

She sighed at the inane prissiness of it all. I commiserated, but in the back of my mind, a little-girl version of me, dressed in pin-curls and petticoats, worriedly wondered, "Where do you get a ha'penny?"

"You're supposed to use a dime," Wei said as if reading my thoughts. "I just don't understand it. I wouldn't do these things at my wedding. It's not like my mom did them at hers. Maybe if it was part of my culture. I guess it is part of theirs."

At this point, Peter roared up, suddenly, surprisingly awake.

"Why," he demanded in exasperation, "does it always have to be about culture with you? Maybe she just likes to do these things. Maybe"—he turned his head from side to side and looked at us—"she thinks it's fun."

He stressed the word "fun" as if we had never heard of the concept.

"Yeah," Wei said. "Maybe you're right. But," she added, "another thing that bothers me—it's going to be all white people. I just won't be that comfortable."

Peter resumed his attack. "God, Wei, white people. It's not a big deal."

The strange thing was that Wei was the one with a white boyfriend and white friends. Peter socialized almost solely with other Asians.

Wei added the clincher. "East Coast white people," she said.

"Oh." Peter nodded. "East Coast white people. That's different. West Coast white people, they don't care."

Again, I felt the by-now-familiar jolt of our differences crashing against our similarities. Don't care about what? I could only wonder. I had grown up among East Coast white people. For all of the parallels in Wei's and my lives, we really had come from two very dissimilar places. It was only recently that the idea of a wedding full of only Asian people had stopped seeming odd to me.

By the end of the meal, I was paralyzed with food. My digestive system worked furiously to keep up, leaving me able only to stare and mumble. The waitress approached. "Now we are going to have dessert," she told us brightly in Chinese, a nursery-school teacher instructing her flock. "*Hao bu hao?*" she asked us. "Okay or not okay?" There was only one answer. "*Hao,*" we intoned dutifully. We had lost all will of our own.

Dessert turned out to be *ba bao fan:* eight-treasure rice. Unbelievably, I found myself clapping my hands with excitement. The other table must have been contagious.

"It's *ba bao fan*," I whispered to my boyfriend.

"Huh?" he said.

"That's not a real dessert," Peter complained.

I looked at him.

"Not a real dessert?" I was incredulous, not so much that he dismissed the dish, but that he and I both still cared enough to discuss it. I must have had something of the Chinese in me after all. At this point, we should have been having our stomachs pumped at the nearest hospital, not arguing over dessert.

My mother called to me from across the room, "It's *ba bao fan.*"

Her voice was a triumphant echo of my own—or perhaps it was the other way around. She waved her spoon. "Do you like it?"

She asked this knowing full well what my answer would be.

"Yes," I said. "You know I do."

"She likes it." She spread the happy verdict to her own table as if they could not hear for themselves.

"Does Wei like it?" she asked.

"We all like it," I told her. "Except Peter. Peter doesn't like it."

She turned to her own table again.

"Peter *bu xi-huan ba bao fan*," she announced. They nodded gravely.

Peter, Wei, and I looked at each other. Peter shook his head, and at the same instant, we all started laughing.

"What?" my boyfriend asked. "I don't get it."

After the *ba bao fan,* a death pall descended on my side of the room. I swirled the tea in my cup and played with crumbs left on the table. From time to time, someone would ask me a question, and I would respond dully. My tailbone hurt from sitting so long. My dining companions felt as weary as I. But at the next table, the women chattered on, oblivious to our discomfort. In that moment, I felt the years rewind. I could have been 10 again and in a Chinese restaurant in West Hartford, segregated by age with the equally sullen and bored offspring of my parents' friends. I felt the familiar annoyance and resentment I always had in the presence of this older generation—annoyance at what I saw as their tediousness; resentment at the feeling of being so relentlessly chained to them. As in the past, I was seized by the urge to flee. Instead, I went to the bathroom. When I returned, Wei's boyfriend leaned over and whispered, "A major development."

"What?" I asked.

"Wei's mother just turned to Wei and pointed at her watch. Then she mouthed the words 'It's time to go.' "

I turned to Wei for confirmation. She nodded. It was true.

"Oh, thank God," I said. "If your mother wants to go, we're going."

At that moment, Margaret stood up. The next minute, everyone else was standing. I glanced at my watch. It was nine-thirty. We had sat down at five o'clock.

But the evening still had not ended. The party gathered in the hallway, an amorphous mass that remained connected even as it moved through the two main dining rooms. Gradually, we oozed out into the street.

Back in the restaurant, the husbands had thrown various directions at me about how to get home to Manhattan. I was to drive the "children" in my parents' car. The words "turn left," "turn right," "LIE," "Grand Central Parkway," "BQE," "Main Street," "over the bridge" swirled around in my head, vague abstractions with no connection to the Flushing streets. I had no idea how to get home, but I would rather drive randomly or stop at a gas station than spend one more minute with these people. I turned to walk to the car, and Margaret pulled me aside.

"It's hard to drive in New York," she said. "You're not scared, are you?"

Perhaps Margaret was projecting her own fears on me. Perhaps she had noticed some trait in my personality that marked me irreversibly in her mind as an incompetent driver. It was an unfounded suspicion, since she had never actually seen me drive, but I knew my mother judged on even scantier evidence than this. It was always this way. I shrugged Margaret off.

"I'll be fine," I said a little sharply, wondering why they could not just let us go.

I walked to the car. The rest of the young people followed. Wei's boyfriend, who had torn a ligament playing soccer, limped steadily on his crutches and arranged himself in the back of the station wagon without complaint. Wei and Peter climbed into the backseat. My boyfriend sat beside me in the front. I started the car and made a careful U-turn back toward the restaurant. As my headlights swung around, my eyes made out a cluster of people standing on the street corner.

"Oh my God," I said. "It's them."

Instead of going to their own cars, the classmates had huddled together in a giant knot, waiting to see us off. They stood now waving to us as one.

"Goodbye! Goodbye!" they shouted, bare arms flashing in the night air.

Their smiling faces shone in the glare of the headlights. When they saw us looking, they began to wave even more energetically. They lingered on the street corner as they had done so many times before—watching us leave, looking out for us as long as they possibly could. But it was time for us to go. My mother and Margaret stood next to each other, their features spectral in the light. I realized then that, try as we might, Wei and I could never really escape them. I realized too that I no longer wanted to. The women waved and waved, and then, in the car, we all started laughing and waving back. I turned past them and headed for Manhattan.

※

I had grown up feeling rootless, always donning other people's identities in a search for my own. In researching this book, watching my mother interact with her old friends, I realized that I had been wrong. I did not lack roots. I had shunned them.

"We have a saying," Margaret once told me. "We say we close the door when we're in China; open the door we're in America."

America had given them education, opportunities, and even wealth in some cases. It had indeed opened the door. But China had given them their past. When they were with each other, the classmates were back home. The door they closed shut out bigots who would not sell them houses, children who mimicked their accents, indignant adults who told them to "go back to where you came from," and, less obviously, glass ceilings, oldboy networks, and both the praise and the censure that came with being identified only as "the model minority."

That world behind closed doors, which excluded American friends and colleagues, was intricately and tightly woven. It was so tight that practically any mainlander of a certain age who had fled China after the civil war and ended up in America was connected in some way to every other one. It was so tight that when my parents were a young couple in Hartford, there were four Chinese actuaries in the entire state of Connecticut: one was my father; one was a man whose father had worked with my grandfather in the foreign service; two others were brothers whose sister had gone to Beiyinyu with my mother. It was so small that my parents, who met on a blind date, discovered that his father knew her great-uncle. It was so small that Suzanne's two husbands had gone to high school together in Hong Kong. It was so small that my parents could walk into a random party in Taipei made up of Chinese-American expatriates and discover a connection between them and every other guest. The ties even looped back onto themselves. Not only had my mother and Margaret gone to school together, but also my paternal grandfather had worked for Margaret's father. Everything I thought my family had lacked—close connections, deep roots, a vast network of friends—they actually had in abundance.

At the reunion in Hawaii, I asked a woman for her address. She handed me a business card. On the back was her name in Chinese characters.

"That's the ultimate identification," she said. She flipped the card over and pointed to her American name. "This other has nothing to do with this place."

I wondered if I, who could barely pronounce my Chinese name, also belonged in this place. Only the classmates themselves could tell me. I had already retraced the steps of their lives, the history of their relationships with each other, discovering, in the process, how they had come to be. Now, I wanted to learn how their lives had affected others, how they had shaped the generation to follow, which was so different from their own and yet so absolutely intertwined. I needed to know if when the door that Margaret had spoken of closed, it closed also on me.

THROUGH THE LOOKING GLASS

I never knew what I was going to find when I approached Dolores. She could be welcoming and almost overbearingly friendly or she could try to push me away. I remember one phone call when she sounded particularly flustered.

"Oh, Leslie," she said. "Good to hear from you."

Then she immediately tried to get off the phone.

"I'm talking to my broker on the other line," she said. "I'm watching the market. I'm short the S&P 500."

The month before the index had fallen 6 percent, but the market was enjoying a strong bull run. If the index was dropping, it was time to buy, not sell. Dolores reminded me of Wile E. Coyote: the Acme steamroller flattened her, and she just peeled herself off the pavement and started chasing Road Runner all over again.

"I'd like to come see you," I said to her. "Maybe next week?"

"Mmm, maybe," she responded noncommittally. "I'm going to be very busy. I'm going to be teaching part-time this semester."

We talked for a bit more and then she abruptly cut the conversation short.

"I have to sign off now," she said.

The last time I had talked to her, she had gone for a job interview in an attempt to reclaim her old full-time position. Apparently, the effort had not paid off, and after I hung up the phone,

I realized that she would not be teaching part-time, either. She was not lying to me deliberately. She had convinced even herself that she would teach. She could not see the truth, but I could. I knew she would not end up back at her old school just as I knew I would not be seeing her the next week.

In fact, months would pass before I went out to her house again. I took the R train to its last stop in Forest Hills and walked through the gates that marked the private streets of that affluent section of Queens. It always startled me to find stately houses and real lawns in what was still New York City. Dolores lived west of this section, and as I turned off the main street, I noticed the houses get progressively smaller. Detached dwellings gave way to semidetached homes, which gradually turned into row houses. Dolores lived in a brick one of these in a neighborhood dominated by aluminum siding.

At the door, Dolores and her bevy of cats greeted me. She was smiling as widely as she had been the first time we met. It was as if she had a multiple-personality disorder: one minute, charming hostess; the next, distant misanthrope. Later, I would realize that it was because she was torn. She both wanted and did not want to see me. In the same way, she remained estranged from her past yet could not bear to cut herself off completely. I wondered which side, if either, would win out in the end.

"It's so cold outside," she said, and shivered, her plump frame jiggling a little as she crossed her arms in front of her. "We would have come to the station to pick you up, but our car is in the pawnshop."

We walked into the living room, and I noticed cardboard moving boxes stacked against one wall. She had been living in the house for almost four years and still had not unpacked them. It was as if doing so would be admitting defeat. If she could convince herself that her current circumstances were only temporary, then they would be.

Something, clearly, had gone horribly wrong. Dolores's romantic personality and the excesses of New York had proven to be a fatal combination. Dreamers who succeed in New York do so on a grand scale, incomparable in its magnitude to that of anywhere else in the world. New York is a parade of temptations, a revolving showcase of achievements to which the ambitious could aspire. Dolores's first home was down the street from the brick-walked campus of Columbia, an Ivy League beacon of higher education. At Hunter, she found herself next door to some of the world's most expensive real estate, the magnificent apartment buildings and town houses that line Park and Fifth avenues. Everywhere she turned, the American dream called out to her, and in New York, unlike more hidebound parts of the country, it was available to even the most foreign of immigrants. The rest of Dolores's Beiyinyu classmates had gotten a taste of their limits from the moment that they had stepped, conspicuous strangers, onto their college campuses. In New York City, Dolores had never known those constraints. But the dark side of the city is as all-consuming as the bright. Just as one can succeed in New York like nowhere else, so too can one fail.

Her life read like a catalog of missed opportunities. At one point, she had bought a house on Long Island and then decided that the school system was not good enough for her son, who at the time was enrolled in a private school in Brooklyn. She sold the house and never bought another. Many of her decisions had a similar perverse quality, as though she deliberately tried to make the worst choices possible. Most people research the school system of a town before they buy a house there, not after. Even nearing sixty, Dolores showed no sign of abandoning her rash ways or her unrealistic schemes.

"I know," she kept telling me, "that I can do better. I just need more time."

Listening to her, I began to see the wisdom of the famous conservatism of the Chinese. It was a characteristic that had exasperated me when I was young, but Dolores's romanticism seemed dangerously irresponsible. I wondered what consequences it had held for her son.

That evening at Dolores's house, I found out. The first thing I noticed when Mark walked into the room was how absolutely American he looked. The small living room seemed barely capable of containing his overgrown frame. He stood over six feet and had the fleshy padding of athletic muscle turned slightly to flab. When he sat down, I could see the red-and-white stripes of his boxers peeking out from underneath his gray gym shorts. A purring cat immediately jumped onto his lap, and as we talked, he stroked it absentmindedly.

We talked for hours. He had lived all his life in New York City with the exception of two brief periods on Long Island. I was fascinated by his stories of growing up, an experience far removed from the one I had had in Connecticut. His first neighborhood had been a middle-class one sandwiched between wealthy Brooklyn Heights and a public housing project. Mark politely described the kids from the latter as being "rough around the edges." Later, the family settled in Bensonhurst. Mark had not grown up in suburbia like so many of the classmates' children, but he had grown up equally far—if not physically, then psychologically—from Chinatown.

What fascinated me even more was how strongly the trajectory of Mark's young life bore the imprint of his mother's influence. He had attended a private day school in Brooklyn, which ran from the fourth grade through senior year, and was well on his way to becoming a "seven-year man," what in other schools of a similar type is sometimes known as a "lifer." Junior year, he was expelled, two semesters shy of attaining the coveted title. It reminded me of nothing more than the way Dolores herself always seemed to fall just short. In other matters, her influence was even more direct. Mark had wanted to attend college outside of the city, a place with a campus where he could play lacrosse and golf, but Dolores had insisted that he live at home and go to the university where she taught, a bustling commuter school in the middle of New York City. Once there, Mark optimistically tried to re-create a more collegiate environment for himself by pledging one of the few fraternities. His mother argued that fraternities were dangerous. Just a few days shy of completing the thirteen-week initiation, he came home to find her packing his bags.

"We're going to Las Vegas," she announced brightly.

Mark could have stayed behind, but, at that young age, he had lost the will to argue. If his mother did not want him to join a fraternity, he knew that she would eventually get her way. Dolores protected him as assiduously as she had when he was a child boarding the school bus with the ruffians from the projects. The fact that he was nearing thirty and had never lived away from home did not bother her at all. When the family got enough money for Mark to afford his own place, she knew the perfect apartment. It was located in the basement of the house that they were currently renting.

Even during our conversation, Dolores hovered over us like an intrusive waiter.

"Do you want some chips?" she asked. "How about some orange juice? Or milk?"

Each time she entered the room, Mark, who was otherwise extremely relaxed, would tense and cross his arms in front of his chest. He would shake his head no and shoo her from our presence. She always returned, bearing something to ingest. One time it was a bag of chips, which she proceeded to open and eat noisily while we tried to talk. A second time, it was two glasses and a carton of milk. Without even asking, she started to pour.

"Oh," I interrupted her. "I actually don't drink milk at all."

"You don't drink milk at all?" she echoed, stopping mid-pour. The glass was already half-full.

"Yes," I said.

"All right," she said, and resumed pouring. "Mark, you want some?"

"No," he said curtly.

"You sure?"

"Yeah."

She went to put the milk back in the kitchen and returned.

"Why don't you leave?" Mark asked her. "You can talk later."

"What about right here?" Dolores said, motioning to an easy chair behind one of the couches. "Just watching TV?" She asked with a wheedling tone in her voice, like a young child begging for candy in a checkout line.

"No," Mark said. "You're still here. I know you. You're just going to butt in or something."

"I'm not going to butt in," Dolores protested. "I watch TV."

"I can't do it with you here."

"All right, go ahead," she gave in. "I'll do housework."

She left and returned thirty seconds later.

"I'll just take some potato chips. How about that?"

"Okay," Mark said grudgingly.

Dolores leapt at the opening.

"Would you like some orange juice?" she asked. "What do you drink?"

"I'm fine," I said.

"But don't you drink juice?"

She could have continued in this vein for the rest of the afternoon, milking every opportunity to simply stay in the room with us and talk. It obviously did not matter to her what we discussed as long as she could keep Mark in her sights.

"It's always like this," he said after she had left again. He sighed and shook his head.

The thought briefly crossed my mind that Dolores's misfortunes all formed part of a larger plot to keep Mark in her life. If she continued to need him and the money he contributed to the household expenses, he could never leave her. I rejected the idea as absurd. She would do anything to ensure his happiness, which she equated with success. Still, Mark did appear to provide her with her sole reason to exist. Dolores had lost most of her friends long ago. It had been years since she had gone out to see a movie. Occasionally, she and her husband entertained his business acquaintances, but those outings formed the extent of their social life. The vibrant, charming little sister who had captivated her basketball coach in high school and played to packed houses on stage in college now spent her time alone staring at screens. During the week, it was her computer monitor. On the weekends, it was the television set. The commodities market was her sole interest in life. Mark was her only purpose.

It was a strangely Chinese notion, this fanatical devotion to her son, one that was at odds with Dolores's vibrant American ways. I thought of my own mother, who was always pushing me forward and away. Like a brown-headed cowbird, she seemed willing to absolve herself of maternal duties in order to foster a sense of self-reliance in us. It seemed Western rather than Eastern, a philosophy born of the open prairies and endless wilderness, where a person could only count on herself for survival. Dolores had grown up counting on other people.

She bustled back into the living room, where we were sitting, face wreathed in smiles, and bearing two oranges.

"Now can I come?" she asked.

Mark sent her away again. She returned a few moments later and leaned furtively against the entry to the small dining area as if she were trying to hide. Her son stopped in mid-sentence and glared at her.

"What," he asked rudely, "are you doing?"

"Oh," she wailed anxiously. "When can I come?"

Dolores could not recognize that her behavior was driving Mark away. In college, he had arranged his classes to free up Fridays and Mondays. Every Thursday night, he left town, heading north to SUNY Binghamton to the floor of a friend's room or south to another friend at American University in D.C. During one visit, he stayed at SUNY Binghamton for ten days. He was there so often that other people naturally assumed that he was a student. These days, he had a full-time job selling television advertising space. He stayed at the office as late as possible and often persuaded his colleagues to join him for a round of drinks afterwards. On the weekends, he left the house the moment morning broke to hit the links. To my amazement, he reeled off the name of every golf course in New York City and the relative merits of each. I had not even known any existed.

"Oh, sure," he said. "Manhattan's the only borough that doesn't have one."

After eighteen holes, he ducked briefly back into his house for a quick shower and then went out again with friends. He was doing his best to pretend that he was on his own. When he was home, he spent the time holed up in his room. He even took his meals there. The time he and Dolores spent talking to me in the living room was probably the longest conversation they had had together in years.

Dolores blamed the distance between them on his friends. "He runs around with these kids," she said. "Italians."

It was true I heard the faintest hint of Bay Ridge in his speech. He boasted to me of his pasta sauce. "I make pizza from scratch," he said to me, wistfully adding, "I like to think that I would have been a great chef."

Such words made his mother despair. "Italians . . ." She

groped for an explanation. "They're very big on social . . . They're not so big on intellectual pursuit. Okay?

"Mark has a good heart," she quickly added. "I want everyone to know that, even though he's not a high achiever."

Mark snorted. "Thanks," he said sarcastically.

As Dolores talked, Mark paced in one corner of the room, his head hung down. He looked like a caged grizzly bear. He flipped a Frisbee in the air and caught it again. He twirled it on his finger. Two of the cats purred at his feet. He stroked them both with his two hands.

There remained one aspect of Mark's life that Dolores could not control: his friends. The fact clearly bothered her. She told me mournfully and repeatedly: "I wish he had some Chinese friends." It was an odd comment, given that she had turned her back on all of her own; but in spite of her isolation, Dolores remained connected to the land of her childhood. As surely as Mark had been formed by her, she had been formed by it.

Dusk had already fallen when I rose to leave. Dolores insisted on calling me a cab to the train station. I insisted on walking. When she saw that I would not budge, she told Mark to walk with me. No argument would dissuade her. Finally, we simply gave in to the inevitable. Mark ran upstairs and put some jeans and hiking boots on. To carry the farce that he was actually going to walk with me one step further, he grabbed a jacket. We went down the front walk together.

At the end of the small yard, we stopped.

"Well," I said, "it was great to talk to you."

"Yeah," he answered, smiling, all traces of the sullen adolescent gone again.

I thought about something he had told me back inside. Dolores had just come in to close the shades even though the afternoon light still glimmered palely through the window. After Mark sent her away, he had leaned back against the couch and sighed. "These are the little things," he had said, "that are always getting on my nerves. God forbid I close my door, you know? Can't keep it closed. Close my door at night? Nope. Can't do that."

Anxiety flitted briefly across his face. I remembered the open

door from my last visit and the sound of the football game that
emanated from it.

"One of the problems I have right now," he continued, "is that
I feel I need to move out, but I can't, because, then, what hap-
pens to them? I don't feel comfortable enough yet that I feel I can
leave here and everything will be fine."

"When will you feel that way?" I asked. "What has to happen?"

Over our heads, Dolores stomped loudly to make her presence
known. She was pretending to do housework, but I sensed that
she was eavesdropping.

"I don't know," Mark said, and paused. He hung his head for
a moment. "When . . . when the two of them start actually bringing in a steady paycheck." He paused again and added, "Which
could be never."

Finances and filial piety kept him bound to his parents in spite
of his American ways and his crowd of friends, which had jok-
ingly dubbed itself the United Nations because it included people
of Jewish, Arab, Italian, African, and Greek descent. His parents
had isolated themselves socially at such an early age in his life
that he never grew up going to Chinese gatherings the way I had.
He had never had to suffer through Chinese school. I had never
considered myself particularly Chinese when I was young, but he
seemed to be someone even farther removed from his roots. Yet
here he was, still living at home, an arrangement that would surprise no one in China today.

But Mark was American after all, not Chinese. His easy gait,
hearty build, and lacrosse skills all marked him as such. Standing outside his house, shuffling from foot to foot, he looked like
a draught horse longing to break free from the harness that
bound him to duty. He stuck out his hand, and I shook it. I felt
sure that his mother was watching from the window.

"Good luck," I said, and smiled back. "I hope you get your
own place."

"Oh, I will," he said. "I will."

I wished that I could believe him. I turned to walk back to the
station, and he turned toward the house.

After that visit, a long time passed before I talked to Dolores
again. When she answered the phone, she sounded so weary that

I didn't recognize her voice. I asked to visit her, and, typically, she put me off.

"Let's see," she said, and named a time that was three months away.

Mark still lived at home. A change in their landlord's situation had caused the family to move to another house. The rent was five hundred dollars more. Dolores had taught a class at her old school the previous semester. I sensed a new desperation in her voice. I asked her how things were going.

"All my aspirations are gone," she admitted. "All my life, ever since college, I've worked, worked, worked. I work so hard to lose money, day and night. It really doesn't make sense anymore. Now, I don't even want money anymore. I just want to relax.

"I'm so tired and burned out," she added. "Finally, I come to reality."

The long illusion had finally vanished, leaving her, as illusions do, with nothing. Before it had disappeared, Dolores had forever changed the course not only of her own life but of her son's. She did not know if she was waking up from a dream or a nightmare.

The thing that intrigued me most about Suzanne's story was its outcome. I could understand her incompatibility with Tan, the desire for a new life, even Richard's allure, but not the deep, violent rift that emerged in the wake of her divorce. She had not spoken to her son in nearly six years. He had not invited her to his wedding, and when the invitations were sent out, only Tan's name appeared as Jim's parent, as though Suzanne had already died. Her voice dropped to a whisper when she told me this, embarrassed and hurt by the omission. I wondered how this woman, so sensitive to the standards of social propriety, to the duty and tradition with which she had been raised, could have slapped them all so violently in the face.

"See," she told me, "when you're writing something, sometime you can erase it. Sometime, it's better to tear the whole page off."

Her new home was just that, brand-new, with every modern convenience, from the automatic garage doors outside to the ice maker and trash compactor within. Like Dolores, Suzanne lived in a three-bedroom house, which should be a warning to every potential home buyer about just how little information is conveyed by that description. The two dwellings could not have been more different. Suzanne's house was situated in a new executive development of the type which will all be gated twenty years from now. Though her neighborhood was not, the basic blueprint existed intact: overgrown houses with showy but unlovely architectural details sitting fattened cheek by fleshy jowl on minuscule, manicured lawns.

Inside, the decor indicated a complete absence of children, pets, or spastic adults. The color cream dominated the furniture, walls, and carpets. Any other hues remained muted pastel shades of blue, pink, and green, as if they did not dare assert themselves too vigorously in this sanitariumlike setting. Even the outside of the house was an ivory stucco. Light poured in from the cathedral ceiling in the living room. The kitchen contained pretty maple surfaces crowned by a white-tiled prep island in the middle. The master bedroom was bigger than the entire layout of the first apartment I had lived in after college. A glass-fronted fireplace set into the wall separated that room from a marble bathroom complete with Jacuzzi.

Not a hint of her past remained in this comfortable but anonymous home, not even a photo on the wall. One time, Suzanne gave me a file folder packed with clippings and other memorabilia from before. In it, I found her résumé, a ream of correspondence with one of her old publishing houses, and photos of Jim printed in the local newspapers when he graduated from high school. He had been salutatorian of his class. He had given a speech entitled "Embrace the Future." For all I knew, the faded newspaper shots represented Suzanne's only remaining photographs of her son. When I told her that I wanted to photocopy some of the material, she told me to take the entire file.

"Are you sure?" I hesitated. I knew that she would offer me anything that she thought I wanted, whether or not she wanted the material for herself.

"Yes, yes," she said. "I don't need it anymore."

I do not know when a mother stops needing her son. I thought of Dolores and her almost unbearable attachment to Mark. Whenever I visited Suzanne, she always treated me like a favorite pet. I felt as though I were staying in a hotel. Fresh sheets and towels waited for me in the guest room. To complete the atmosphere, a basket of miniature soaps and elfin bottles of hand lotion and bath gel, culled from the couple's various trips, sat on the counter in the bathroom. And in the morning, I came downstairs to a breakfast already laid out for me on the kitchen table and still steaming, which made me wonder if Suzanne had been listening for my footsteps. It would not have surprised me. Neither did the arrangement on my plate: three bagel halves, thick slices of ham, and carefully cut fruit. The amount probably represented more than Suzanne ate in an entire day.

"Pineapple's not very sweet, I'm afraid," she said as soon as I sat down. "I'm sorry."

She treated other friends' children the same way, inviting recent transplants to the area in for weeks at a time while they hunted for an apartment. Once, when I was staying there, I had had to assure her that I could get my own lunch. She had been insisting on leaving work to make sure that I was being fed. When she learned of my predilection for See's candies, unavailable on the East Coast, she began buying some for me whenever she saw my mother. She had confused the type, though, and, when my mother tried to explain the difference, the confusion only mounted. She thought that I wanted the same candies that she had been sending all along but packed in boxes, but that kind of candy did not come in boxes. The next time she went to See's, she bought the same candy and asked for some empty boxes, meticulously hand-packing them herself when she returned home. She seemed born to be a mother. More than any of my mother's other classmates, she still carried the aura of old China about her. Her every action seemed to revolve around pleasing other people in as unobtrusive a way as possible. I could not understand how she had let Jim go.

The answer turned out to be far more complicated than I ever imagined.

Part of the answer lay with Richard, of course. Suzanne regarded their relationship as fated.

"First love and love at first sight," she explained to me. "That's two things combined you really cannot escape."

When he reappeared in her life, after she had tried so hard to forget him, she knew how incredibly kind destiny was being. She would no longer deny herself what she had always wanted.

"I have a sense," she said, years later, "that time is running out. If I don't do it, the first time I already regret. The second time, I have this chance. I don't take it, I don't have the chance anymore."

These days, Richard and Suzanne shared everything. She worked as a secretary in his medical practice. They saw friends together for dinner and on the weekends. Richard played tennis with the fervor of a zealot. When Suzanne had first moved to California, she had never picked up a racquet before. Now she went to lessons twice a week and displayed a far superior game and form than I, who had started tennis lessons at the age of six, ever did or will. But even more than their other activities, their interests meshed when it came to gardening.

In the evenings, Richard would grab his trusty flashlight and stride vigorously out into the night. "Time to kill snails," he would announce.

When he returned, he would give us the casualty report: "Only six tonight."

He could talk about them without pause. His hatred knew no bounds.

"They're all over the place," he told me in a nonstop monologue. "They eat up all the flowers. They love orchids. I search all their favorite hiding places. You think snails are slow? Not slow. Wow, they can move fast. Next minute, you don't know where they go. But," he added ominously, "I can find them."

So greatly did he love his garden that he willingly crushed the snails into his driveway, leaving their crippled remains a permanent blight on the otherwise pristine paving stone. Perhaps they were like scalps to him, guerrilla gardener that he was.

I have never seen my own parents as content in each other's presence as I have seen Suzanne and Richard together in their garden. One morning, I watched them from the kitchen while I ate my breakfast. I felt like Jane Goodall observing chimps, so foreign was their behavior to me. She wore khakis, a cream-colored turtleneck, and a nubbly red sweater with cables. He had on a blue pullover and black pants. Both wore glasses. Their tall, lean frames matched perfectly.

They carried their duties out separately but remained together in spirit. She tied orchid stems to a stick with a bit of green string. He used gardening shears to clip the stems of dead irises. The wind ruffled the leaves. A man had come in to mow the lawn that day, and I heard the sound of the engine rounding the corner from front yard to back. When the man appeared, Suzanne and Richard straightened and moved slightly apart, as if they were still two teenagers caught in some forbidden act. But they had not even been standing that near each other to begin with. Later, when they moved to the front lawn, and I could no longer see them, the phone rang. It was for Suzanne. I went outside to find them holding hands. They startled; their fingers flew apart as if they had been shocked.

As a result of all their attention, the garden looked spectacularly healthy. In a space of not more than six hundred square feet, the couple had created an orderly profusion of blooms. A frivolous but charming azalea tree shook its pink ball of a head in the breeze. A patio shaped like a spiral held glazed pots of bonsai. The oldest was over thirty-five. Accenting them were a red Japanese maple and a wooden plaque Richard had brought from his family's home in Hong Kong that read "Spring comes" in Chinese characters. An Australian willow tree grew against the fence. Its long branches drooped gracefully to the ground. Richard loved this particular type. "Doesn't shed its leaves," he said happily.

But he reserved his greatest enthusiasm for a juniper tree that he had somehow tortured into curving around a pole. He pointed it out to me. It looked like it belonged in a botanical print from eighteenth-century France. Its blue-green bristles spiraled up and up.

"Used to be three and a half turns," Richard boasted. "Now five."

It was an interesting piece of information, but became far less so when repeated many times—more times, in fact, than the tree itself had curves. Still, there was something enchanting about

Richard's enthusiasm. Whatever he did, he did with zest. When Suzanne was with him, a side of her long buried by the years and circumstances of her life emerged: the tomboy who had gone bowling with her grandmother and dribbled a basketball to school. Richard liberated Suzanne from staidness. He was as far from Tan as California was from Pennsylvania. Suzanne had left her old life far behind.

It was not surprising, then, that when I told Suzanne that I intended to visit Tan, she looked pained. What did surprise me was her next reaction.

"He won't hurt you," she said.

Her following statement was odder still, a half-explanation that raised more questions than it answered.

"He's a strange man," she said. "When I went back to Reading for the divorce trial, my lawyer was so worried. He had them search Tan every time I meet with him."

The divorce had brought all the unpleasantness of their marriage to light.

"In court," she told me, "he accused me that I had spent so much money, so whatever money left is his. Every weekend, I go home, I have to give him money. It's getting pretty ridiculous. I just want to pacify him. He asked for half of my paycheck at least. This has been going on for many years. He would nag, nag, nag. That's the one thing I can't stand."

She told me also that two of her own sisters had testified against her. She no longer spoke to them. For a long time after she left Tan, she severed all contact with her family except for one sister.

"I'm really afraid," she explained to me, years after the fact, "my father get somebody to kidnap me or do something drastic. Then, through my sister, she say she saw my father cry, thinking of me. My father never want to talk about me, turn his back when people mention me."

Divorce had hit her tradition-bound family so hard that it had ripped them apart—so hard, she hinted, that for my own good I should not visit Tan.

I drove out to Reading anyway, uncertain of what I would find. Just past the exit for Bethlehem, a contraption out of Dickens spewed soot into the air. It was summer and so hazy that the air was practically visible. Big metal boxes of buildings and concrete smokestacks crowded together, all engaged in the task of pumping heavy smoke into my lungs. In the middle of all this industry, a deer-leaping sign flashed by. As I approached Reading, the land and its inhabitants grew more harmoniously together. Cornstalks fluttered green banners in the humid air. Poplars shaded the road beside tidy frame houses and red barns. Then I hit Reading itself. Victorian flights of fancy mixed with stern stone facades. The winding main road even reminded me a little of San Francisco as it twisted its way up and down the hills. It surprised me. I had not expected to find it so charming.

But later, sitting in a small café, watching the rain pelt down on passersby, it became decidedly less so. The women wore denim skirts with fringe. Bad perms came from all directions. White pumps appeared to be the fashion accessory of the moment. I counted four pairs in the short span of time that it took me to eat a bagel and down a cup of coffee. Two men wore ties and short-sleeve shirts. I remembered something my father, who likes to keep track of such things, once said.

"The Midwest," he had proclaimed, "really starts in Pennsylvania."

I now believed him. Suzanne always strove for a certain elegance that seemed woefully out of place in this environment. Although I did not always agree with her sartorial statements, she did not look amiss in New York. Here, the only person who would have blended into a Manhattan cityscape was a seedy-looking black man who was wearing a stained tan jacket and carrying a torn plastic shopping bag. A cigarette dangled from his mouth. His walk clinched it for me. He walked at the speed of the average homeless person in New York, which was to say twice as slow as everyone else in New York and twice as fast as everyone else on the Reading streets.

When Suzanne left Reading in 1990, all of Berks County, where Reading is located, had just 2,334 Asians out of a total population of 336,523 people, or 3.5 percent of the total population. And that number had risen 90.4 percent from the 1980 census. The town's largest industries consisted of mushroom-packing plants and outlet stores. The median value of a home was $81,800. Now Suzanne lived in Cupertino, an average town in Silicon Valley. Even so, only 2.4 percent of its homes were worth less than $100,000, while 80.4 percent cost over $300,000. 22.8 percent of the population was Asian. In fact, there were nearly four times as many Asians in Cupertino alone as in all of Berks County. Emotions and personal circumstances aside, those bare statistics went a long way in justifying Suzanne's decision to leave.

There was no doubt that finances had played a part. In fact, Suzanne had confided to me that money was the reason Jim no longer spoke to her. She said that when she originally asked for a divorce, Tan had replied, "Okay, you can go, but just don't take any money." At first, she agreed to give up everything, but after Richard's divorce settlement had left him with half of his previous worth, Suzanne decided to sue.

I stopped by the Reading courthouse to look up their divorce file. The lobby had marble floors and brass fittings, like practically every other courthouse in the Northeast. The most interesting feature was one that few people bothered to look at—a painted wood ceiling that belonged in a Bavarian country house. Vines and flowers wove around the delicate wood beams that crisscrossed above my head. The panels themselves had geometric shapes in pink, green, and white.

Upstairs, generic reigned again. I asked for the file and sat in an anonymous carrel to look it over. It was as dry as its surroundings. No testimony existed, only documents—Inventory and Assessment of Property, Vital Statistics, Notice of Election to Resume Maiden or Prior Name, Interrogatories and Request for Production of Documents, Answer to Petition for Special Relief, and the divorce settlement itself. Each one seemed unremarkable in itself, but taken together, they told the story of the end of a marriage. In the Answer to Petition for Special Relief, Suzanne claimed that Tan had gotten the date of their wedding wrong. It was not June 6, 1961, but June 16, 1962. The mistake, whomever it belonged to, summed up the enormous chasm that had sprung up between the two parties. They could not even agree when they had married.

The divorce proceedings lasted from the first motion, filed on July 9, 1991, to the final settlement, on October 7, 1994, a span of three and a quarter years. In the end, it looked like a simple fifty-fifty proposition. Suzanne received $165,000, mostly in the form of certificates of deposit. Tan received the property, which just about equaled their savings in value. Three and a quarter years seemed a strangely long time to reach such a basic decision. Everyone told me that the fault lay with Tan. He had contested the divorce until Pennsylvania law required a judgment. I wondered what he had been fighting for.

I went to see Tan the next day. I nervously scanned the block lined with modest Cape Cods, ranch houses, and split-levels. I wanted to find the house but feared doing so as well. Then it stood before me on a corner lot, the door fronting a small dead-end, more of a large driveway than a street. I parked the car—the same car, in fact, that my mother had used to drive Suzanne to Reading that one time. I wondered if Tan would recognize it. I hoped not. On the phone, he had sounded nervous but friendly, but Suzanne's warning echoed in my head as I walked up the path to the front door. No one knows that I'm here, I thought to myself in a momentary flash of panic. I rang the bell.

An old man, the same height as I, opened the door. He wore baggy gray pants and a blue polo shirt. I immediately felt relieved. He reminded me of my father.

"Come in," he said.

I stepped inside the cramped hallway. The shades were drawn, as I knew they would be. We walked into the kitchen, and he poured me a glass of water. Plastic wrap covered the stove. A plastic top protected the dining-room table. I shivered at how narrow his world seemed. A baking sheet leaned against the wall behind the stove. It still bore the greasy imprint of its last victim, a frozen croissant.

I had stayed with one of the Chinese families in the area the night before. The wife had told me about Tan's reaction after Suzanne had left him. "He used to have a belly," she said. "Now, when you see him, he looks so thin. He lost so much weight that his pants is all torn because now the pants is too long for him. He didn't hem it."

We sat down in the kitchen, and his story gradually emerged. He spoke a rich English, more finely nuanced than that of his wife and more fluent. Frequently, he punctuated his speech with short bursts of nervous laughter.

He sketched his childhood out for me briefly. Like all Chinese of his era, he had moved about a great deal when he was young. To my surprise, I discovered that he had spent his earliest years in Hong Kong. He had even attended high school there.

"So," I said, "you must have spoken Cantonese with your wife."

"No," he said emphatically.

"But," I persisted, "she's Cantonese, isn't she?"

"Yes," he agreed. "She's Cantonese. We spoke Mandarin."

Their communication had been faulty from the start. When he remembered the infamous note Suzanne had written when she had packed up her things and vanished, its contents did not surprise me.

" 'I'm divorcing you,' " Tan repeated to me from memory. " 'I'm going on a trip, and I'll have my lawyer talk to you.' I only saw her twice after that, in the courthouse."

"So," I said, "you never talked to her."

"I never talked to her. I said, 'Let's talk it over.' But then she wants everything I had. I worked for thirty years, and she took basically all the money I had. They filed something called no-fault divorce. It's called equity distribution. Her family has plenty of money, and both my parents died. Whatever's left from them is already put in the bank, so she got that too. I thought the decent thing to do is at least talk to me, and she's running around with someone else."

"Why didn't she want to talk to you?" I asked.

"Because," he spat out angrily, "she want money. She want all the money she can get. I find that very distasteful. I came here with nothing. I work my way. I'm not very rich, as you can see. I work thirty years, and she take it all."

I looked around his modest home. It too had three bedrooms, but the whole of it could have fit into Suzanne's downstairs. I knew also that he had been recently laid off. The house pretty much summed up all the money he had.

Then I remembered what Suzanne had told me. "She told me that she gave you all her paychecks."

Tan laughed without mirth. "I never saw a penny from her," he said.

"So," I said, unable to believe what I was hearing. "She's just lying?"

"She's just lying." He nodded his head. "She pay for the groceries. Yes, she pay for it. Everything else I pay for, including Jim's tuition."

In the divorce settlement, I had noticed, Tan had agreed to finish paying off his son's student loans. Now he was telling me that not only did he not deprive Suzanne of her salary, she had not even contributed it to a general pool of family money. Instead, she had kept it to spend on trips and clothes. I remembered what others had told me of shopping sprees at Donecker's, the area's most expensive clothing store. I remembered what Suzanne herself had told me of numerous trips abroad to Asia and Europe. I no longer knew whom to believe.

Afterwards, we wandered outside. Tan's mood abruptly changed. He proudly showed me the trees that dotted the landscape—dogwoods, a weeping cherry, a maple, various pines. In a garden plot, he had planted begonias, onions, and tomatoes.

"There was nothing here when we moved in," he said. "I planted all of this when I come."

Back in California, when I had remarked on Suzanne's garden, I had asked her if she or Tan had ever done any planting in Reading.

"No," she had said decisively. She had laughed at the thought of Tan doing yard work. "He just sit inside on the computer."

I wondered again who was lying.

As we left the yard, I stopped in front of a tree. Two empty dark-brown husks that had once contained what looked to be ferocious insects clung to the bark. "What are those?" I asked.

"Locusts," Tan said. "They come out every seventeen years."

The husks looked so lifelike poised on the tree, except for the fact that they remained completely still.

"These are dead," Tan said. "Nothing left."

He reached a hand up and brushed one of the husks to the

ground. It disappeared into the summer grass. The other one remained, hollow and dry, against the living tree.

Our conversation surprised me. Where I had once viewed Tan
through Suzanne's eyes, I now viewed him through my own. I
found that I pitied and even liked him. Certainly, I did not fear
him, as Suzanne had seemed to suggest I should. I could not
make sense of the contradictions in their two stories. I decided
that I would have to find Jim.

I asked Tan where his son was.

"Oh," he said. "See, I don't want to tell you that."

I realized that, in his own way, Tan was as melodramatic as
Suzanne. Throughout my visit, he had been waiting for this moment, convinced that my intention all along was to find Jim, to
snatch him away, as though his son were a five-year-old child
and not a full-grown, married adult.

"Maybe later you'll tell me," I said.

"Maybe," he said doubtfully. Then his face brightened. "If you
are ever here again, come see me."

I hounded Tan for months, and he always put me off in his
quiet, well-mannered way. In the end, I found Jim through a
friend of their family. He was toiling away in an electrical engineering lab at Princeton. I thought he would refuse to see me,
but, like his father, he was polite, if puzzled. We arranged to meet
at his office.

When I walked into the building Jim had mysteriously described as E-Quad to me over the phone, a sea of male faces
stared out at me. I mounted the stairs and headed for the wing
that Jim had described as being "perpendicular to the street." At
least I had not had to ask what that meant. The door to his office was closed. When I knocked, an awkward-looking Asian
man with bed head and bad skin greeted me.

"Jim?" I asked, smiling in greeting.

"Uh, no," the awkward man said, becoming, impossibly, even
more awkward. "Over there."

I looked in the direction of where he was pointing. An athletic-
looking man in faded jeans and a green chambray shirt was rising out of his chair.

"Hey," he said. "I'm Jim."

He stuck out his hand.

"You want to get something to eat?"

As he led me down the street to a noisy diner, we talked about his future. He was almost finished with his doctorate and had not yet decided what to do with his life.

"I might stay on the East Coast," he said. "I might move to California."

His indecision baffled me. I knew his wife was doing her residency in San Francisco. I assumed he would be joining her, but I said nothing. We sat at a table against the wall, and I studied him head-on for the first time. He had his father's fleshy nose and thick lips, but they were set into his mother's angular face. His wiry frame had been modeled on his mother's, but the nervous laugh that filled the pause between his sentences came from his father. I remembered that he had played basketball in college, but he was an engineer like his father. He seemed evenly split between his two parents in terms of looks and interests, but there was one important difference. He had not spoken to his mother in almost six years.

He did not circle around the conversation like his father had. He calmly told me that his parents' marriage had been disintegrating for a long time, that fundamentally they were different. Suzanne wanted to leave Reading. She wanted to move to a bigger house, to go on trips, to eat out. Tan wanted to stay put. He hated change in any form. Suzanne's desires threatened his own. To compensate, he began to belittle her in public. He criticized her in front of their friends and made fun of her intelligence. She responded by managing to spend as little time with her husband as possible. Even at a young age, Jim recognized that his parents' relationship was not working. He was thirteen when his father received the phone call from the airlines telling him that his wife's plane to San Francisco had been delayed. He did not begrudge his mother for marrying another man. He begrudged her for not telling him the truth.

"When I see my parents split," Jim told me, "I clearly understand why, and I clearly understand why my mom would leave. But my feeling is, you've got to be honest about it. You can't just pack up and leave and demand whatever settlement. I think she just went about it completely wrong. I mean, if she had just said, 'Look, we're clearly different people now. We've got to move on with our lives. I'm going to leave. We should talk about how we're going to split things up,' I would have been totally cool with that. I would have maintained a relationship with my mom."

"But," I said, "her claim is that she was just so afraid to tell people where she was or say what was going on. She told me she thought her father was going to try and kidnap her."

Jim screwed up his face in disbelief. "Come on," he said, and snickered at the absurdity of the thought.

I then told him what Suzanne had said, that he had broken off their relationship because she had changed her mind about not taking any money from Tan and had decided to sue for a settlement.

"No," Jim said adamantly. "I mean, I don't even remember her telling me that she wasn't going to take any money. I mean, that wasn't the straw that broke the camel's back. I mean, it was the whole thing.

"You see," he continued, "the thing is, the last time I talked to her, I told her to come stay with me. She was saying, 'Who knows? I might become a bag lady.' That's what she said. And I was like, 'Well, you know you can always come here.' But, you see, the thing is, she knew. What bothers me is that she knew exactly what she was going to do. She had it all planned out from a long time ago. She knew she was going to leave. She knew she was going to go to California. This was all part of her scheme.

"You know," Jim added, "I remember the last time I talked to her because what I was trying to do was, I was trying to mediate between the two of them in terms of the financial settlement, and I basically told her, and I got angry, which I shouldn't have, but I was like, 'You know, why are you asking for all this? You should be doing the right thing.' And her answer was, 'Well, that's the law. The law entitles me.' "

"So," I said, trying to puzzle something out in my mind, "she never said anything to you like, 'Well, that's my money because your father took all my paychecks'?"

"No," Jim said. "She never said that to me, and I find that very hard to believe."

"She told me," I said, "part of the reason she felt she ought to get her settlement is that when she was working, she gave all her paychecks to your dad. And your dad says that's not true; she never gave him a single paycheck."

"Well," Jim said. "I don't know. But if I had to believe somebody, I would believe my father. My father can't lie. That's just one thing he can't do. He can't lie. He doesn't have that ability."

He told me a story about his father that happened years ago. One of Tan's best friends was a physicist who was filing for a patent. He asked Tan to come meet him in Boston. There he explained that he needed someone to verify the date that he had come up with the idea. The date was a lie. Tan agreed to sign the form and left. He spent the entire trip back to Reading in a moral quandary. When he arrived, he called his friend.

"I can't do it," he said. "It isn't right."

As a result, the friendship had ended.

"Things are not black-and-white to my mom," Jim said. "They are very black-and-white to my dad."

Jim seemed to have taken his father's side, but he did not speak with his father's bitterness. Even as he recounted his mother's crimes against him, his voice never rose in anger. He sounded disappointed more than anything else. I had assumed that his testimony would be biased, that he would automatically defend his father, but he did not appear to be a man who did anything automatically. He had asked himself a lot of questions. The answers he gave me were ones he had come up with on his own.

"What is your relationship like with your dad?" I asked him.

"We don't really talk," he said, surprising me.

"How often do you see him?"

"Not too often. Probably once every two months."

Princeton was a two-hour drive from Reading.

"Do you spend holidays with him?"

"Uh . . ." Jim hesitated. "Some holidays."

A very different picture was emerging of their relationship than the one I had envisioned. I had imagined them as passengers from a shipwreck, clinging to each other on a life raft for survival. Instead, they sounded almost as estranged from each other as they were from Suzanne.

"One of the things he told me when I went home," Jim said, "was, 'All the happiness I'm going to get is going to be derived from you.'

"You see," he continued, "that's such the wrong way to look at life. You have your own life, you know? You can do things. And my dad's always been like that. He wallows in his own pity. One of the things I can't understand is, I'm not sure he learned anything from this whole experience. You know what I mean? It's almost like he feels like it's always somebody else's fault. Like he was punished. My feeling is, 'Okay, well, you've had a bad experience. But what can you learn from it? Maybe it's something about you that you have to change. Maybe it's something about you that you can learn from or try to grow from anyway.' I don't think he's done that. It's always, 'These are the circumstances, and she did this wrong, she did that wrong.' He won't go beyond that. And I wish he would look at it in terms of our relationship too, as to how our relationship could change, and possibly try to grow."

I understood what he meant. My own father was that way. When my mother confronted him with proof of his affairs, he simply denied it and continued to deny it even in the face of my mother's pain. The situation was slightly different. Tan was the wronged party when it came to affairs. But something in their attitudes struck me as similar. They had both remained children in a way. Tan was obsessed with an unrealistic notion of justice. My father thought that pretending nothing had happened was the same as nothing happening. He did not have to explain his actions or worry about how they affected others. They were not bad men; in most ways, they were very good. But they were out of place. Where they had come from, people rarely married for love, and a man ruled his household absolutely. The idea of cheating on one's spouse did not exist. Women simply did not; and men, whatever they did, were not cheating but merely exercising their rights as men. In America, the situation turned nearly on its head; but, educated and assimilated as they were, on some level Tan and my father refused to accept the change. Confronted with a cheating wife, Tan remained flummoxed, at a loss as to how to preserve his marriage. Rather than trying to figure out why, he had concentrated on how. Caught cheating, my father could accept no blame for his actions, preferring instead to assign it all to my mother's neglect, and if she was to blame, then he was certainly not going to be the one to apologize. They were decent men who might have made wonderful husbands under different circumstances and with different wives, but no one could blame their actual wives for wanting more.

I did not wonder at Suzanne's desire to get a divorce. I wondered at the way in which she chose to do it. It came from some part of her that perhaps I will never understand. She felt that she had lived all her life without options. This time, she would leave nothing to chance.

She constructed a fable, tailor-made for American ears. It featured villains: the narrow-minded father who insisted she marry someone from a good family; the stingy, mean-spirited husband who had taken her money; the unforgiving son who would not let his mother have her own happiness. She was the heroine of the piece, the woman who had come to America and become an American. She had found the strength and independence to throw off the shackles of the old world. And she had been willing to sacrifice the ultimate that a mother could. Her saga inspired admiration, respect, and sympathy in others. It was a touching tale, except for the fact that it wasn't exactly true.

The truth, as always, proved much more complicated. Suzanne and her family had indeed become Americans. Halfway through lunch, Jim revealed that he and his wife of four years were now separated and in the process of getting a divorce. He and his father remained distant. Suzanne now lived in a place where the grocery stores burn incense to the gods for luck and the Chinese restaurants have become so specialized that one can eat the Muslim food of my mother's youth in Xi'an. All her friends were Chinese. But the way she had cut herself off from her only child was not. In many ways, Suzanne had achieved the American dream. She lived in California and drove a BMW. She went on trips to Greece and Hawaii. She married for love, and he was a doctor too. Her life sparkled, as bright and shiny as a stage set. In true American form, she had reinvented herself. But behind the scenes lay the set from the last play, splintered into fragments, the old cast members adrift in their own isolation. This too was American.

At first, Suzanne's lies had angered me. Like Jim, I had wanted her simply to be honest. But Jim and I were products of a different time and place. I came to see that Suzanne needed to lie. She had woven her myth in self-defense, unaware perhaps of what she was even doing. It was not enough that she was unhappy with Tan and in love with Richard. Divorce ran against everything that she had ever been taught. She needed to justify her decision to herself and others, and she did so by shading the story in a more dramatic light, one in which she emerged as the only victim. In a way, she was right to embroider. Her own son, who admitted to me that he had gotten along better with her than with his father, had stopped talking to her, simply because, Suzanne believed, she had dared to be greedy. She remembered her grandmother, the one who had found her husband another wife when she could not bear him a son. No one had ever let Suzanne be selfish. She did not even know how to be. But running away would make her happy, and so it naturally seemed selfish to her, an act justifiable only in the most extreme cases. In order to free herself, she had invented just such a case, capping it off with the ultimate penance. She needed to make an enemy of her husband. She needed Jim to pick sides. Losing her son was a form of reparation for what she and many of her relatives still viewed as a betrayal to her family and her upbringing. I had been terribly wrong. Suzanne had not slapped tradition in the face after all. She had chained it to her heart.

Of the three women, only Margaret treated me as I expected to be treated—like the daughter of a friend. By this, I mean that she acted like a mother, or, rather, like my mother. She treated me casually—I remember one dinner she concocted almost entirely from canned food products, while Suzanne once brought home an entire live fish to cook just for me—but with a fond affection. Of the three families I had met in the course of researching the book, Margaret's was the one with which I felt most at home. In some ways, I even began to wish it were my own. They lived life on a more even keel. Confrontations did not escalate into the conflagrations that threatened to consume my own family almost constantly. Wei and Peter did not appear to suffer from the same insecurities that plagued me. From where I stood, at least, growing up Chinese in California was far preferable to doing so in Connecticut. I would soon discover, though, that the grass is seldom, if ever, greener on the other side, particularly when the other side is a desert.

It is an understatement when people say that Los Angeles is unlike any other city. Even the ride from the airport filled me with wonder. We passed an oil refinery. It looked like a magical forest in the dark. The distilleries stood like spindly trees. The lights shining on them were glowing leaves. Clouds of smoke poured from stacks that dotted the sky. The sight was both mystical and ugly. As we drove farther out on the Palos Verdes peninsula, where Margaret lived, the landscape began to change. The terrain became hilly, almost mountainous. The ocean swept along one side of the road while cliffs rose up on the other. Million-dollar houses stuck grimly to the sheer drops, like foolhardy sightseers at the Grand Canyon, risking any danger to get the best view. The streetlights disappeared. The car hummed quietly along. Palms loomed in the distance.

At length, Margaret broke the silence.

"A friend of mine picked up a mainland Chinese at the airport," she said. "They're driving to her house, and the Chinese says, 'Americans are so orderly! When they drive on that side of the road, they all use white lights. When they drive on this side, they use red.' "

We laughed together. That could not have been the only thing that had fascinated the visitor. I was undergoing culture shock of my own.

Margaret lived on a quiet dead-end street in a white rectangle of a house, set, like most of her neighbors' homes, into the hillside. The garage, through which we entered, housed a white BMW, a white Infiniti, and, waiting for me, my very own Infiniti, the color of ginger ale and shaped like a sleek bullet. Driving a luxury car appeared to be a prerequisite to living in Los Angeles.

Dan, Margaret's husband, went through them too quickly to ever buy them. He preferred to lease.

"I get tempted by the new things," he explained. "Don't want to have the same car five, six years."

I thought of my family's trusty Volvo station wagon, going on its tenth year. Its lemon yellow had faded to butter. The left side bore witness to the inept driving of the person who rented the parking space next to ours.

Peter was home from college that weekend. We sat in the kitchen while he told us his plans.

"I'm going to Universal Studios tomorrow with some friends," he said.

"You're going to be back in time for dinner?" his mother asked. "My old classmate's coming to town."

"I don't know." He shrugged.

"But," his father said, "Sunday, you visiting at home."

It was half question, half command.

"Yes," Peter said good-naturedly.

"That's okay then," Dan said with satisfaction. "Tomorrow I have to take my first Chinese opera lesson."

The Tai Da alumni association was putting on an opera, and they had asked Dan to play a small part.

"They must be very impressed with your voice," I said.

"No," Margaret interrupted. "He's a joke."

"She always say that," Dan said, shaking his head with mock sorrow.

"It's true," Margaret said decisively. "They ask you for a joke."

Instead of getting angry, he simply nodded. "Still," he said, "you need comedians, make people laugh."

My own family would have exploded by now. If Peter were my brother, he would have hissed at his parents to stay out of his life. He would come home when he wanted. If Dan were my father, he would have lashed out at his wife. She would have responded. Raised voices and slammed doors would have inevitably ensued. Instead, the Lis all remained sitting calmly.

Margaret folded the newspaper she had been reading. "Well," she addressed me, "I'm going to bed. Tomorrow I'm going to take an aerobics class, if you want to come."

I could see that I had more than a time change to adjust to. I woke the next morning to a view of the vast Pacific Ocean below and the endless sky above—indigo meeting cornflower. Beneath Wei's window, a high hedge of oleander was blooming with bright red flowers. Everything grew spectacularly in this weather. Tall eucalyptus trees shed papery strips of white bark. Magnolia trees exploded with fat white blossoms. But they belied the hard truth of the desert climate. The vast expanse of brush that clung to the cliffs and ran along the hillsides was the color of wheat. It turned green for only three months of the year. Joshua trees brandished bristly cudgels. Wraithlike pines stood in sorrowful clumps lurching, ghostly, towards the road, branches outstretched like so many slender Grim Reapers. Squat palmettos burst from the ground like grenades. Used to the gentle green lawns of Connecticut and the asphalt of New York, I made a mental note to take careful heed of my surroundings. The prevalent attempts to tame nature in the form of in-ground pools, tennis courts, and intricate sprinkler systems did not fool me. This landscape could kill. Even the seductive oleander contained poison in its soul.

I was not just being paranoid. The next day, we drove downtown, taking Palos Verdes Boulevard south to the freeway. The cliffs rose steeply upward from the churning waves. The view inspired silence.

"Yeah," Peter said casually, waving his hand, "this is all falling into the ocean."

Landslides. We crawled agonizingly slowly over the next quarter-mile. The moving earth had twisted and buckled the road so that it resembled hot candy in cold water. I added this new danger to a list that included earthquakes and raging forest fires. The impermanence of things out here no longer surprised me. Everything was disposable, from the Lis' leased cars to the warehouselike malls that lined the main roads. None of Wei's schools existed any longer. From elementary to senior high, they had all been closed over the years. Even if they no longer amazed, the transient ways of California still disturbed me. My high school back east, founded in 1843 and considered fairly young by New England standards, was older than Berkeley itself.

But nature in the Northeast eroded the spirit gradually, a combination of harsh winters and hot summers that wore the life out of a person over the years. In California, nature smiled upon humanity until it frowned. Then fire and brimstone rained calamitously down. It was all beauty or it was all hell. It only made sense to live in the present.

This lack of reflection suited the Chinese in the area perfectly. They lived for pleasure, forgetting, or perhaps remaining unaware of, the past. Margaret and I were driving in northern California once when abandoned railroad tracks met the road we were on and began running alongside it. "So many Chinese died," she said, "building this railroad. Well, Chinese life is cheap."

It was the first and only time I heard any Chinese in California comment on the subject. Instead, they mostly dined and shopped. In Los Angeles, they even had their own suburb, Monterey Park, just for those twin purposes.

The mall in Monterey Park is standard-issue southern California fare. Faux Spanish mission touches decorate the stucco walls. Arches and bright trim speak of hot climates and lazy days. But inside, everyone is Asian. In Monterey Park, according to the 1990 census, a full 56 percent of the population was Asian. The numbers could only be higher now. But the place bore no resemblance to the Chinatowns of my youth. True, everyone was Chinese, and I still could not read the store signs, but instead of rinky-dink plastic toys and tourist T-shirts, the stores sold Versace, Polo, and Moschino, specifically tailored for the more petite Asian frame. The mall even had its own banquet halls. The afternoon that I was there, two weddings were occurring. I had seen the limousines in the parking garage, one decorated in red and white streamers, the other in pink crepe rosettes. Errant guests wandered around the hallways, looking perhaps to pick up a last-minute present for the happy couple. The women, encased in slinky evening gowns that sparkled with beading, teetered on stiletto heels. The men wore dark, double-breasted suits. At a store that sold laser discs for karaoke, the Lis ran into a friend.

"She's going to a wedding," Dan said after she left.

"She's always going to a wedding," Margaret said.

In the Chinatowns of New York and Boston, the two I had spent the most time in as a child, trash littered the streets. Hunched old women walked wearily, flip-flops flapping and heads bowed. On the sidewalks, fish lay on beds of ice, gasping to death in the open air. Ancient, tubercular men coughed and spat noisily without caring whom they hit. Those Chinatowns had reeked of poverty and ignorance. My family only drove in once every few months to stock up on goods that had not yet found their way to the tiny Vietnamese grocery in Hartford. I had hated and feared Chinatown when I was little—the noise, the crowds, the dirt, the grating click-clack of a language that I had never heard anywhere else before. Chinatown was a ghetto, and like most ghettos, it was ugly and depressing.

The Chinese who did not live in Chinatown inhabited tidy suburban homes. Alone in a sea of white faces, they clung tenaciously to whatever minute Chinese community existed near them. I despised them too for their timidity and joyless soberness.

I was in college before I spent much time with Chinese kids from the West Coast. They fascinated me with their exuberance and lack of self-consciousness. They surfed, went to parties, and wore the latest styles. But unlike me, self-hating Asian that I was, they were not slavishly imitating white culture, they were creating their own. I had envied their self-confidence and freedom. Looking around the mall in Monterey Park, I began to understand where it had come from. I remembered a time when I had picked Peter up at his apartment in Berkeley. He was living in a house that had been cut up into several smaller units. Standing on the porch, I noticed the names on the mailboxes lining the entryway: Inouye, Chao, Choy, Cheng, Sui, Li. At the time, I had felt like my brother Derek once had helping me move into my own room at Columbia. At that point, he had been educated entirely in New England. I lived in a perfectly ordinary dorm with the usual assortment of students milling around, but by my brother's second trip down in the elevator, he was shaking his head. "Jesus Christ," he had said, "what is this? Fucking Asia House or something?"

Equally disconcerting was my experience later at a gathering of women that Margaret was hosting at her house. A Chinese artist was giving a lecture on painting. I arrived late to find the women already seated around the dining-room table, talking and laughing as they ate.

Margaret introduced me as her *"xiao ke-ren,"* or little guest. The women greeted me politely but with a distinct lack of interest. In Hartford or Reading, they would have devoured me like a pack of nosy coyotes, desperate for news from the outside world, from the younger generation. Here, they ignored me. *Xiao ke-ren* ran amok in southern California. I represented one of the countless many. They already knew all about me. I drove a sporty little BMW or Acura. I had probably studied marketing at one of the UC schools. If my parents were lucky, I was dating a nice Chinese boy. If not, the boy was white. It did not matter. They had better things to talk about—like their own daughters.

"My daughter just got engaged," a woman in a polka-dot shirt said.

"Who is he?" asked her neighbor.

"Oh," Polka Dot said, shrugging and waving a manicured hand. *"Yang ren."*

I had not heard this term before. I wrinkled my brow, and my neighbor leaned over. She was wearing a silk Escada blouse festooned with pictures of medals hanging from ribbons. They said "glamour" and "love." I remembered what Margaret had said about the woman the night before. Dan had asked if she was coming, and Margaret had shrugged. "I don't know," Margaret had answered. "She says she's interested, but I don't think she really is. She's interested in shopping and going to restaurants."

"Do you understand?" Escada now asked me. On one of her fingers sat a giant ruby ring. The stone was at least five carats, the size of a small dumpling. It glowed softly in the dim lighting.

"No," I admitted.

"Yang ren," she said, "is another word for 'foreigner.'"

Polka Dot clearly had no interest in her newest relation. He was white. That was as specific as she needed to be. But her neighbor did not give up so easily.

"What's his name?" she asked.

It was Polka Dot's turn to wrinkle her brow. Her own future son-in-law's name escaped her. After a long pause, she brightened up and slowly spelled, "K-I-N-S-L-V-E-R," and then hesitantly said, "Kinslver."

The other women looked perplexed. No one appeared to notice that Polka Dot had skipped a vowel.

"Kinslver?" Escada asked, and then slowly said it again, as if it were some strange mantra. "Kinslver."

"Mmm," Polka Dot said uncertainly. She tried again. "K-I-N-S . . ." She faltered. She thought hard. "O!" she said triumphantly. "*Hai you yi ge* O." She recited the rest quickly, afraid she might forget again: "L-V-E-R."

"Kinsolver," the table said in unison, relieved that the ordeal had come to an end. I sat in astonishment. They cared and knew as little about white people as white people have traditionally cared or known about minorities. This revelation pleased me. Margaret and her friends lived complete and satisfied lives, wholly apart from the mainstream that had dominated my own existence. But my pleasure could not last. In spite of all of the Chinese in the area, Margaret still lived in America. Her separateness commanded a price, and she paid it in her relations with white people and, more importantly, in her relations with her own children.

It never failed to surprise me when Margaret, whom I usually thought of as so fearless, quailed in the face of confronting white people. One time, we had just finished a day of skiing when she realized that she had left her sunglasses at the lodge. Dan turned the car around over his wife's many protests. "We can come back tomorrow," Margaret kept saying, which puzzled me. Tomorrow, we planned to ski a different mountain. We should just go back right then, since we had nothing better to do.

Peter echoed my thoughts out loud.

"Maybe," Margaret replied, "they're closed."

"Just call them," he said.

There was no answer at the lodge.

"See," Margaret said, "closed."

"We might as well go," Dan said. "Just take a look."

"Waste of time," Margaret said, but we headed back to the lodge anyway.

I wondered why she was so reluctant. It was six-thirty when we pulled up the drive. A lonely handful of cars sat in the parking lot. Most of the lights had been turned off. In front of the lodge, a solitary workman was brushing snow off his pickup truck with a broom.

"There's someone," Peter said, pointing to the man. "Go ask him."

Margaret hesitated. "Yeah," she said slowly. "But maybe they won't let me in."

"Ask him," Peter said impatiently. "Don't just . . ."

His words trailed off. I realized with sudden recognition that the woman who often intimidated me and others with her imperious irritability was actually afraid or embarrassed or even both to ask a stranger a simple question. She had probably even toyed with the idea of just leaving her glasses behind. Her timidity endeared her to me. For the first time in our relationship, I felt like she was the child and I the adult. A protective instinct made me want to run out of the car and ask the man myself. Instead, I watched solicitously as she slowly got out of the car and disappeared into the lodge with the workman. When she reemerged, holding her glasses aloft, I silently cheered.

Another time, the family took me to see a play, *The Heiress*, at the Ahmanson Theater in the Los Angeles Music Center downtown. When we arrived at the theater, Dan went to the bathroom while the rest of us looked for our seats. I noticed a quartet of white women look up when we entered from a side door.

"Uh-oh," one of them whispered to her friend.

They were sitting in our seats. But Margaret did not notice them, or she pretended not to. She led us all the way around the back of the theater and down another aisle to check the numbers on the other side. They did not match. We trooped back to where we had started. Margaret still ignored the women, who had obviously stolen our places. She pointed to the empty row behind the four.

"Are those our seats?"

I looked. Our row was V. She was pointing to W.

"No," I said, and, exasperated, I turned to the interlopers, who had known from the beginning that they were sitting in seats that did not belong to them.

"Excuse me," I said. "I think you're sitting in our seats."

"Oh," Margaret said, as if noticing them for the first time.

The four women did not even say "Sorry." They rose as one mass of jiggling flesh and pushed rudely past us.

"Jeez," one grumbled to the others so that I could hear. "Now we have to find new seats."

Their gall infuriated me, but it did not intimidate. Margaret was different. If she had been alone, I would not have been surprised if she had simply sat quietly in row W. And if someone had claimed the seats in row W, she would probably have gone to row X. It was not a question of being raised an American. I had learned how not to be pushed around from my mother, who spoke worse English than Margaret but who would have kicked those nervy women out on their fat asses in two seconds. She had quickly discovered how to swim in Hartford. In Los Angeles, one simply floated.

It was this difference, this distance that made the generation gap even greater between Margaret and her children, exacerbated as it was by a cultural one. Nothing illustrated this more clearly than her reaction to the play that followed. *The Heiress* is based on a Henry James novella about a painfully shy New York heiress who falls prey to the first gold digger who woos her. When her father threatens to cut her out of his will if she marries the man, she takes the one defiant stand of her life and plans to elope. The gold digger, not surprisingly, disappears. The heiress is reinstated, and later, when her father dies, she becomes a rich woman. The gold digger, again not surprisingly, returns. The heiress pretends to still love the man, then leaves him in the street to bang helplessly and hopelessly on her door. The development of the weak girl into a strong woman engrossed me. I clapped loudly at the end of the final scene, when the heroine blows out the light and heads upstairs, deaf to the pleas of the man outside.

As we walked to the car, Margaret was the first to speak.

"Hmm," she said. "You'd think most people would just pretend everything's okay. He came back, so okay, why not marry him?"

"What?" Peter and I said simultaneously. "He was a jerk."

"Yeah," Margaret said. "But it's better than nothing."

"But," I said, "in the end she could have anyone she wanted."

"Yeah," Peter said. "That was the whole point, that she became stronger."

Dan had remained silent during the discussion. We looked to him now.

"I was thinking," he said sadly, "maybe he's going to strike it rich and come back for her, that he loved her all along."

At that, Peter and his mother exchanged glances. They rolled their eyes simultaneously and sighed. The incurable romantic, the unsentimental pragmatist, the self-empowerment junkies—together we formed as unlikely a crew as any. We were products all of our own particular circumstances and environments, unable to understand one another's point of view.

Margaret's pragmatism took on a deeper shade when seen in the light of her children's aspirations. She had a particular, cynical philosophy of life, born of her own frustrating experiences and antithetical to those of her young, hopeful offspring. She outlined it during a drive with Peter and me one day.

"You might as well pick the easiest career," she said. "If you are really talented, like Mozart or Picasso, of course you're an artist, but most people are not. In that case, you are better off to be a mediocre doctor than be a very bad artist, because you can make a living."

Peter, who was driving, broke in. "I disagree."

"You'll see my point when you get older," his mother said.

"So what if you're a horrible artist?" Peter demanded. "If you like it, you like it."

"But," Margaret said, "most people don't really especially love this or love that. If you like something, you're good at it. If you're good at it, you like it. If you're no good at it, you're not going to like it."

"That's not true," Peter said.

"There are plenty of people who aren't good at things who love doing them," I said. "So you're saying that someone who isn't a really good musician but really loves it should give it up because they're no good?"

"In a way," Margaret said. "Yeah."

"Because," Peter said, sighing, "it's more practical."

"It's more practical," his mother agreed. "I'm saying most people don't know exactly what they like or what they're good at. Most people can be like this and like that too. Eighty percent of the population. Very few really know that they passionately like painting pictures. They just mediocre in everything."

It was a very different style of parenting from the rah-rah one that American parents favor. I know one white mother who promotes her own children so blatantly that it makes me embarrassed for her. One time, she described her son to me as "highly exceptional." That was one thing all of the classmates shared. They would rather die then let such shamelessness leave their lips. Margaret was her children's worst critic.

One time, Peter casually mentioned that a public-policy journal had published one of his papers.

"Is that a good journal?" his mother asked, voice immediately full of doubt.

"It doesn't matter," Peter said. "It got published."

She muttered something disparaging under her breath but did not say it loud enough to hear. To Peter, she said: "Is that by yourself or with someone?"

He did not answer.

"They only let three undergraduates publish," he said as nonchalantly as possible.

Now it was Margaret's turn not to reply. Perhaps to show that she was a fair mother, she instead began disparaging Wei's work as well. Wei had been selected to present one of her papers at a conference in Las Vegas.

"It's a small society," Margaret said about the organization holding the conference. "They study 'Why is Madonna so popular?' 'What is the significance of Michael Jackson's moonwalk?' "

I stifled the laugh that I knew Margaret wanted to hear. I had too much sympathy for her children to give her the satisfaction.

"I saw Wei's paper," Margaret continued. "It's called 'Pop Singers,' 'Chinese Pop Singers,' or something. What does she know?"

"I don't know," Peter cautiously ventured in defense of his sister. "I think it's cool."

Cool did not carry much weight in Margaret's circle. Her attitude nicely jibed with the stultifying conformity of her set, which liked to produce smiling, professional automatons who would marry each other and live happily ever after. When I asked one mother what her daughter did, the woman rolled her eyes. "She wants to be in film," she said in a tone of utter gloom.

"A lot of my friends, their parents tell them what to do," Peter once explained to me. "They don't have any choice. You've got the Asian parent thing: engineering, business, law, or medicine, you have to pick one." He held up a hand and ticked the careers off on his fingers.

"But," he added hastily, "my parents aren't like that."

I wondered. True, his parents had sent Wei to New York after graduation to become a dancer. Four years later, they were still helping pay her rent, but a difference remained between her and Peter.

"We made it clear," Margaret had told me, "it would be nice if she go to law school straight from college, but we can't force her."

Medicine and science, they knew, were already beyond her grasp. One evening, we watched a Schoolhouse Rock video one of Peter's friends had given him as a joke birthday present. Margaret walked in the room just as Interplanet Janet was visiting Mars. She had clearly never heard of Schoolhouse Rock, because she watched for a few moments and then sniffed with disdain. "This is real kids' stuff," she said. "Grade-school level of science."

"That's Wei's level of science," Dan said.

They all laughed, and I remembered another conversation that had occurred over dinner. Peter had been talking about a scientist with whom he might study. "He does agriculture," he said. "He works on this flower."

And that had been the extent of my ability to follow the conversation. From then on, it became a serpentine creature, the likes of which I had never encountered before. I heard phrases: "G protein," "transmembrane signaling," "cryogenics," and a host of other words whose spelling I could not even begin to reproduce. The discussion lasted throughout dinner. I said barely a word. Science occupied a different realm, one that spoke of years of training designed to isolate its master from the rest of humanity. Anything one of the Lis wanted to share with me, they would have to explain from the beginning. When I later recounted this conversation with Wei, she nodded in recognition.

"Sometimes," she confessed, "I kind of feel like an outsider."

I realized that none of her family had the faintest idea what she did. It satisfied them simply to be able to put a label on it. My parents did the same to me. When I announced I was going to journalism school, my mother looked puzzled and then said happily, "Oh, like Connie Chung." When I got my book contract, her first comment, after "How much did you get?," was "I can't wait for the movie." Wei had gone somewhere her parents could not follow. She would never go to law school, and they knew it.

Peter was different. He was premed. He did well in science. He occupied a world that his parents knew well. All his friends were sweet Asian kids, budding business executives and baby engineers. He would be safe there, if only he would stay. The question was whether or not he would. Recently, Peter had become interested in public policy. Much to his father's dismay, he kept putting off taking his MCATs. It seemed that whenever I was with him and his parents, the conversation inevitably turned toward his future. He might not think that his parents were telling him what to do, but it was obvious that they were trying.

One night, we ate at a restaurant which Dan called "new Hong Kong" and Margaret described as "a Chinese diner." East and West mingled on the menu—BLTs and red bean shakes, coconut rice and spaghetti, Hong Kong borscht, curry fried chicken and bo-bo iced tea. The last was a sweet, chilled Southeast Asian concoction that featured giant globes of tapioca and a wide, thick straw for sucking them up. I was still studying this mystifying menu when Margaret spoke up abruptly.

"Peter's not sure he's going to medical school," she said. "But he doesn't dare tell his father."

She was not actually speaking to me, but to the table in general. Peter looked fatigued, his father resigned.

"I know already," Dan said. "What can I do? I let him do what he wants."

Peter's eyes widened a little at this last remark.

"But—" Dan continued.

"There's always a but," Margaret interrupted dryly.

"Dad," Peter snapped suddenly. "If I enjoy public policy more, shouldn't I do that?"

"I'm just saying," Dan said, "it's only two years of science. You're interested in social welfare? This is social welfare. You interact with patients. You help them. I never go to a lab. Let me tell you, if you're going to be a social worker, who do you think is going to be above you? Doctors. Social workers," the doctor proclaimed grandly, "is second tier."

He changed tack. "Also," he said, "public policy's not going to fit your tastes." He pointed to Peter's shirt. A small polo pony pranced on the upper right side. Dan turned to me. "He has expensive tastes."

"Dad," Peter said, ignoring him, "I don't enjoy biology. I'd rather write a paper than take a test."

"It's only two years of science," Dan said again. He had known he wanted to be a doctor since he was a boy in Hong Kong. His son's attitude baffled him.

"But," Peter protested, "I already know I don't want to do it. I don't like it."

"That's what you say," Dan said. "But what I hear is you want to take the easy way out."

"So?" Peter asked.

It was a child's rejoinder and beneath him, but Dan's remark had stung. Peter was not trying to take the easy way out, and everyone at the table knew it. He had held two demanding internships the summer before. He was applying for a Rhodes scholarship. He played varsity volleyball at Berkeley and, notwithstanding his inclination toward public policy, managed to remain premed.

"So, okay, Peter," Dan said, exasperated, "take the easy way out. You do what you want. But you get what you pay for."

The issue remained unresolved. For the first time since I had met him, Peter acted visibly annoyed. I could not blame him. Later, trying to park the car, he circled the lot, looking in vain for a space. Dan suggested using the underground lot, but Peter ignored him.

"There's one right there," Peter said, pointing to a couple getting into their car.

Two other cars had already lined up.

"Peter," Margaret said impatiently, "why don't you just use the underground?"

"You don't want to listen to experience," Dan said. "Use the underground."

Peter sighed with defeat and pulled into the underground.

Later that same night, I overheard a conversation between Peter and Dan. I could not help it. The two tried to speak softly, but they sat in the television room, a wall away from me. They were still puzzling out their differences.

"Other people say you should hope for the best," Peter said. "But what you and Mom are saying is prepare for the worst. This is the way our family is, but I think it's better, if I have a friend who's trying, it's better to encourage them. It's good to give them self-confidence to think maybe they can get it, and it's bad to think someone doesn't have enough self-confidence to handle defeat."

"The parents are the ones who need to be realistic," Dan said. "If you say you're going to get it and you don't, you'll be very ashamed."

"You're not listening to me," Peter said. "I'm saying that's okay. A lot of things you guys have said over the years—like Mom saying I'd be lucky if I got into a place like Cal State for college—your reason is not to give us false optimism. But I'm saying that encouragement can be positive.

"You know," he continued, "in psychology, you learn if you have a young child, you need to build their self-esteem."

"Psychology is a Western science," Dan said.

"But . . ." Peter said. Frustration charged his voice. "I'm a Western kid."

"But," his father reminded him gently, "I'm not a Western parent."

It was then that I stopped envying Wei and Peter. I saw now that growing up Chinese in California was a mixed blessing. On the one hand, Wei and Peter belonged to a vibrant, successful, and close-knit community. On the other hand, they belonged to a vibrant, successful, and close-knit community. They had never felt shame at being an outsider the way I had, but they had never known the freedom of being one, either. Their community's claustrophobic nature and conventional expectations had caused Wei to flee to the East Coast. Its isolation had made Dan unable to see things from Peter's more Americanized point of view. The Californian Chinese could keep their sunny weather and temperate ocean. I vastly preferred having an East Coast edge and an outsider's heightened awareness. Except for one thing, I would never willingly trade places with them.

I went to visit Margaret while she was on sabbatical at Stanford, and she drove me to her parents' house in Palo Alto. They were just sitting down to dinner when we arrived.

"*Lai le, lai le*," her mother said, ushering me into the kitchen. "Come in, come in."

She reminded me of the Chinese grandmothers of my youth, the elderly women who seemed to live in everyone else's home but my own. Her face looked as soft as a kid glove. She had smoothed her white hair into a neat bun.

"Do you want something to eat?" she asked me, automatically heading for the stove to fix a meal.

"Oh no, no please." I was anxious for her to sit down. I feared she might break, she looked so precious and fragile.

Her husband sat at the table, eating noodles and strips of tofu stir-fried with vegetables. He had two furry white exclamation points for eyebrows, half the length of normal ones. They shot up the sides of his face like stunted cypress trees. He resembled a koala bear.

"Eat, eat," Margaret's parents cried at me in unison.

I demurred. I would eat later. They shook their heads sadly.

"This is the daughter of my classmate," Margaret told them. "You knew her grandfather."

It was true. Years ago, before the war, my paternal grandfather had been on the faculty of the university that Margaret's father had headed in Manchuria. She began to feed her father the details. He shook his head. He sucked his teeth. He did not remember.

"I had three hundred twenty faculty," he apologized. "I can't remember them all."

Her mother pointed to me and said in Chinese as if to compensate for her husband's poor memory, "She's pretty."

"Yes," Margaret replied, also in Chinese. "Cute."

Her mother asked me if I spoke the language.

"No," I said, making my usual pantomime of apology and embarrassment. I shook my head, shrugged my shoulders, and smiled like a dope.

"But," Margaret's mother said with great kindness, "you understand some."

I nodded and, this time, smiled with pleasure. Each word I understood represented another fragile link back to China. I suddenly realized that when my parents die, I will never be able to taste my favorite dishes again. I do not know their names to order them in a restaurant. And here before me sat two representatives of the generation beyond, the one that I had been deprived, by war, cancer, and my own resistance, of knowing. In their day, they had dragged their country into the twentieth century. They had founded modern China. They had created its first republic. They had banned foot binding and sent their best scholars abroad to study. They had fought for democracy, progress, and enlightenment. But to me, they represented tradition, a faint echo of what had come before and existed now only in books and poems.

Margaret's parents stared at me, smiling happily. They looked like apple dolls, small, round, and gentle. I wanted to live with them. Margaret turned to her father.

"Leslie wants to know," she said, "what books to read about China."

Her father thought for a long time. A significant tooth suck later, he pronounced: "Fairbank. Fairbank is good. Very fair."

He lapsed into silence.

"Edgar Snow?" Margaret prompted him.

He turned to her, disdain dripping from his voice.

"Edgar Snow," he said, drawing the syllables out as if he wished to torture each one. "Yes, he wrote a book."

His tone implied that it was not one whose title he cared to remember. Of course, he knew it. Everyone did. It was *Red Star over China,* Snow's manifesto for Mao. Margaret's father furrowed his stubby eyebrows as if trying to drive all thoughts of Edgar Snow out of his mind. He succeeded by replacing Snow with his antithesis.

"Henry Luce!" he declared triumphantly. The way he pronounced it, it sounded like "Hen-ree Loo-seh," as though he had bestowed a Chinese name upon the missionary's son.

Listening to him speak, I felt the weight of history. He was ninety-five years old. He had been alive for an entire decade when the Qing dynasty was overthrown in 1911. The saga of twentieth-century China was the saga of his life.

Slowly, the old man rose from the kitchen table and went into another room. He was carrying a worn address book when he returned. He thought that he could find my grandfather's name inside.

"No," Margaret said. "He won't be there."

But her father persisted, wanting to help me. He paged slowly through the book. And then head shake, tooth suck. I knew the routine.

"No," he said sadly.

I too was disappointed. I stared greedily at him, willing him to remember my grandfather, to establish a link between us. I wanted to memorize the lines of his face. If I could keep him with me always, maybe I could find the past. It was only for this that I envied Wei and Peter. The last of my grandparents had died when I was seven. I realized that I had been searching for them ever since.

Like Alice, I had tumbled through the looking glass and into three alternate sets of reality. There everything turned upon its head, distorted but familiar. Enough of my mother existed in each of her friends and enough of me in their children for me to see how, with just the slightest twist of fate, my own life might have been. As Peter Li said to me, when I was telling him about my research: "Wow, so you get to go around and be like everyone's kid?" The reality was slightly different.

I had a different relationship with each of the women. Suzanne treated me like an honored guest. She always behaved with the utmost generosity and graciousness towards me, but it was with a formality that made me feel slightly awkward. Dolores provoked an entirely different response. With her, I felt like a therapist. Our meetings always seemed to end in tears and sympathy, the former coming from her, the latter from me. Even Margaret, who treated me most like my own mother did, was just a looking-glass substitute.

The differences that existed between us were too vast. Their lives did not offer any of the answers I had been seeking. But even if none of these women held the key to the mystery that was my mother, they had given me new insight into our relationship. Comparing their different worlds had helped shade my perspective on my own. It was with new eyes that I turned my vision back to home.

CHINA AGAIN

The only problem was that I no longer knew where home was. My parents had announced that they were moving to Hong Kong. My father was being transferred. One spring afternoon, a few months before they would leave, my mother and I drove out to my parents' house in Westchester to clear out my things for the new owners. It was the last time she would have to do so. She had spent the day before there with my oldest brother Tim. My other brother Derek wanted his boxes shipped to him in San Francisco.

"No problem," he told me with his typically breezy confidence. "I'll just go through them here."

My sister in London expected my mother to sort through her boxes for her.

"You know," she instructed our mother, "just keep the things that have sentimental value and throw everything else away."

As the oldest child, she should have known better. My mother ran into trouble on the very first try. I caught her holding a piece of gauzy white fabric.

"Do you think," she asked me, genuine uncertainty in her voice, "your sister wants to keep her wedding veil?"

Not a sentimental woman, my mother. Turning her attention to an old trunk that smelled of cedar, she quickly discarded a silky pile of brightly colored *qi pao* that had been made for her right before she came to America. Her ruthlessness did not surprise me. What happened next did.

"There's another trunk," she said suddenly. "Where is it?" She started burrowing under the piles of boxes that still remained. "Where is it?" she asked again.

The inflection in her voice surprised me. It sounded almost like panic. I wondered why she was so upset.

"Here it is," she said. The relief was audible in her voice.

She raised the lid of the wooden trunk. Inside were more layers of silk, but of a finer, heavier grade. I fingered a *qi pao*.

"Whose is this?" I asked.

"Your grandmother's," she said, and pulled it out. Underneath it lay a black silk jacket which had faded to a dark brown. I unfolded it. It was stuffed with cotton batting and had cloth buttons running down one side and little loops along the other. Woven into the fabric was a subtle pattern of flowers and trees.

"Good quality," my mother said.

She pointed to a band of cloth buttoned into the inside collar.

"That's to protect it," she said. She wrinkled her nose at the yellowing fabric. "Dirty."

Instinctively, I reached into the front pocket of the jacket and pulled out another band, which had been folded and fastened to the inside flap with a button. It was identical to the band on the collar except that it was clean and white.

"Oh, good," my mother said. "Replacement."

She said this automatically. She did not marvel at the cunning design or the fact that after fifty years, the replacement band had remained in its proper place for me to find.

I tried the jacket on. It just fit. I ran my fingers down the front and felt the cool silk against my palms. It was soft and smooth like newborn skin.

"How does it look?" I asked my mother.

"Nice," she said. She always said that.

I mounted the stairs to look in a mirror. As I climbed, I envisioned myself in it gliding down the streets of my East Village neighborhood on a misty evening. In my mind, I wore red lipstick, little black pants, and my hair in a sleek chignon. I stepped out of a snapshot from Shanghai, circa 1930. Then I faced the

mirror and shattered the illusion. My hips bulged an unacceptable shade too wide, ruining the jacket's fall. The jacket itself
puffed me into the Michelin man, a look that had been worn
successfully a few seasons earlier by feline Parisian women but
which only seemed hopeless on me.

I stared at myself. I sucked in my stomach and tensed my leg
muscles. I brought my shoulder blades together. That was better.
But the minute I moved, the image vanished. I longed to look like
the lithe Asian beauties who haunted the restaurants and bars
near my apartment. They appeared almost without substance in
their slenderness, but they were not bone-thin the way anorexic
white women were. Rather, they looked as if they possessed no
bones at all. They were held together with some more supple
fiber, which was simultaneously stronger and finer than the un-
gainly compositions of calcium carbonate that made up the rest
of us.

What I saw reflected in the mirror was one of those overblown
Asian-American women who made me shudder whenever I encountered them in classes, at parties, on the street. They were the
kind who wore large silver earrings and denim shorts which
hugged their chunky thighs. They giggled too loudly and tossed
their permed hair to attract attention. They slung dainty pocket-
books diagonally across too-ample chests. In the summer, they
wore huarache sandals. In the winter, they clomped about in
black leather ankle boots with elastic along the sides. In college,
they hung large collages on the wall that consisted of photos of
them and all their friends from high school. Their friends were
always white. The person in the mirror would have done the
same except she had had so few friends in high school that a col-
lage would have been embarrassing. She looked baffled and big
in the black silk jacket. She shook her head no.

"It looks terrible," I said when I returned to the basement. I
handed the garment back to my mother. "I don't want it."

She looked at it. She hesitated.

"Keep it anyway," I said, and she nodded.

No matter how much I had wanted it to fit, the black silk
jacket would never look right on me. Still, I would keep its image
in the back of my head, a point of desire, the way my own seem-

ingly unsentimental mother had kept the jacket itself, safe from harm in a battered wooden trunk, all these long years.

My mother's move to Hong Kong marked the close of a chapter in our relationship. With the exception of a brief period of time at boarding school, I had always lived in the same city as her. Now, the next time I saw her, it would be in Asia.

My parents had been living in Hong Kong for just two months when I went out to visit. My mother had agreed to take me and my boyfriend, Ben, around China for two weeks. After that, my mother and I would continue, by ourselves, to Taiwan.

To prepare, I decided to reacquaint myself with my mother's past. I drove up to Massachusetts to visit her sister, the one who held the family's secrets. I regarded her as a Pandora's box of sorts. I feared what she might unleash if questioned. As I explored my mother's past, each new layer that revealed itself to me made me want to stop searching. Each new revelation tore a hole in the carefully constructed image—fantasy, I now admit—I had held of my mother's family. I joked to friends that researching the Kuomintang was like finding out my grandfather had been an SS officer, but the reality terrified me. My heroic grandfather had died in the service of a corrupt and hated army. I could only infer that, as a leader in that army, he too had been corrupt and hated. My mother's older brother, a person I had barely realized existed, had stuck a gun in his mouth and blown his head off. My modern, college-educated grandmother had, in the end, been too weak to protect her own children from her own greedy sister. Cancer had eaten away at her beauty too, turning her body into a rotten melon. The loyal concubine had fled as soon as she could find a way.

My mother had explained away such events glibly. She had been too young to remember. It did not matter. The past was the past. I could discover her pain only through the pain of my aunt, a woman who whitewashed nothing that had happened to her. Again and again, the stories of the two sisters had diverged, and the discrepancies exhausted me. One glaring contradiction remained, and as much as I dreaded the prospect, I needed to hear my aunt's version. She holds the key to the repository of bad family memories. While my mother glosses over facts and events like a stone skipping on water, my aunt burrows into the ground after them like a terrier chasing a rat. She emerges from the earth snapping and snarling, and shaking some vile reminder of the past in her teeth. The day I saw her in Massachusetts, I asked her about the uncle who had come from the mainland to take care of them after their mother died. My aunt's eyes narrowed, and she spat an answer out at me.

"My uncle?" she said. "He's sick."

I had asked my mother the same question.

"He help us when we have no one else," she had said. "I am grateful for that."

She had revealed nothing more.

My aunt and I sat on the front porch of an old Cambridge Victorian. It was a lazy August day, and bees buzzed among the tall blades of grass and the wildflowers that grew sporadically in the yard. In that peaceful setting, the stories I heard took on an unreal quality. I did not know whether or not to believe them.

In my aunt's version of events, the faithful uncle who had risked his life and gone to jail for wanting to help his nieces had proven to be the worst of all their betrayers. Tales of his abuse pushed their way out of my aunt's mouth as if she were retching them up. Each incident was more evil than the one before. Her uncle, she told me, emerged from prison a mean and bitter man. Verbal abuse came daily. Slaps on the face were common. He stole their mother's money. He locked his youngest niece in an outhouse. He made his nephew, the baby half-brother who was born after my grandfather's death, sleep on the floor like a dog. As for this aunt, the one telling me the stories, she claimed she received the brunt of his abuse. She was too old to lock in a closet, but he beat her often, once for receiving a letter from a secret admirer. She intimated that he did far worse, abuse she cannot bring herself to remember. The kind of abuse that drives her to take three showers a day and wash her hands constantly. My aunt is working towards her doctorate in psychology now, a field she finds fascinating. It has helped her understand many things about her past. But there is one body of case studies she cannot bring herself to read. Every time she tries, she ends up vomiting in the bathroom. The case studies are Freud's.

Something else my aunt told me surprised me almost as much. She believed that her uncle treated my mother better than the other children. He took her to the movies. He gave her spending money. Together, they rode in pedicabs. An image I had of my mother began to vanish too, like a photo fading from improper storage. Perhaps she was not the savior of her sisters and half-brother that I had envisioned. The way my aunt tells it, home life ran like something out of the antebellum South. The uncle presided over the plantation while the younger children slaved away in the fields. My mother worked in the house, a favored pet, who tacitly complied through her silence with all that went on.

"She was only a girl herself," my aunt said as if reading my thoughts. "What could she do? I don't blame her."

"Your mommy and I, we're sick," my aunt continued. "We have scars in ourself. We feel low self-esteem. We feel constantly helpless."

I caught a disturbing glimpse of my mother's world, one that I was not sure I wanted to see. I knew then that, no matter what others might say, she did blame herself. She had failed her siblings and her parents. She would never forgive herself. I was beginning to understand the source of the current of despair that seems always to course within her. It makes her veer erratically from one mood to another, to lash out at others, to be intently focused one day and despondent the next. I had reasons for my interest. As surely as I had inherited my mother's height and wide hips, I had received this same current within myself.

I began to have blank dreams that nevertheless left me feeling disoriented and hopeless when I woke. During my conscious hours, I grew frantic, haunted by the irrational fear that my mother would die before I reached Hong Kong. I had never worried about her before. I did not quite know what to do with this new emotion.

The Hong Kong airport teemed with people. Amazingly, only one exit existed for us all. Ben and I walked out, dazed with jet lag and culture shock. A stern policeman motioned us to walk along the side, a position that would surely obscure us from my mother's view. We found ourselves in the taxi line before we found her. We hastily stepped out.

"I'll watch the bags," I said anxiously to Ben. "You go look for my mother. You stand out more."

He returned less than five minutes later, my mother clutching his arm and trotting to keep up with his long strides. She walked into the taxi line, got into a fight with another traveler, and hustled us all into a cab. I sank back in the seat. My fears of the past few weeks had all vanished. My mother rapped on the plastic divider that separated us from the driver.

"Take the Old Tunnel," she commanded expertly.

"Oh," the driver shook his head mournfully. "Old Tunnel, very much traffic. Much, much traffic."

"Now?" My mother was incredulous.

I broke in hastily. "Why don't we take—" I began to say.

"New Tunnel?" the driver asked hopefully.

"No," my mother firmly insisted. "Old Tunnel." She turned to me and said, "It's faster this way."

And, of course, it was. As we approached the mouth of the Old Tunnel, she whipped out a cellular phone. She had already gone native—or so it seemed. Before, I would have taken her instant adjustment for granted. Now I wondered.

We drove through the tunnel into Hong Kong proper. The road twisted like a narrow canyon bed surrounded on either side by towering skyscrapers. Not a blade of grass appeared to exist. It felt like some stage set for a movie about the soulless future. The feeling persisted when we pulled up to my parents' apartment complex. It looked like a hotel. A security guard presided over the front desk like a concierge. Marble and wood paneling predominated. And, like a hotel, the place had its own restaurant—two, in fact—along with a swimming pool, a video arcade, and a gym.

I stepped out of the elevator on the thirty-second floor and into my parents' apartment. The view left me reeling. Floor-to-ceiling windows made up one entire wall. I felt that if I took one more step, I would fall down into the vast expanse of Hong Kong, the bay, and Kowloon that stretched below me. The city was a giant, intricate web of lights. In the dusk, the Bank of China's giant white X's softly gleamed. Hong Kong and Kowloon practically touched across the narrow bay, which had fallen victim to enthusiastic developers.

It so happened that my brother Tim was celebrating his birthday poolside with a gaggle of friends. A level 8 typhoon warning sent them scurrying back inside. We joined them in one of the complex's function rooms. They were all bankers in their thirties. Most were expatriates, with a few Hong Kong natives sprinkled in. With the exception of two men, all the guests were Asian—Chinese Americans, Korean Americans, and Japanese Americans. They had all come to Hong Kong for one reason: to make money.

"It's too bad you're not staying longer," one sleekly groomed woman said to me. "We could go out on the Morgan Stanley junk."

It was a year before the Asian crisis would hit. Money was the only game in town. I watched people arrive for a party at the Grand Hyatt. Valets in white gloves ran up to park the cars as they pulled up one after the other. A parade of wealth on wheels rolled by: Mercedes, Mercedes, Jaguar, Bentley, Rolls-Royce, Mercedes. This was about as hard as these beauties were ever worked. There's just so far a person can drive on an island.

Another time, my brother and a friend were desultorily hitting golf balls at a video simulation of Pebble Beach. A cellular phone rang. My mother, my brother, and his friend all automatically turned to see if it was theirs.

"There's nothing to do here," my brother complained as time ran out on the video game. "We're always trying to entertain ourselves."

I wondered just how my mother managed to amuse herself in this static, opulent playground. The oppressive weather forced everyone inside to the comforts of air conditioning. My mother had not even walked up Victoria Peak yet, even though its base lay just outside her door. As I suspected, she too was discontent.

The day we left for China, we ate dim sum in a restaurant on the Kowloon side. I asked her if she liked Hong Kong.

"I don't know," she admitted. "It's different."

She bemoaned crooked shopkeepers who refused to take merchandise back. She complained about laws that gave every advantage to landlords.

"If a typhoon blows out our windows," she said in disbelief, "it's our responsibility fix it, not the building."

The Hong Kong matrons who populated the island mystified her.

"They bring their maid everywhere," she said. "Even to lunch so they can take care of the children. Some restaurants, now they have signs: No Maids."

It always annoyed me when people referred to my parents' move to Hong Kong as "going back home." It was like telling an Englishman who had lived in America for forty years, become a U.S. citizen, and was being transferred to Ireland by his company that he was "going back home." In fact, the difference was even greater. At least the English and the Irish speak the same language. My mother had nothing in common with people in Hong Kong. She, who adapted to every new situation with ease, was having a difficult time adjusting to this one. Perhaps she was too old and too American.

Now we were on our way to China, back, for real, to her home. I wondered if she would fit in any better there.

"I'm never going to China again," my mother announced on our third day in the country.

"Why not?" I asked.

"Because you can't go to the bathroom."

It was true. As my mother said, pointing out one particularly gruesome building at a tourist attraction: "That must be the bathroom. It's dirty, and people are coming out of it."

The place turned out to be a gift shop. Not only did the bathrooms reek and look filthy, but the people who ran them had the temerity to charge for their use. After the glamour of Hong Kong, China could not have presented me with more of a culture shock. We landed in Chongqing, the provisional seat of the Kuomintang during World War II. Barely a trace of that old city remained. In its place stood a jumble of gray buildings with concrete facades. In other words, the quality of construction ranked so low, developers did not even use concrete, that lowliest of materials, but only pretended to. In the meantime, they slapped up buildings as fast as they could, all in the name of progress. China, I was coming to discover, could overwhelm with such contradictions—the new juxtaposed with the old, the beautiful with the ugly. In the densest of urban sprawls, we saw the most

archaic of scenes. In Chongqing, population three million people, Ben witnessed a man riding a motorcycle one early morning.
Thrown over the back, like some kind of macabre Hell's Angel,
was a giant dead pig. In Wuhan, population four million people,
I watched a road crew bore through bedrock. Instead of an electric drill, they used old-fashioned pickaxes and manual labor. In
Xi'an, population three million, we saw a goat casually climb
one side of the ancient wall that surrounds the city. As it mean-
dered, it leisurely nibbled on weeds growing between the jutting
stones.

We traveled down the Yangzi River through the Three Gorges
area, the inspiration for many of the country's classical landscape
paintings. As we entered each gorge, the mountains straightened
up and rose above our heads, sheer and vertical. Wispy green
plants and slight trees clung to the rocks, which tumbled elegantly down to the water. The water itself rolled calmly on, the
color of toffee. In some places, a road had been cut into the side
of the mountain, cinching it like a rubber band around a person's
forearm. These roads dated from centuries past and were used,
in the days before engine power, to pull barges up and down the
river. We passed hidden caves where artists and poets had once
dwelt in quiet contemplation of the spot. We saw the famous
Kong Ming tablet, which recounted the deeds of a Chinese leader
from the third century. Stone pagodas nestled in the peaks'
craggy embrace. Where the gorges petered out, the mountains
sloped gently back down into arable land. These plots looked as
if they wore the softest of green chenille sweaters, trimmed with
strips of terra-cotta-colored ribbon. Glossy-leafed orange groves
grew in bumpy rows. It was all so beautiful, and it was all about
to disappear with the building of a giant dam whose hydroelec-
tric production, the Chinese government boasted, would equal
one-fifth of the country's entire current output. The project
would cause the relocation of some two million to three million
people. Entire villages would vanish, as would much of the natural and historic splendor of the gorge area.

The Chinese toed the government line. "We need the power,"
they told me.

Foreigners decried the loss of so much beauty at the hands of governmental bombast. "A shame," they said. "They could build several smaller dams and get the same power. They just want to make a statement."

I began to see the dam merely as inevitable. The flooding of the gorges seemed a pity, but it also seemed so Chinese. I did not know how they could not build the dam. Throughout its long history, the country had built and destroyed, destroyed and built. If it was not in the name of the Cultural Revolution, it was in the name of economic progress. And that was just recent history. The ancient city wall that once surrounded Beijing, the looming fortification that my mother remembered from her own childhood, was torn down by the Communists in 1950. But the walls themselves only dated back to A.D. 986, a full two thousand years after the city's founding. Americans cling to totems of their past—a cracked bell, a piece of parchment—because they have so little heritage to celebrate. The Chinese have no such problem. The loss of one priceless item means little in the face of so many riches. The Cultural Revolution destroyed countless temples, monasteries, and works of art in an attempt to erase the corrupt and feudal past. Even so, treasures still abound.

My mother embodied this indifference. At the Forest of Steles in Xi'an, she walked by a sign that said the tablets had a history of 900 years.

"Only nine hundred years?" she said, as if it were not worth her while to enter. "We've seen things older than this."

How little she knew about China dismayed me. On the journey through the Three Gorges, it had also left me in a state of perpetual ignorance. My mother had booked us on a Cantonese tour, a language that she did not speak, either. It was left to Klaus, a German tourist and one of the four white people on board, to explain things to us in his broken English. One afternoon, the three of us walked back to the ship together after seeing a temple.

"That place is very old," my mother said. "From Ming period. That's two thousand years."

"No," Klaus gently corrected her. "That makes six hundred years."

I remembered something Peter Kwong, the Asian-American

scholar, had said to me about my mother's generation. "These Chinese," he had reflected, "they don't know anything about their culture. They turn to food, to speaking Chinese, to very superficial things as replacements. There's a lack of self-reflection, an immaturity in terms of philosophical development that is very boring.

" 'The old temples,' " he had continued in imitation of what a Chinese might say, " 'the old houses, these are all junk. They're ugly and dirty. We want modern houses. Chinese furniture is stiff. We want wall-to-wall rugs.' "

It was true. In Hawaii, my mother's classmates had been able to talk about the quality of their papaya for half an hour. At Pearl Harbor, the same women had mutely sat through a documentary which featured footage from the Japanese invasion of Nanjing. Of course, there was no self-reflection. Self-reflection was too painful. The women did not want to think. History was tragic. It had ended their childhood, killed their parents, driven them from their homes. Culture was useless. It had not given them rice when they were starving or found them a place to sleep when they were homeless. Better to come to America and forget the past. Success meant washing machines and air conditioning, college education for the children, and well-paying jobs. My mother and her friends had been too busy surviving life to ponder its mysteries.

In Xi'an, where my mother spent her earliest years, two incidents encapsulated the strange and complex relationship she had with the land of her birth. It was not the first time she had returned to China or even to Xi'an. She had first gone back in 1986 and had since traveled in the country several times. My father's business often took them to Beijing and on the occasional boondoggle to other areas. My mother had arranged the current tour for my benefit alone. She had not even wanted to come. She made it plain that she would serve as a translator and little else. Nothing so far had moved her—except to outrage or disgust. Flickers of interest stirred within her only when either Ben or I appeared taken with some new scene or other. It was our interest that delighted her, not the object of our interest.

But there was one thing that seized my mother's attention that had nothing whatsoever to do with us: shoes. As we traveled through China, she hunted every market stall for a particular sort of shoe. They were handmade of layers of cotton. She had worn them as a child, but they appeared to exist no longer. They were the most comfortable shoes she had ever owned. She had a legion of walking shoes in her closet—Reeboks, Nikes, New Balance. None of them measured up. Her one mission in China, besides shepherding us around, consisted of procuring a pair of cotton shoes. Each time she thought she had found them, she would quickly turn them over. A look of disappointment would cross her face.

"Rubber," she would say, pointing to the soles, and toss the substandard pair back into the heap.

She tried in Chongqing and in Zi Gui, near the memorial hall to the poet Qu Yuan. In Wuhan, my mother pulled aside our waiter to ask him if his shoes had cotton soles.

"No," came the inevitable answer. "Rubber."

But in Xi'an, we were walking to the mosque in the old part of town when we stumbled on the largest shoe stall yet. My mother ran over to one of the bins and began sorting through them. She held a pair of shoes triumphantly in the air. Cotton soles! The peddler found her size then retrieved a stool from under a table, set it on the sidewalk, and dusted it off. My mother sat down. She tried a pair on. Too small. The next pair was also too small. Another pair hung oversize from her feet— too big. By this time, a crowd of people had gathered to watch. The woman who ran the stall was amassing a giant heap of shoes by my mother's feet. No luck.

The woman pointed to a pair of corduroy shoes. They also had cotton soles. My mother began trying those on. The bystanders laughed and pointed as the piles of discards grew. They began commenting on each pair.

"Too big," they muttered as one.

"Too small," they grumbled.

"That one fits," one man said.

"No, no," his friend disagreed.

Finally, my mother pulled one more pair on. Miraculously, they fit. She stood up on a worn piece of cardboard the peddler had given her. She wiggled her toes. She looked around. The crowd waited expectantly. She frowned. They groaned.

"They just don't feel the same," she said, and sat down.

She took the shoes off and handed them back to the salesperson. "Sorry."

The bystanders shook their heads and began drifting away. My mother slowly pulled on her black cross-trainers. I knew she would never find those shoes. Even if someone magically produced the same exact pair she had worn as a child, the shoes would never feel as comfortable again. She had outgrown them, both literally and figuratively. The person she was when she once wore those shoes no longer existed.

At our next stop, I saw how that child had disappeared. We were walking through the nearly empty grounds of the mosque. It was late September, and the trees were already starting to lose their leaves. We passed one tourist, a white man whose head was buried deep inside his guidebook. Otherwise there was no one. Then we stepped over a stone threshold, through an archway, and into another courtyard. Off to the side, an old man was sweeping leaves with a large branch. He had tied several smaller twigs to the bottom of the limb to form a sort of broom. He bent over his labor, rhythmically raking leaves that had fallen under a gnarled tree. The twigs scratched against the stone pavement of the courtyard. The air felt cool and fresh. My mother pulled my arm.

"The day my mother died," she said, "I get up in the morning and I don't know what to do, so I start sweep like that man. Then my mother's friend come, tell me I better go to the hospital."

Together, we stared at the old man for a moment. He did not look up.

My own relationship with China was different but equally complex. On the same day that my mother declared that she would never go back to China because of the bathrooms, I announced that the country made me allergic. It did. The food gave me diarrhea. The heavy mix of coal and diesel that hung everywhere made my eyes burn and my lungs wheeze. When I blew my nose, the mucus came out black. On the Yangzi, when we left the ship to go ashore, people followed us about peddling green oranges and grimy bottles of water. A child with white hair and open sores all over his face sold Ben a glass egg for ten cents. In Wuhan, I saw fifteen construction workers living in a room that was little more than a lean-to. It had a sagging tar roof and nominal walls made of tin. They had jury-rigged a shower in the middle of the place. It sprayed water everywhere when it was turned on. Life on board the boat had its own unsavory side. Something about the smell—the mixture of engine fuel, human sweat, and old cooking grease—made my stomach turn. People threw all sorts of trash in the water—beer bottles, Styrofoam containers, a lone plastic flip-flop. One day, a dead man even floated past us, facedown in the muddy water.

Even as China repulsed me, it also thrilled. The stately old monuments and the bustling energy of people trying to make up for lost time created a heady mix. In Xi'an, the solemn rows of terra-cotta soldiers stared blankly into history, while on the street, a man dressed in a suit and bicycling to work reached into the briefcase dangling from his handlebars and pulled out a cellular phone. But when I reached out to embrace the country, I discovered that China did not feel the same about me. At one museum tour, the guide turned to our group and asked, "Who speaks English?"

"These three," my mother said and pointed to Ben, Klaus, and me.

The woman looked at me askance.

"She doesn't understand, either?" she asked my mother in Chinese.

I shook my head no in embarrassment. In a way, it seemed worse that I had understood the question, as though I were affecting not to speak Chinese. The woman wrinkled her brow and turned away. She did not know what to make of me. None of the Chinese did. My mother could pass as one of them and often did, slipping in for the local price to exhibitions and monuments. She would buy my ticket too, and as long as I said nothing, I also passed. But the minute I opened my mouth, they sent me back to buy the full-price fare.

Ben was hopeless, of course. A child sitting on his mother's back in Xi'an had turned to him and screamed with a look of utter delight: *"Mei guo ren!"*

"Yes," his mother had said, "that's an American."

And what benefits Ben received as such! People showered him with presents and special attention wherever we went. Our tour guide on the boat did a brushstroke on a rock and gave it to him. One of the cabin boys held special tai chi lessons just for him. A woman who took us around Xi'an handed him a jar of special hot pepper just before we left for Beijing.

At one hotel, we went for an early-morning run, and Ben returned just ahead of me.

"You have nice exercise?" the clerk asked him with a smile.

"Very nice," he responded.

She tittered, blushed, and waved goodbye when he turned for the elevator. When I walked by, she looked at me disapprovingly and said not a word. When we had trouble with our travel arrangements, the hotel faxed our agent and listed us as "Mr. Ben and party," even though my mother had made all the arrangements and paid all the bills. The hotel had simply assumed we were in Ben's employ. There could be no other explanation. My mother must have been his translator. As for me, it was obvious what I was.

I did not know if I had lost China or China had lost me. It was in Beijing, center of Chinese life, that I felt the distance most deeply. More specifically, it was, I'm embarrassed to say, at that cliché-ridden site, the Temple of Heaven. I fell immediately in love with its perfect gray symmetry, the hushed awe that descended on the tourists as they gazed on its beauty. Circle upon circle upon circle of white marble reached up to the gods. Ceramic roof tiles, glazed a deep blue, shimmered intensely in the sun. The emperor who ordered its construction was so pleased with the result, he promoted every last person who had worked on the project. I could see why. Up until this moment, I had been willing to forgo China. Then I came face to face with this splendor, and I wanted it to belong to me. But I had forsaken my claim a long time ago. Now China turned its proud back to me. Wherever I might belong, it was not here.

Beijing was the city my mother remembered best. It was the

last permanent home she had lived in before the family left for Taiwan. It was here that she had learned of her father's death and here that her brother had killed himself. But so much of the city had changed. The station where they had gone to meet her father's funeral train had been torn down just like the city walls. She tried to show me where she used to go skating but could not locate the pond. We went to her old elementary school, on a busy street right by the Forbidden City. There, she cajoled her way in past a stern guard. Almost all the buildings had been constructed after she had left. It did not matter. Her most vivid memory was of the coal stoves that still heat the classrooms in winter. On the way back to our hotel, we drove past Tiananmen Square. Somewhere under the paving stone lay the foundations of what had once been her house, a piece of property to which she still held the deed. A display outside the museum counted down the seconds until Hong Kong reverted to Chinese territory. My mother had said that she never wanted to go back to China again. Soon, she would be living there.

One Beiyinyu classmate of hers already was. Her husband had been transferred from San Diego to Beijing. We met them for dinner. Together, the two old friends complained about their new lives. My mother's friend had worked for immigration in California. She was now trying to get a job with the U.S. embassy.

"I don't like the system here," she complained. "You have to know someone before they even look at your application. I hate doing that. In San Diego, whenever a congressman writes a letter for someone, I always put it to the very bottom of the pile. Everybody go through the same channels. Why should you get special treatment?

"I don't know," she added hesitantly. "Maybe I'll go back."

My mother nodded sympathetically. They no longer belonged in China. They had become Americans. Or had they? I remembered the phrase "bamboo generation" that a friend of my mother's had used to describe their type of immigrant. "Hollowed," she had called herself, neither Chinese nor American. And then she had added, "Either way, you're not good enough."

On our Yangzi River tour, we had eaten a special fish for dinner one night. One of the waiters had told us that it was called "the king of breams." It came from a tributary that spilled jade green into the Yangzi's milk-coffee waters. "If you take this fish," the waiter had said, "and put it in a different river, it will become a different fish."

We flew back to Hong Kong. I was relieved and heartbroken. My mother was just relieved. Ben left the next day. Alone for the first time the entire trip, my mother and I went to take afternoon tea together at the Mandarin Oriental. We wound up there after stopping at the Peninsula, where a waiter had asked us to queue in a different part of the restaurant.

"Why?" my mother had demanded. "What about all those other people?"

Without waiting for a response, she then turned to me. "Let's go."

Before the trip, I would have argued with her. Now I simply gave in. I just wanted to make her happy.

A woman led us to a round table with two soft armchairs. My mother sank into one.

"This is real nice," she said, smiling. I relaxed.

We ordered finger sandwiches and jasmine tea. As heavy silver clinked against fine bone china, my mother leaned in toward me and apologized for her behavior at the Peninsula.

"I am sorry," she said. "I get so angry. I hates to be taken advantage of."

"Why are you like that?" I asked her. It was not a question she would ever answer. I did not think she even knew how.

"I don't know," she said, and lapsed into silence. She raised her teacup to her lips and looked around. Then she surprised me.

"It's hard for Mommy," she said. "I have no one tell me how to raise children. I don't know what to do. I'm insecure, living with all these white people. I want to fit in, want to succeed. I'm always giving parties. Don't spend enough time with you guys. I made a lot of mistakes.

"Every time we sit down to dinner, we fight," she continued. "That's because of me. I'm too impatient. We live in that long house, and we're always screaming at each other down the hall.

"Our family," she concluded, "is really screwed up."

"We're not that bad," I protested feebly.

"But," she said, "you could have been better."

It was the first time she had ever talked to me in this way. The pat answers, surly "no"s, and uncommunicative shrugs had disappeared. She was trying to explain herself.

"I think the family is the family," she said. "It's like one person. If I do something good for one of you, it's like it's for the whole family. Now I know I should have treated you all fair, like individuals. Now I try, but maybe it's too late."

Now I understood why she had taken me to China, why she let my boorish brother use her apartment like his personal club, why she planned to spend a month in London helping my sister with her two children. It was a grand apology that I had been too callous to recognize. Not anymore.

"My life," my mother said, "is all a waste."

She wished for absolution, and I, who had sinned no less than she, could only give it to her.

"No," I said. "It's not."

The next day we went to Taiwan. For the first time, we traveled as friends. We walked around an upscale mall in Taipei and marveled at how sophisticated Taiwanese tastes had become. Seven years before, when I spent a summer there, the women had favored midriff-baring tube tops and orange pants. Now the stores carried Max Mara and Jil Sander. My mother and I shared a shaved ice in the basement food court, and she let me in on a secret.

"I hate my name," she confessed. "It's so tacky. Man-li. Anything that ends in li is tacky. Sometimes I hate tell people my name."

We were like schoolgirls sharing confidences. It only made sense that the next day we went to Beiyinyu. Its appearance from the street had not altered. It still presented a modest face to the outside world, hidden behind a high brick wall. And the board in the front hall continued to post bad-conduct notices.

"She wore earrings," my mother said, chuckling as she read down the list. "She has the wrong shoes. She wore a bracelet. She was rude to a teacher."

But things had changed. Microwaves sat in every classroom to heat the students' meals. I presumed the old tin lunch boxes had disappeared along with the giant mesh bag that was once used to carry them down to the kitchen. The girls now wore gym shorts to athletic practice instead of the wide bloomers of my mother's day. The students could even wear their hair slightly longer. There were telephones in the hallway. The old pool where my mother had learned to swim had long since metamorphosed into a courtyard. The school now had an indoor pool.

Things had changed beneath the surface as well. Teachers no longer lived on campus. In my mother's day, Beiyinyu had been both a middle school and a high school. It just served as a high school now. Most astonishing of all was the student body. Of the cluster of ten or so girls I spoke with, no one wanted to be a scientist. "Too dangerous," they said. They all wanted to be lawyers.

"No one wants to be lawyer when I was in school," my mother said. "They all look down on them."

The girls all wanted to study in America after college, but they did not want to live there. "Taiwan is more exciting now," one student said. "That's where the money is."

In fact, many of them had already traveled to the United States, Europe, and Japan. In the years since my mother had left, Taiwan had blossomed into a country of considerable economic strength. Its best students no longer fled for opportunities elsewhere. Back in 1955, no one could have guessed this provincial backwater would accomplish so much. I wondered how many of my mother's classmates would have left had they known. Now the majority of them lived lives of middle-class obscurity while the native Taiwanese, who had always been treated as second-class citizens in their own country, grew rich. Yet not a single classmate I spoke to had expressed regret. "I have a good life," one had said to me. "What do I do in Taiwan? I don't know anybody. I have no place to live." After all, their generation had never regarded Taiwan as a home.

The same held true of my mother. As in China, she showed little curiosity about the school and how it had changed. Her indifference surprised me. I knew how much Beiyinyu had meant to her. But the woman I had seen in Hawaii was nowhere to be found. The person who had clapped excitedly each time an old classmate walked into the room now strolled along with a bored look on her face.

I asked her outright: "Is this interesting to you?"

"No," came the frank response.

But on the way out, we stopped in the alumnae office, and my mother joined the alumnae association. It finally dawned on me why she cared so little about being there. The Beiyinyu of today and the one of yesteryear might differ in some respects and remain similar in others. It did not matter. The first existed in her mind: the latter held no relevance. The physicality of a place meant nothing to my mother. She had lived in thirteen different cities and towns by the time she was twenty-one. In her movable feast of a life, it was the people who mattered, not the places.

With that in mind, I went farther back into my mother's past. The first person I met was the daughter of my mother's great-aunt, a woman she instructed me to call Auntie Eva. Eva was a few years younger than my mother, and the two had played together as children. My mother had not seen her since 1960.

My mother and I walked in the rain to meet Eva on a street corner. Taipei had changed so much that my mother had to stop every few feet to ask directions of the passersby. The rain in Taipei does not fall so much as pelt. We hurried along, shoulders hunched and head down. Flush with money, the Taiwanese had paved many of the sidewalks with marble. The rain turned them into ice rinks. We skidded and slid along their wet surfaces. My mother had the hood of her green windbreaker up as she barreled along, intent on getting to our meeting spot in one piece. She almost mowed down a short, calm woman standing in her path. The woman opened her arms.

"Man-li," she said simply.

It was Eva. The two women embraced and immediately started talking. Eva's mother had been very close to my grandmother. Eva's mother was the wife of General Tu, the famous war hero who had been captured by the Communists.

"I never know," my mother had said to me earlier that day, "why she did not help when my mother died. She didn't even get my uncle out of prison."

Over dinner at a nearby restaurant, Eva told us the story.

"My mother was very sick with gall bladder," she said. "She knows your mother is dying but couldn't see her even though they were so close. She really wanted to see her to discuss the children. By the time she got better, it was too late. Your aunt already has her hold on the money.

"Also," she added, "we lived in Hualien, not in Taipei. There was not much she can do."

Eva tried to change the subject. She entertained us with stories about my great-grandmother, who, in spite of her age, her stocky build, and her bound feet moved surprisingly fast. "Your grandmother," Eva said to my mother, "was so funny. She was always chewing ice cubes." She tottered around in imitation of the old woman.

"I liked my grandmother," my mother said wistfully. Memories that had been still for so long came rushing out of her. Images that she had tried to suppress now appeared, unbidden, in her head.

We left the restaurant and walked out along the damp, dark streets of Taipei. The recent rain had cooled the air only slightly. The heat still ran up along my neck, making me sweat, as I listened to my mother speak about those old, awful days.

"One day," she said, "I came home from school, and my uncle was gone. It was the most terrible feeling. There was no note. The maid had to tell me soldiers came and took him away."

I hated myself then for dredging up this pain. My mother had visited Taipei several times since she had emigrated to the United States. She had never bothered to find Eva before. She had done so only for me. Eva represented a past that my mother had not wanted to face—a past she had spent the last forty-five years trying to forget. I had no right to force her to remember. But I could not stop what I had started.

"Oh, Mom," I said, and put my arm around her.

She had never been so far away from me as she was at that moment. Eva looked at the ground and said nothing.

We arrived at a dingy apartment building. Steel bars closed all the windows off from intruders. A listless guard watched television in the lobby. He jerked his head toward the elevator when we entered to forestall any questions that might arise. We went up to the fourth floor. Four is an unlucky number in Chinese. It is a homonym for the word "death." The high-rise where we were staying with friends did not even have a fourth floor.

No one had explained to me whom we were about to see. Eva rang the doorbell, and I heard a shuffling noise coming closer. The door opened to reveal an ancient woman dressed in a pink, tie-dyed muumuu. She peered at us suspiciously like a cranky old tortoise coming out of its shell.

"Guess who's here," Eva said, smiling.

The woman looked directly at my mother. She frowned. My mother smiled a wide, strained, uncertain grin. I had seen that look before. The woman shook her head.

"*Shi Man-li,*" Eva finally said. "It's Man-li."

"Man-li?" the crabby woman said in disbelief. She folded her arms across her chest.

My mother pushed me forward. "This is my littlest daughter," she said.

The woman looked at me. She touched my face.

"But," she said, "you were just a baby. You were so little."

Gradually, I realized this cantankerous old woman was my mother's aunt, the very one who had stolen her own sister's money and denounced her brother to the police. She had met me once before on a trip to the States that she had taken in the early 1970s. I had no recollection of the visit and now watched in disbelief as my mother led her aunt to the most comfortable chair and plumped her cushions. In turn, the old woman queried her.

"You've been here before," she said. "How come you don't know how to find it?"

She meant that we should have stayed with her. I shuddered at the thought. I still could not quite believe that we were there at all.

While the three older women spoke in Chinese, I glanced around the room. Framed pictures of her family sat on an end table. My mother's aunt appeared in many of them, a squat, unsmiling figure wearing shaded glasses, surrounded by a handful of well-fed grandchildren my own age. The men stood with arms folded, wearing smug expressions. The women had doused themselves in hairspray. I thought of the old woman as a demon and her glossy, self-satisfied descendants as her spawn. I hated them, and I hated her.

"How pretty," she said to my mother, referring to me. "She has grown so much."

I smiled grimly.

"Do you have any questions for Auntie?" my mother asked.

I could not think of a single innocuous one. I asked the first question that came to me.

"What was my grandmother like?"

The old turtle paused and wrinkled her mouth down in a small frown.

"Stubborn," she said in a raspy voice.

"What was my grandfather like?"

"Playboy," she said.

"So," I said, gathering my courage. "You and my grandmother did not get along?"

"*Hao*," she said. "We did. She was very . . ." The old woman paused and groped for a description.

"She was very good to me," she said finally. "She took care of me."

On the wall hung a familiar picture. Eva had had a similar one in her home where we had briefly stopped after dinner. My mother did too. It was a picture of Chiang Kai-shek and another officer in uniform. In Eva's case, the photo showed her father. In this instance, it was my mother's uncle. At home, the man was my own grandfather. The war had personally and tragically touched every one of those families. Eva and my mother had lost their fathers. I did not know what horrors might have befallen the old woman in front of me. I, product of upper-middle-class suburbia that I was, could not even begin to imagine. In any case, I was in no position to judge her or her actions. The responsibility of hating her did not belong to me. It belonged to my mother. To me, she was merely old while I was young. She lived in solitude; I did not. Every day, she puttered about this dim apartment, straining to see in spite of her failing eyesight. Her children had scattered around the globe. Her grandchildren spoke English better than they spoke Chinese. Her husband may have survived the war, but the old woman was all alone now.

When we finally rose to leave, she followed us into the hall-way.

"Call me," she said to my mother. "I'll take you out to dinner."

My mother nodded.

Her aunt turned to me. "So pretty," she said again.

This time, I managed a weak but real smile.

The next day my mother and I drove out to the Shrine to Martyrs near the Grand Hotel on the outskirts of the city. The day had dawned typically hot and humid. The bright sun hurt my eyes as I stepped out of the car into the wide plaza that marked the memorial's entrance. I shielded them and stared up at the building in front of me. It was divided into three long hallways, a three-sided square of a monument designed in imitation of the old imperial style. Red lacquer pillars rose to meet green-tiled eaves. Wood panels lined the ceilings.

I had come to this place to find a person who had never set foot on the island of Taiwan, a person who was no longer alive. It was here that the Republic of China honored its war dead. It was here that I hoped to find my grandfather.

We walked up the stairs and down the silent corridors. One wing contained memorials to civilians. The other was devoted to the military. We went in. Rows and rows of wooden plaques stretched the length of the room, from shoulder level to the ceiling. The ones toward the front featured just one name. Farther back, the tablets contained dozens of appellations, line upon line upon line of characters that had once represented living people. My mother scanned the room. We walked up and down as she searched for her father's name. I could not help her. I did not know what his name looked like.

At last we gave up. There were too many. We went back out to the plaza to the administrative office. A sharp-eyed lieutenant greeted us. When my mother said that she was looking for her father's name, he invited us to sit down, offered us tea, and disappeared into a backroom. Sitting across from us was a young man barely out of his teens. He carried a small canvas traveling bag.

Another soldier entered the room. He looked at the boy. "What regiment was he in?" he asked.

The boy shrugged.

"Well," the soldier said gently. "What division then?"

The boy did not know. All he had was the soldier's name and the province where he had died: Guangdong. The officer went back into the other room. The boy fiddled with the straps on his bag.

"Are you trying to find someone?" my mother asked.

"Yes," he said. "My grandfather."

"Her too." My mother pointed at me.

"I came from Hong Kong," the boy said. "If I can prove my grandfather was a war veteran, I can get some scholarship money. But they can't find his name."

The soldier came out and shook his head at the boy. "I'm sorry," he said.

The boy sighed and stood up. He would return to Hong Kong that night. He had just reached the door when our lieutenant appeared in the room. He was holding a slip of paper. The boy turned to look.

"Any luck?" the boy asked us.

We looked at the lieutenant. He nodded. I looked back at the boy. He too nodded, smiled wanly at me, and then disappeared into the sunlight.

The office maintained as complete a record as existed for the 3.3 million troops who had died in combat, but only 10 percent of those men were honored at the shrine. My grandfather, the officer told me, was one of them.

Again, we walked out to the memorial. This time, the lieutenant accompanied us. He looked at the slip in his hand and then at the rows of tablets. He walked slightly left of center, stopped, and extended a finger.

"Here," he said and pointed to a plaque in the front row.

"The front row," my mother whispered. "It's in the front row."

The soldier took the tablet down and set it on a table in front so that we could get a better look. The marker was long and narrow with a frieze on top. It contained just nine characters.

" 'Han Tsin-tong,' " my mother read to me. " 'He died a patriot for his country.' "

It was just a piece of wood. No doubt some nameless bureaucrat had ordered it made many years after my grandfather's death. But still we bowed before it, first my mother and then me. Three times she bent from the waist with her eyes closed. I followed suit. I wondered what my mother was thinking. I knew that she had only come here for my sake. When we turned to leave, she looked at me happily.

"It was in the first row," she said again.

We linked arms and walked back out into the blinding white of the plaza. With each step, we put to rest another fragment of my grandfather's ghost.

The night before we left Taiwan, my mother woke me at three o'clock.

"I'm going to miss you," she said. "It was a real good trip."

Five months later, it is early February, the second day of the Chinese New Year. Wei and I are throwing a party at my apartment. It is the first time I have ever thought to celebrate the New Year on my own, without my parents. I have sent out invitations in envelopes with red foil linings. The cards are marked with a rubber stamp of a cow in red ink. They do not sell ox stamps at the local art supply store.

Margaret has mailed Wei a package full of treats for the party: sour plums, spicy beef jerky, peanut candies, and pineapple cakes. They sit on platters on my dining-room table. Peter, in town for a visit, supervises the cooking of the red bean soup. Wei makes noodles with hot sauce and vinegar. I have bought pork buns in Chinatown. We are just about finished. Only one task remains for us to do. I bring out a large platter and set it on the butcher block in the kitchen. Wei fills a bowl with water. In front of us sits another, larger bowl, which contains a mixture of ground pork, salted cabbage, and minced scallions. A pot waits at the ready on the stove.

For the next half hour, before the guests arrive, we make dumplings together. Each of us uses a different technique. I have learned mine from watching my mother, who pays little attention to beauty of form but who always makes sure the wrapper is tightly sealed. I do not know where Wei has acquired her own delicate touch; Margaret is notorious for not knowing how to cook. Perhaps she managed to pass this one culinary lesson on to her daughter. Indeed, Wei's movements have the precision of a scientist. Each small package she produces is the same shape and size as the one before. The dumplings go around the platter in concentric circles. When the next layer begins, we decide to cook a few.

They bob up in the boiling water almost immediately. Wei peers into the pot.

"Mmm," she says, "when they float, you're supposed to add cold water. When the water boils again, they're ready."

We look at each other. We shake our heads and shrug.

"Whatever," we say.

I point to the kitchen timer.

"We could," I suggest.

Wei nods.

"Ten minutes should be enough."

As we ladle our miraculous, delicious dumplings out, I wonder what Jim and Mark are doing. Perhaps Mark is catching a movie with friends, oblivious to the fact that it is even the new year. Perhaps Jim has holed himself up in his lab, pleading work as an excuse not to go home to visit his father this holiday weekend. I wish for a moment that we could all be here making dumplings together, like our mothers used to do in Taipei.

I know it will never happen. We each of us have struck out on our own paths, as different from one another as the lives are that our mothers have made for themselves in America. True, Wei and I only met because our mothers once went to school together, but that fact alone could not suffice to make us friends. We accomplished that on our own. It was as it should be. In giving up part of who we were to become who we are, we had struck a fair exchange. If our mothers were the frogs of poetry, valiantly continuing to sing in spite of their broken pasts, then we, their children, had reaped the rewards of that courage. We were all kings of the bream, taken from the dead water of our ancestors and given life in a new stream. We would never turn into the same fish.

ACKNOWLEDGMENTS

My first and deepest thanks must go to the women and their families featured in these pages—without whom this book would not exist. They have generously and openly shared their lives with me, and I hope they know that I have tried to do their stories justice.

I would also like to thank the many other members of the Beiyinyu class of 1955 who welcomed me into their homes and who often made me feel that I had not one, but a multitude of mothers throughout the country. I interviewed a number of other people as well, and, although I mention only a few by name in the book, I am grateful to them all for their time, their memories, and their opinions. It is with sadness that I particularly note the contribution of my mother's dear friend, Betty B.C. Yang Low, who died just as this project was nearing completion.

I relied upon numerous texts to provide background information and to re-create for me eras and places in which I have not lived. To the various scholars, journalists, editors, and writers whose works proved so helpful, I owe a debt beyond price. I would also like to acknowledge the staffs of the many different libraries and archives where much of this research occurred.

Writing a book is one thing; getting it published is quite another. For the fact that this book is actually a book and not just a pile of papers under my desk, I would like to thank Rosemary Ahern for giving so unsparingly of her deep insight and intelligent criticism; Mary Evans for having the courage and generosity to view me in a new light; Sam Freedman for being the first to agree that this vague idea of mine could one day be a book; and Kari Paschall, Jenny Lee, Laura Albritton, and Tanya McKinnon for keeping things running with professionalism and good cheer.

It goes without saying that my debt to my mother is enormous, but I owe an equal, if different, thank you to my father, Yuan, who has been one of my most important instructors in life. Not least of his lessons was teaching me the value of the past. Thanks also to my sister, Christine, and her husband, Bill, for keeping the world in proper perspective; and to my brothers, Tim and Derek, for constantly forcing me to prove myself.

Finally, to Ben for making me laugh even when I thought I couldn't.